Understanding Music

Understanding Music

Second Edition, Revised and Enlarged
An introduction to
music's elements, styles, and forms—
for both the layman and the practitioner

WILLIAM S. NEWMAN, Ph.D.
Professor of Music and Chairman of Instruction in Piano
The University of North Carolina

HARPER COLOPHON BOOKS
Harper & Row, Publishers
New York, Evanston & London

To Claire

Contents

Preface by Glen Haydon   *xiii*
Author's Foreword   *xv*
Foreword to the Second Edition   *xxi*

I. Prelude

1. Your Road to Musical Understanding   3

2. A Historical Frame of Reference   11
   HISTORICAL VIEWPOINTS, PAST AND PRESENT
   WESTERN MUSIC VIEWED IN HISTORICAL CYCLES
   THE STYLE PENDULUM IN ART HISTORY

II. The Elements and Styles of Music

3. The Nature and Instruments of Musical Sound   29
   SOME ELEMENTARY ACOUSTICS—PITCH, INTENSITY,
      TIMBRE
   ORCHESTRAL INSTRUMENTS CLASSIFIED
   STRINGED INSTRUMENTS
   WIND INSTRUMENTS
   PERCUSSION INSTRUMENTS
   PIANO, ORGAN, AND OTHER KEYBOARD TYPES
   THE HUMAN VOICE

4. Rhythm: Its Notation, Patterns, and Tempos   *49*
    NOTE VALUES
    "SIMPLE" METERS
    FURTHER VALUES AND METERS
    RHYTHMIC PATTERNS, NEW AND FAMILIAR
    TIME AND TEMPO

5. Melody: Its Notation and Pitch Organization   *64*
    KEYBOARD CONCEPTS OF PITCH AND SCALES
    STAFF NOTATION
    THE TANGIBLES AND INTANGIBLES OF MELODY

6. Harmony and Tonality   *78*
    INTERVALS, BOTH CONSONANT AND DISSONANT
    CONSTRUCTING CHORDS FROM INTERVALS
    THE PRIME DIRECTIONS OF HARMONIC MOVEMENT
    KEYS AND KEY RELATIONSHIPS
    TONALITY AS AN AGENT OF LARGER ORGANIZATION
    NEW TONAL VISTAS

7. Texture and Sonority as Style Clues   *105*
    MONOPHONY IN EXOTIC AND WESTERN MUSIC
    HOMOPHONY, OR MELODY QUALIFIED BY ACCOMPANIMENT
    POLYPHONY AND ITS APPEAL TO THE INTELLECT
    VOCAL GROUPINGS
    INSTRUMENTAL GROUPINGS
    SONORITY PER SE IN RECENT MUSIC

III. Forms Based on Inner Laws of Music

8. What Is Musical Form? (A Problem in Aesthetics)   *133*
    "VARIETY WITHIN UNITY" AS THE STARTING POINT
    STRUCTURAL ASPECTS OF A "TIME" ART
    PROGRESSION BY MOTIVIC PLAY
    PROGRESSION BY PHRASE GROUPING

STANDARDIZED DESIGNS BASED ON REPETITION AND
CONTRAST
MODERN TRENDS

9. Forms Woven Out of Motivic Play   *156*
THE MOTET AND THE MADRIGAL
FUGAL FORM
BINARY DESIGN IN BAROQUE INSTRUMENTAL PIECES

10. Hierarchic Designs Based on Phrase Grouping   *171*
BINARY DESIGN IN HOMOPHONIC MUSIC
TERNARY DESIGN (A-B-A)
THE RONDO IDEA
"INTUITIVE" ARRANGEMENTS OF SECTIONS

11. Variation, a Compound Process   *186*
SIMULTANEOUS REPETITION AND CONTRAST
THE RECURRING BASS LINE
THE RECURRING HARMONIC PATTERN
THE RECURRING BINARY MELODY
OPTIONAL PRINCIPLES IN THE THEME-AND-VARIATIONS

12. Instrumental Cycles of the Baroque Era   *202*
THE GROUPING OF CONTRASTING MOVEMENTS
SUITES OF DANCES
TRIO SONATAS IN CHURCH AND AT COURT
THE CONCERTO GROSSO

13. The Classic Sonata, Prototype of Modern Instrumental
Cycles   *214*
SYMPHONY, CONCERTO, QUARTET, AND OTHER MEDIUMS
THE CHOICE AND ORDER OF MOVEMENTS
"SONATA-ALLEGRO" FORM

IV. Forms Influenced by Extramusical Factors

14. Instrumental Fantasy and Description   *235*
PROGRAMME VERSUS ABSOLUTE MUSIC

FREE FORMS BORN OF MUSICAL AND TECHNICAL FANTASY
TONE POEMS THAT REFLECT MOODS
TONE POEMS THAT DESCRIBE LITERALITIES

15. Allegiance to Text in Song and Opera   247
CURSIVE ART-SONG
THE VICISSITUDES OF OPERA
CONFLICTS AND COMPROMISES INHERENT IN OPERA
OPERA'S DELIGHTS

16. Sacred Choral Cycles Governed by Text   263
OFFICE AND MASS IN GREGORIAN CHANT
THE POLYPHONIC MASS AND REQUIEM
ORATORIO, PASSION, AND CANTATA

V. *Postlude*

17. The Pursuit of Music   283
AN IMPORTANT AMERICAN INDUSTRY!
"DE GUSTIBUS NON EST DISPUTANDUM"
THE EVALUATION OF MUSIC AND PERFORMANCE
IN SEARCH OF MUSICAL TALENT

Appendix I. Some Biographies of Great Musicians   *301*

Appendix II. A Coordinated List of Music to Hear   *308*

Index   *317*

List of Music Examples

FIGURE

1. Ranges of women's and men's voices   47
2. Note values from whole- to 16th-note   50
3. A rhythmic pattern in simple meter (*Frère Jacques*)   52
4. Rests in a rhythmic pattern   55
5. A rhythmic pattern to clap and count   55
6. A rhythmic pattern in compound meter (*Sailing*)   56
7. The rhythmic patterns of nine dance types, chiefly Romantic and Modern   57
8. Alignment of the keyboard and staff   64
9. Middle C in four clef positions   69
10. Three steps in building a major scale   71
11. Prout's example of an unmelodic series of tones   73
12. Typical traits of melody (Mendelssohn)   74
13. The first sixteen partials of great C   79
14. From triad to thirteenth chord by adding thirds   83
15. The seven most common chord forms   84
16. A number and name for the triad on each scale degree   85
17. The fourteen standard key signatures   92
18. Modulation through remote keys for the sake of harmonic color (Schubert)   97
19. Extended horizons in Modern harmony (Shostakovitch)   *101*

FIGURE

20. Styles of musical texture: (a) polyphony (Fresco-
    baldi); (b) homophony (Chopin); (c) mono-
    phony (folk song)   *106*
21. Harmony as a qualifier of melody—the climactic
    chord (Mendelssohn)   *112*
22. Two styles of accompaniment in homophony: (a)
    Alberti bass (Mozart); (b) two-against-three
    (Brahms)   *114*
23. Motivic play (Bach)   *142*
24. How the same motive might have been treated in
    different eras   *143*
25. How the same phrase might have been treated in
    different eras   *147*
26. Procedures in a motet (Lassus)   *158*
27. The subject and countersubject in a choral fugue
    (Haydn)   *163*
28. Procedures in a fugue (Bach)   *166*
29. The "gallant style" in harpsichord music (D. Scar-
    latti)   *169*
30. The main themes in an "intuitive" design (Chopin)   *184*
31. Four variation techniques as they might be applied
    to the opening of *Drink to Me Only with Thine
    Eyes*   *188*
32. A recurring bass line (Bach)   *192*
33. A recurring harmonic pattern (Brahms)   *195*
34. The decoration of a recurring melodic outline (Paga-
    nini)   *197*
35. Variation treatment in a chorale prelude (Bach)   *201*
36. Patterns of the dances in a Baroque suite (Loeillet) *207*
37. A passage from a church sonata in trio setting
    (Corelli)   *208*
38. The opposition of *tutti* and *soli* in a concerto grosso
    (Vivaldi)   *212*

FIGURE

39. Thematic relationships within and between the movements of a sonata (Beethoven) — 222

40. Dualism of themes in a Romantic sonata: (a) "masculine"; (b) "feminine" (Brahms) — 225

41. Dissection of a theme as a process of development (Beethoven) — 229

42. Idiomatic writing in a piano fantasia (Liszt) — 240

43. Impressionism as exemplified in a fragmentary theme (Debussy) — 243

44. Literal description in music (R. Strauss) — 245

45. Styles of lieder accompaniments (Schubert) — 251

46. Vocal styles in Classic and Baroque opera (Mozart, Lully) — 258

47. Types of plainchant: (a) syllabic; (b) melismatic; (c) sequence — 267

48. Contrasting styles in Bach's *Mass in B Minor*: (a) chromatic fugue subject; (b) diatonic fugue subject — 270

49. Word painting in Handel's *Messiah* — 278

List of Plates

(The plates follow page 42.)

PLATE

1. An Early Christian church under Byzantine influence
2. A Renaissance palace (Romano)
3. A Baroque church (Longhena)
4. A Classic government building (Gabriel)
5. A Romantic opera house (Garnier)
6. A Modern industrial building (Wright)
7. (a) Pathos: The actual photograph of a motif; (b) Ethos: The same scene idealized in a painting (Cézanne)
8. A concert of Medieval-and-Renaissance music (Vielle Trio)
9. A string quartet (Kroll Quartet)
10. A "woodwind" quintet (New Art Wind Quintet)
11. A "unit" pipe organ with two manuals and a pedal keyboard (Aeolian-Skinner)
12. A cutaway model of the action on a grand piano (Steinway)
13. A full symphony orchestra (New York Philharmonic-Symphony Orchestra)
14. A concert band (United States Marine Band)
15. A performance of Baroque chamber music (Vanloo)
16. Opera in a Baroque theater (Panini)
17. Impressionism in painting (Monet)
18. Expressionism in painting (Kokoschka)

Preface

Here is a new introduction to music, carefully planned to meet the interests of the general reader and of the college student alike. That the general reader—the concertgoer, record collector, amateur performer, or other music lover—will welcome this addition to the literature intended for him may safely be assumed from a knowledge of its solid content. It is about the college student's need for such a book that further comment is offered here.

One of the prime responsibilities of a department of music in a liberal arts college is to bring music significantly into the lives of as many students as possible. The band, orchestra, glee clubs, choral groups, and other organization activities afford opportunities for many who are not specializing in this field to pursue their musical interests. The various concert series annually presented on the campus bring music to the whole student body, and certainly make a valuable contribution to the cultural life of the American college. But all these activities are commonly thought of as extracurricular and not as an integral part of the undergraduate curriculum.

For many years there has been a growing feeling that a so-called liberal education is distinctly lacking when it fails to include some systematic training in the arts. This thinking is reflected in the various courses in music and art appreciation that have long been offered as electives in numerous colleges. More recently, required courses in the arts have come to take their place alongside the required courses in language and literature, natural science, and social science. But the fundamental difficulties of adapting a subject matter whose essential values rest rather on immediate awareness than on the more intellectual processes of thought have badgered the footsteps of those who have worked on this problem. On the one hand is the danger of superficiality, leading to "snap" courses, and on the other the danger of an overly intellectualized approach at the risk of factual dullness and a possible stifling of any real art appreciation.

It was with a keen awareness of these and the many attendant problems, backed by some twenty years of experience, that Dr. Newman undertook the difficult but rewarding task of working out a satisfactory course and bringing it to fruition in the present text. That he has been remarkably successful is attested by the wide endorsement of this course on the campus. Faculty committees have cited its worthy content; and students, rising to the challenge that it presents, report great enthusiasm for their increased understanding of music.

Designed for the musical layman, this book does not talk down to the reader. It takes its point of departure from the actual music example. Technical terms are introduced, defined, and illustrated in the natural, organic development of its central theme. Skillful, enthusiastic instructors of the sort to be found in increasing numbers throughout the country will find exceptional opportunities for effective teaching here. *Understanding Music* certainly provides the factual knowledge systematically motivated so as to encourage independent thinking, a growing understanding, and increased appreciation of fundamental principles and values in music. Thus it makes a real contribution to the teaching of music in the liberal arts college.

GLEN HAYDON
Head of the Department of Music
The University of North Carolina

Author's Foreword

Books on the understanding and appreciation of music abound on library shelves. Why, then, has it seemed necessary to write a new one? The answer is simple enough. Styles, tastes, standards, and attitudes change in music as they do in all living. Thanks to a twentieth-century heyday of musical scholarship that is permeating the field at large, new, more fundamental approaches to music itself have emerged. New organization, new techniques of presentation, new subject matter have developed. And what is more, music's place within the humanities has become clearer in the light shed by wider, overlapping cultural interests.

When it comes to books that reflect these changes, then one must speak of a dearth rather than an abundance of material. Numerous introductory books have been written around the lives of great composers, numerous others around the historical periods of music, and still others around running accounts of some of music's best-known masterworks. But there have been remarkably few attempts, for example, to make music's very elements, styles, and forms serve as the points of departure—which, indeed, is the object of the present book.

Primarily, I have wanted to provide a book that gets at the inner workings of music in a more fundamental manner, in explicit terms accessible to all intelligent readers. The present book seeks to explore not only the how but the why of music's basic operations. Such an aim is, of course, a large order in any field. To describe how tan-colored grass seed grows into something that is green is one thing; to explain why is quite another matter. One might suppose that the problem of explaining music's basic operations would be merely a routine task for the professional writer on music. Actually, the musician who faces squarely up to this problem must come to grips with the most vital, yet elusive, elements of his subject. No wonder music's scholars have generally preferred to commit themselves to books on almost every aspect of music but its prime ingredients, rhythm and melody.

For my own part, I found it necessary to write this book not once but several times before I could resolve or at least reconcile numerous fundamental questions that I had previously side-stepped or neglected. During the throes of this musical self-analysis a considerable interchange of philosophies took place between the present book and *A History of the Sonata Idea*, which has been in progress for many more years. The chief results of this interchange may be found here in Chapters 8 to 13, where the object has been to approach musical form as a generative process.

Understanding Music is addressed both to the layman and to the musical connoisseur—to the layman who wants an introductory survey and to the connoisseur who seeks to put his knowledge in perspective. The practicing musician may wonder that something so rudimentary as note values and something so abstract as the aesthetics of a time art appear in the same volume. But he must remember that to the layman these concepts present about equal challenges. And to the connoisseur they are both necessary, since all the main aspects of music must be presented or re-presented in just proportions if his need for a rounded and coordinated view is to be met.

How may the individual reader, pursuing music on his own initiative, use this book to best advantage? It is hoped, first of all, that he will want to read it in its entirety and in sequence, since every effort has been made here to survey the subject in an organized, comprehensive, and consistent manner. Certainly if he has no background in music he will do better to read at least the first eight chapters in sequence, for this much is approached inductively, starting with music's elements, proceeding to its styles, and arriving at the all-important matter of form. However, the reader who has reason to skip about will find that each chapter is planned as a separate unit, with cross references to other chapters where necessary. He will be able to orient himself further to the general plan by frequent reference to the synoptic table of contents, which was designed with this use in mind. In any case, without such orientation learning becomes as inefficient as the fireplace in which most of the heat goes up the chimney. Such facts as do get noted must rattle around loosely, unassimilated, unrelated, and without that perspective or interpretation that fixes them in the memory.

Thanks to an extremely cooperative publisher, it has been possible to include numerous other aids that should be of special value to the individual reader. Among these are charts, diagrams, tables, photographs, and music examples in sufficient number to amplify or illustrate every main point discussed in the text; lists of supplementary readings at the end of each chapter and of musicians' biographies (Appendix I); and a comprehensive, balanced list of "music to hear" (Appendix II), plus many other references in the course of the text, which will suggest a basic library for the enthusiastic record collector. Finally, it is hoped that the reader will put to the test the various clues to styles and experiments in sound that are suggested throughout this book. Then, whether he gets his music by way of the concert hall, radio, television, phonograph, or performances of his own making, he will have a better understanding of what to listen for and a better idea of how music feels "from the inside," as it were.

As a college text, *Understanding Music* is intended, on the one hand, for the general college student who wants a broad survey course in music, and, on the other, for the music "major" who needs a preliminary overview of his subject. The instructor may want to know that the following schedules have worked out in practice:

Chapter	One Semester, 3 Hours a Week for 15 Weeks No. of Class Hours	One Quarter, 5 Hours a Week for 10 Weeks No. of Class Hours	Two Semesters No. of Class Hours	Two Quarters No. of Class Hours
1	1	1	1	1
2	2	2	4	4
3	3	3	4	4
4	2	3	4	4
5	3	3	4	5
6	3	3	5	5
		Test, 1	Test, 1	Test, 1
7	2	3	4	5
8	2	2	4	5
	Test, 1			
9	3	3	4	5
10	3	3	4	5
11	3	3	5	5
		Test, 1	Review, 1	Review, 1
12	3	3	6	7
13	4	4	8	9
14	2	2	6	6
			Test, 1	Test, 1
15	3	4	8	8
16	2	3	8	9
17	1	1	4	5
	Review, 2	Review, 2	Review, 4	Review, 5
Total hours	45	50	90	100

If two semesters or quarters are devoted to the course, then a slightly larger proportion of the time may be spent on the later chapters, which occupy somewhat fewer pages but invite more extensive illustrations in class. It is in these later stages and in the final periods of review that the recognition of historical styles can best be developed. In the last analysis, such recognition is the crux of discriminating listening by the layman.

While planning their schedules, students should beware the usual chief pitfalls in the study of any such introductory text as this: underestimation of the time needed to read and digest chapters that are relatively short yet concentrated; failure to see the details in perspective—that is, in the larger view outlined by the table of contents (as previously mentioned); insufficient attention to the new words or jargon that every new subject must introduce; and not enough actual listening to the music under discussion.

Here is a list of abbreviations used in this book that may not be self-evident:

Fig.	any of the numbered music examples
Plate	numbered photographs appearing after page 42.
S.A.T.B.	soprano, alto, tenor, bass
K.	Köchel-Einstein index of Mozart's works (3rd ed., Leipzig, 1937) or Ralph Kirkpatrick's listing of Domenico Scarlatti's keyboard sonatas (Princeton, 1953)
S.	Schmieder index of Bach's works

Roman numerals are used both to identify certain chords and to designate the respective movements of a work in several movements.

I wish to thank the many students whose helpful reactions in class have found their way into this book, and the several graduate students who have put certain of the more original ideas to the test in their research work. Among persons who have given special counsel I am indebted to Professor G. S. Dickinson of Vassar College and the late Professor Emeritus Arthur Shepherd of Western Reserve University for their keen and detailed comments on the treatment of musical form; Mr. Almonte Howell, Jr. of the University of Kentucky and Professor Edgar Alden of the University of North Carolina for careful reviews of the entire manuscript; Professors L. C. MacKinney, J. E. King, Clemens Sommer, W. P. Friederich, L. A. Cotten, and J. V. Allcott, all of the University of North Carolina, for extended advice on the preparation of Historical Chart II and the separate era descriptions in Chapter 2; and Professors Glen Haydon, Wilton Mason, and Lowell Ashby, and Mrs. Myra Lauterer, of this same University, for other valued suggestions and assistance.

WILLIAM S. NEWMAN

Foreword to the Second Edition

Like many another book revision, this Second Edition of *Understanding Music* began in all innocence as a simple plan to bring the subject matter up to date. But it was not completed until many portions of the text had been rewritten and all of it reset. A fair share of the revising has been directed toward further clarification and a certain amount of aeration of the more concentrated discussions. And a fair share of it is actually new material, showing up especially in expansions of such diverse topics as atonality, folk song, concerto, hymn, cantata, transcriptions, and art-song. Also, more masterworks have been examined in some detail.

The lists of readings at the end of each chapter and of biographies arranged by eras in Appendix I have all been reconsidered and expanded to include outstanding books from the past eight years. Let the lay reader not be troubled by the addition of certain more basic studies (other than biographic). These are offered especially to the instructor who may feel the need to fortify his own background, and to those graduate students who seem to be finding this book helpful as a broad but consistent introduction to problems of musical style and form.

With all these changes there has been *no* change in the fundamental approach, if only because I am more than ever convinced of its rightness and effectiveness for the serious lay reader, whether he reads independently or in a formal college course. The book is still factual and non-sugar-coated; it still emphasizes not history, great men, or peripheral tidbits, but elements, styles, and forms; and it still proceeds inductively in that order.

May I once more thank my colleagues at the University of North Carolina. They have again given many valued suggestions, especially Doctors Glen Haydon, Edgar Alden, Joel Carter, and Glenn Watkins. And may I take this opportunity once more to salute my dedicatee Claire, who certainly is getting no chance to lose her command of either motivic play or phrase grouping on our clattering yet metric Royal portable.

WILLIAM S. NEWMAN

November, 1960

Part I

Prelude

Chapter 1

Your Road to Musical Understanding

If those who look to world federation as a solution to the world's ills could limit their aims to a world-wide society for music, they might rest assured of early success. We call music the universal language—universal in that it has the same meaning and appeal for peoples the world over, without needing to be translated anew in each different land. Even the line-and-staff notation and much of the terminology of music have become universal, succeeding easily while Esperanto and similar attempts at common speech and writing have scarcely advanced beyond their promoters. Furthermore, at a very time when national barriers and differentiations are being sharply accentuated, the styles of music have become *inter*national as never before, probably more so than the styles of sister arts like painting and sculpture.

There could be no better evidence than this universality to show that music is a basic human experience. Enjoyment and appreciation of music are the norm among all peoples, not the exception. Recall among your own acquaintances how general is the interest in music—how many persons can boast the makings of a phonograph record collection, for example. Yet, curiously, the layman often greets the invitation to learn about music with extraordinary diffidence and misgivings. "Really, I've never had a lesson and don't know one note from another," he warns, as if his confession blocked all prospect of learning (not to mention that applied music lessons seldom can get to the sort of thing

3

you will be reading here, anyway). But he fails to realize how much he already does know of music, even if he is one who has never made a conscious effort to understand it. For unless he has led a remarkably cloistered life, this layman has been literally steeped in the sound of music—on the radio, on television, and in the movies; at school and at church; in community and in social gatherings. In fact, his conditioning and emotional response to the sound of music will be about as matured as that of the trained musician at the same age. Only in his ability to identify music's materials and to perceive their relationships will he fall behind at the start, and he will be pleased to discover with what relative ease this handicap can soon be overcome.

Similarly, anyone entering newly into deliberate contact with any other art for the first time is in for a pleasant surprise if he supposes that he must grope about in wholly inaccessible or foreign territory. All art depends in some way on human experience. The first time you went to the theater to see a play you were already well prepared to appreciate its dramatic excitement by those real-life dramas that everyone experiences right from the time of his birth. You were similarly well prepared when you made your first visit to an art gallery. To be sure, music does not reproduce so literally the very actions and scenes of everyday life. In this sense, it is a more abstract art than any of the other arts, with only such indirect resemblances in the world around us as the rhythms of bodily movements, the pitch fluctuations of speech, or the sounds of nature may afford. Yet, as we have seen, music does occur abundantly in daily experience.

Perhaps the fact that music is generally so abstract an art explains the misgivings of some about to explore it for the first time, and not only the misgivings but a characteristic, almost superstitious awe of music's "sacrosanct mysteries." Unfortunately, this awe is furthered by the sentimental bosh that too often colors motion pictures about composers' lives and works, by the ethereal terms without which some writers will not or cannot describe music, and by the popular notion, exploited in much music publicity, that composing is a privilege reserved for only a chosen few. Then it becomes necessary to remind ourselves that musicians are people, too, and that music is by and large a very tangible art with a literature, history, theory, and practice open to all who want to enjoy it.

Now what can you hope to learn about music from a book? Mainly you can be introduced to those same tangibles. And with their help you can expect "to listen to seriously conceived music without bewilderment, and to hear with pleasure music of different periods and schools and varying degrees of complexity," which is the often quoted goal that the Englishman Percy Scholes sets for music appreciation study. In short, your taste for music can be cultivated and refined. But note that your likes and dislikes cannot be determined for you. "I've read about Beethoven until I think I am familiar with his methods in music; now what can I read that will help me to like the music itself more?" This is a familiar question. The answer has to be, "Nothing," for likes and dislikes depend not only on knowledge but on conditioning and association (as discussed in our final chapter).

Furthermore, music has its intangibles as well as its tangibles. Or rather, there are aspects of music that can only be expressed in the language of music. The literally millions of pages that have been written about the subject can go only so far, after which nothing but hearing the music itself will suffice to complete an understanding of it. This is equivalent to saying that the whole in art equals more than the sum of its parts. Thus, a critic once wrote that he had worked his way through John Ruskin's detailed description of a Venetian cathedral, almost stone by stone as it were; now all he needed was the cathedral itself so that he could get the general idea!

You might do well to stand off a moment and consider your road to musical understanding as it lies ahead here, much as a motorist will consider his route map before starting on a trip. The present book is meant to guide you toward an understanding of music as our Western civilization has known it. Elements, styles, forms, and literature are introduced in a way that should give meaning and perspective to this music when you hear or study it. In addition, correlations between music and the other humanities are emphasized.

To cover the ground efficiently and directly, and to start with a foundation in music's rudiments so that something more tangible than vague generalities can follow, this book takes an *inductive* approach—that is, it proceeds from the parts to the whole, from the small to the large. Aside from the over-all view taken in Chapters 1, 2, and 17, which make up a "Prelude" and a "Postlude," the book is divided into three sections. First come four chapters devoted to the main elements of music (sound itself, rhythm, melody, harmony), then one chapter on the styles (or "textures") in which these elements are combined, and finally nine chapters on the forms that grow out of these elements and styles, whether determined solely by them ("absolute" music) or influenced in some degree by extramusical factors such as a story or a painting ("programme" music). To use a familiar analogy, if we were to watch a building go up we would observe first its elements or materials (brick, wood, glass), next the styles or manner of putting these together (mortaring, nailing, puttying), and last the total form or design that results (ranch house, store, church).

This organization is based not on any order of history or succession of great names, but rather on the various styles and forms that are inherent in the very nature of music. Once the elements of music have been explored here, each interesting in its own right, our object will be to get into the core of complete musical forms. A mere tourist's guidebook to the scenic points that stand out in these forms will not suffice. Our hope shall be to apply in a modest way the methods of the trained researcher—chiefly to divide and conquer, as it were, considering one element at a time, then the synthesis of these elements in the complete form. In other words, instead of taking everything or anything as it comes along in a musical work—perhaps an oboe melody in the first ten measures, then a rhythmic pattern in the next two measures, then a strange chord in the next measure—we should be able to get into that work more meaningfully by first giving separate consideration to the melodic treatment throughout, then the rhythmic treatment, then the harmonic treatment, and so on.

Every approach of this sort must be made at a consistent angle. Here the angle is found in a bond between certain styles and forms, and the essence of that bond appears in Chapter 8, "What Is Musical Form?" If we were in fact exploring architecture, this question of what *is* form would hardly arise. But architecture is perceived visually whereas musical form must be perceived aurally—a method that may be no more difficult in the long run but does presuppose some clarifications at the start. In particular, we shall see that two styles of musical "progression" are found to be the processes out of which three main classes of musical forms grow (Chaps. 9, 10, and 11). These processes, described as "motivic play" and "phrase grouping," concern what might here be called the connective tissue that binds the musical skeleton. They are to music what processes like knitting or sewing are to fabrics, or—to bring in still another, and more dynamic, analogy—what motoring, flying, or sailing is to transportation.

At the same time, remember that a consistent approach has some built-in hazards along with its advantages of greater clarity. No art has ever evolved quite so neatly and systematically as its historians would seem to imply. Nor have the great artists seemed to worry unduly about the historical patterns into which posterity might want to fit them. Not Bach, nor Beethoven, nor Brahms had the "advantage" of reading this book before he created his music! Otherwise each would have decided against various master strokes that do not happen to tally with the present approach. It was Beethoven, by the way, who remarked, when critics questioned a license in one of his pieces, "Yes, yes, then they are amazed and put their heads together because they never found it in any book on thorough-bass."

Biographies of great composers and performers are always intriguing. Along with your explorations into music you will enjoy and profit from reading one or more of the excellent biographies that are listed alphabetically by eras in Appendix I. Most musicians seem to have moved about in lively circles, so that any one biography should give you a chance to meet many of their important contemporaries as well. Other supplementary readings for those who wish to delve further into particular aspects of music will be found listed at the end of each chapter.

It should go without saying that no aspect of your explorations into music is quite so important as the actual listening that you can do. In Appendix II is a list of musical works selected so that the principal eras, forms, composers, styles, and mediums of music are represented. Other representative works are cited in the text as the occasions arise. Insofar as the activities of the fast-moving record industry can be predicted, these are all works that you should be able to hear on recordings. Many of them you will want to procure for yourself at some time or other, for these are also works that bear repeated hearings. Consider, too, the possibility of examining the scores of the same works in some adequate music library. If you do not play the piano you may still be delighted to discover, after you have reached Chapter 6, that you can at least pick out main themes and other melodies. No harm and perhaps a lot of good can come from this much enterprise and from some other firsthand, inside experiences that are suggested to you from time to time throughout this book.

Examples of music from before the middle of the eighteenth century are likely to be less accessible to you than later ones.

Here are the titles of seven anthologies of earlier music that have very few duplications in their contents. (The dates are those of recent editions or revisions.)

Parrish and Ohl, *Masterpieces of Music Before 1750*. New York: W. W. Norton, 1951; also available on recordings issued by the Haydn Society.

Carl Parrish, *A Treasury of Early Music*. New York: W. W. Norton, 1958.

Johannes Wolf, *Music of the Earlier Times*. New York: Broude Bros., 1946.

Arnold Schering, *History of Music in Examples*. New York: Broude Bros., 1950.

Davison and Apel, *Historical Anthology of Music*, 2 vols. Cambridge: Harvard University Press, 1946 and 1950.

Alfred Einstein, *A Short History of Music* (including 39 complete examples). New York: Alfred Knopf, 1938.

Gerald Abraham (general editor), *The History of Music in Sound*, 10 record albums (RCA Victor) and 11 handbooks (Oxford University Press), from ancient and oriental to present-day music (published in conjunction with *The New Oxford History of Music*, listed at the end of Chapter 3).

Reading about music may tempt you to look further into many special topics. Among standard reference books on music that you are likely to find in most libraries, the following are especially helpful (with dates of recent revisions):

Baker's Biographical Dictionary of Musicians, 5th ed. New York: G. Schirmer, 1958.

Willi Apel, *Harvard Dictionary of Music*. Cambridge: Harvard University Press, 1950.

Percy Scholes, *The Oxford Companion to Music*, 9th ed. New York: Oxford University Press, 1955.

The International Cyclopedia of Music and Musicians, 8th ed. New York: Dodd, Mead, 1958.

Grove's Dictionary of Music and Musicians, 5th ed., 9 vols. New
    York: St. Martin's Press, 1954; supplementary volume scheduled
    for 1960.

For a further discussion of the philosophy underlying the present approach, reference may be made to this author's article,
"Roads to Musical Understanding—an Apologia," in *Bulletin*
of the American Association of University Professors, XXXIX
(1953).

Chapter 2

A Historical Frame of Reference

HISTORICAL VIEWPOINTS, PAST AND PRESENT

Although we do not approach music here by way of its history, a preliminary bird's-eye view will help in several ways. For one thing, it will afford an opportunity to tie music in with the other arts and with history in general. For another, it calls attention to pendulumlike changes of style in all the arts, changes that seem to accompany if not actually stimulate corresponding shifts in the pattern of society. And third, it provides an essential frame of reference to which the various facts, names, forms, and styles of music can be oriented as we come to them.

In taking any such sweeping view we may remind ourselves that history itself is never absolute. Our understanding of it must depend on how the historian chooses to view it. In the nineteenth century, music history was viewed as a kind of "evolutionary" process. Every event was seen as a link in one single chain of events, or as an organic seed out of which the next event blossomed. Thus, a sentence from *Beethoven and His Forerunners,* published by the American Daniel Gregory Mason in 1904, reads: "In the countless centuries before Palestrina, music grew slowly and uniformly, like a plant; in the short three hundred [233!] years between Palestrina's and Beethoven's death it had its inconceivably rich and various blossoming." Other writers spoke of continuous, steady, orderly *progress,* often implying a constantly more complex music. According to these views, Palestrina was a fine enough composer in the sixteenth century; yet only a forerunner of Bach, who was a still greater composer; yet only a forerunner of Beethoven, who was still greater, yet, after all, only paved the way for Brahms and Wagner. Fortunately, the opposite or "devolutionary" view was never applied by music historians, as it was by those art historians who venerated the ancient Greeks above all others and recognized after them chiefly a gradual deterioration.

More recently, in keeping with general historians, music historians have come to feel that music has not necessarily progressed for the sake of posterity, nor followed any one logical continuum throughout its history, nor evolved toward ever greater complexity. Rather, in what men like Spengler and Toynbee have made known as the *cyclic* theory, music is viewed merely as undergoing ceaseless changes from era to era, each change originating in the special needs, tastes, and satisfactions of its particular *era*. Bach is considered to be as great in his way and for his day as Beethoven in his way and for his day. Furthermore, all events are not now regarded as related in a single chain. Some of them seem simply to have coincided in time. And historical truth itself is seen to be not absolute but only relative. Facts are capable of different interpretations depending on the interpreter's time, place, and circumstances. An amusing repercussion of this idea in Modern art is Luigi Pirandello's clever drama *Right You Are, If You Think You Are,* in which each character offers an explanation for his actions that is at once honest or false, depending on whose viewpoint is accepted.

WESTERN MUSIC VIEWED IN HISTORICAL CYCLES

If we agree, then, to regard music history as a series of changes, we will need to know the main cycles or eras in which these changes have taken place. Even the eras will not be absolute but must depend on one's point of view. Were there a completely impartial historian who could stand off and view all of the world's history in a single perspective, he would no doubt decide that eras have succeeded each other steadfastly at almost equal intervals in time. Thus, several music historians observe that the most conspicuous changes leading to a "New Music" actually do seem to have occurred at remarkably equal intervals (every 300 years, especially A.D. 1000, 1300, 1600, and 1900). However, from where we now stand history seems to have sped up. As in the painter's perspective, the closest things loom the largest. Consequently we make a whole era out of the nineteenth century alone, whereas we spread much earlier eras over several centuries because their events seem so much less important at this distance in time. We do this although a scholar concentrating on any one of these eras might see fit to subdivide it into smaller eras— wheels within wheels as it were; and another, writing a broad survey, might prefer to combine several of our eras into one still larger era.

On page 14 is our list, in its briefest form, of the main eras of music in Western civilization. The rough dates at the left indicate how we have viewed the eras as becoming shorter and shorter. Note that they overlap somewhat. The second column— Early Christian, etc.—contains the era names used here and in most recent music histories. These names are used in other arts, too, especially architecture, but do not necessarily correspond in dates. For example, the Classic Era in literature refers to the era of Molière, Corneille, and Racine—more than a century earlier than that of Haydn, Mozart, and Beethoven in music. The remaining three columns suggest other designations that might have been used for these eras, one according to the chief forms, another according to characteristic styles, and another according to great names. As we meet those forms and styles in later chapters a glance back, now and then, at their positions in this chapter's charts should help to keep you oriented.

Note that we begin only with the music of early Christianity.

Era Dates	Terms Used Here and Generally	Possible Form Designations	Possible Style Designations	Possible Great-Name Designations
350-1000	Early Christian	Age of plainchant	Age of monophony	Age of Ambrose and Gregory
850-1600	Medieval-and-Renaissance	Age of the motet and madrigal	Age of modal polyphony	From Guido d'Arezzo to Palestrina
1580-1750	Baroque	Age of the fugue, suite, and early opera	Age of thorough-bass	Age of Bach and Handel
1730-1830	Classic	Age of the sonata	Age of the Alberti bass	Age of Haydn, Mozart, and Beethoven
1790-1910	Romantic	Age of programme music	Age of chromatic harmony	From Schubert to R. Strauss
1890-?	Modern	Age of neoclassic forms	Age of tonal experiments	Age of Stravinsky and Schoenberg

Historical ties have been established with still earlier music, especially that of the Hebrews, Greeks, Romans, and Byzantines, but about the sound of that ancient music we know very little. Exotic music—that of Oriental, primitive, or other non-Western cultures—is generally beyond our scope here. Thus, in the space that we have we shall not attempt to stray far from the mainstreams of Western music.

There follow two, more detailed historical charts (pp. 16–19), which may be studied together. Chart I groups the main styles, forms, and names of music according to the eras just listed. Chart II interrelates other styles, events, and names of Western culture. On the latter chart the vertical lines that define music's main eras are dotted to show that they do not necessarily apply to other fields. On both charts, only the most representative names have been included and only those with some international influence.

Within any one frame these names are listed in approximately chronological order, and sometimes subdivided by nationalities on Chart II. Music terms on Chart I, like the other new terms in this book, will be defined as each makes its first significant appearance (usually in italics). But these definitions may be found at any time by means of the Index, which serves here in place of a glossary and also gives the full names, nationality of birth, and life dates of the main composers discussed. Unfamiliar terms on Chart II may be checked by consulting concise, encyclopedic definitions, such as *Webster's New International Dictionary* gives to main headings in philosophy and the arts. Certain further, broad historical implications in these charts are noted in the final section of this chapter.

Each of music's six main eras has an artistic feel, a cultural climate, a social environment that distinguish it markedly from the others. In conjunction with the historical charts, see the six era summaries given in chronological order opposite Plates 1-6 (after p. 42), the purpose being to suggest something of that feel. By way of further illustration, one representative style of architecture is pictured with each summary—only one, to be sure, out of the several that are embraced in every one of our broad music eras. The intention is not to establish specific parallels, as, let us say, between a Doric order in architecture and a Dorian mode in music; but rather to convey more general parallels of style such as are understood in the terms "ethos" and "pathos"—defined later in this chapter. You can do still more to capture the feel of each era if you listen to representative music as you read these summaries. (See Appendix II for recommended listening.) You will have a still better temporal concept of the eras if you actually memorize the life dates of a few of the greatest masters. Start with the "three B's"—(a too-restrictive label coined by the nineteenth-century conductor and pianist von Bülow)—since J. S. Bach (1685-1750), Beethoven (1770-1827), and Brahms (1833-1897) were obliging enough to be born in alphabetic order in the

CHART I. The Principal

		Early Christian	Medieval-and-Renaissance	Baroque (Rococo)	Classic	Romantic (Early Romantic)	Romantic (Nationalistic and Impressionistic)	Modern
ERA								
YEAR (A.D.)		350 850	1000 1580	1600 1730	1750 1790	1790 1830	1830 1890	1910 ?
CHIEF STYLES	QUALITY	Pathos	Ethos	Pathos	Ethos	Pathos	Pathos	Ethos
	TONAL SYSTEM	Modality	Modality	Major and Minor Tonality	Major and Minor Tonality	Major and Minor Tonality	Major and Minor Tonality	Tonal Experiments
	PROGRESSION	Phrase Grouping	Motivic Play	Motivic Play	Phrase Grouping	Phrase Grouping	Phrase Grouping	Motivic Play
CHIEF VOCAL FORMS	SACRED	Plainchant in the Divine Offices and the Mass	Organum / Superstructure motet / Polyphonic Mass / Fugal motet / Anthem	Chorale / Cantata / Oratorio / Mass / Motet / Anthem	Oratorio / Mass		Oratorio / Mass	Oratorio
	SECULAR		Monophonic and polyphonic verse forms / Madrigal and other part-songs	Masque / Opera / Solo and part-songs	Opera / Solo and part-songs		Opera / Art-song	Opera / Art-song
CHIEF INSTRUMENTAL FORMS			Fantasy and programme pieces / Ricercare / Dances / Canzon	Fantasy and programme pieces / Ballet / Fugue / Suite / Trio sonata / Solo concerto / Concerto grosso / Overture	Fantasy and programme pieces / Sonata in various guises / Solo concerto / Overture		Fantasy and programme pieces / Symphonic poem / Dances, suite / Sonata in various guises / Solo concerto / Overture	Fantasy and programme pieces / Fugue / Sonata in various guises / Solo concerto / Concerto grosso / Overture

Eras of Music History

ERA	Early Christian	Medieval-and-Renaissance	Baroque (Rococo)	Classic	Romantic (Early Romantic) (Nationalistic and Impressionistic)	Modern
YEAR (A.D.)	350	850 | 1000 ... 1580	1600 ... 1730 | 1750	... 1790	1830 ... 1890	1910 ?
QUALITY	Pathos	Ethos	Pathos	Ethos	Pathos	Ethos
CHIEF STYLES — TONAL SYSTEM	Modality		Major and Minor Tonality			Tonal Experiments
PROGRESSION	Phrase Grouping	Motivic Play		Phrase Grouping		Motivic Play
GREAT NAMES — ITALIAN	St. Ambrose Pope Gregory	Guido d'Arezzo Landino Palestrina A. and G. Gabrieli	Monteverdi Frescobaldi Corelli A. Scarlatti Vivaldi D. Scarlatti	Tartini Boccherini	Rossini Verdi Puccini	

FRENCH		Schools of St.
		  Martial and
		  Notre Dame
		Machault
		Jannequin
		Goudimel
			Lully
			Couperin
			
			Rameau
				Grétry	Berlioz
					Bizet
					Franck
					Saint-Saëns
					Fauré
						Debussy
						d'Indy
						Ravel
						Milhaud

GERMAN and AUSTRIAN		Gallus Hasler M. Praetorius	Schütz Buxtehude Kuhnau Bach Handel Telemann	Bach's sons: W. F., C. P. E., J. C. Gluck Mozart Haydn Beethoven	Weber Schubert Mendelssohn Schumann Wagner Bruckner Brahms Mahler R. Strauss	Schoenberg Hindemith

OTHER		LOW COUNTRIES:
		  Dufay
		  Okeghem
		  Isaak
		  Des Prés
		  Lassus
		SPANISH:
		  Morales
		  Victoria
		ENGLISH:
		  Tallis
		  Byrd
		  Dowland
		  Gibbons
			ENGLISH:
			  Purcell
					POLISH:
					  Chopin
					HUNGARIAN:
					  Liszt
					BOHEMIAN:
					  Dvořák
					RUSSIAN:
					  Mussorgsky
					  Tchaikovsky
					NORWEGIAN:
					  Grieg
					SPANISH:
					  Albeniz
					FINNISH:
					  Sibelius
					AMERICAN:
					  MacDowell
						RUSSIAN:
						  Scriabin
						  Stravinsky
						  Prokofiev
						HUNGARIAN:
						  Bartók
						ENGLISH:
						  Vaughan
						  Williams
						SWISS:
						  Bloch
						AMERICAN:
						  Gershwin
						  Copland

CHART II. Concurrent

MUSIC ERAS (for comparison) YEAR (A.D.)	(Early Christian) 350 850	(Medieval-and-Renaissance) 1000 1580	(Baroque) 1600 1730	(Classic) (Rococo) 1750 1790	(Romantic) (Early Romantic) 1830	(Modern) (Nationalistic and Impressionistic) 1890 1910 ?
LITERARY	Manuscripts of the New Testament, the Church Fathers, and the ancient classics	Epic romances of Roland and Arthur; Liturgical drama; Lyric and narrative poetry and prose: Walther von der Vogelweide, Dante, Petrarch, Boccaccio, Chaucer, Ariosto Satirical romances: Rabelais, Cervantes Sonnets and odes: Ronsard	Comedies and tragedies: Shakespeare, Jonson; Corneille, Molière, Racine; Vega, Tirso de Molina Epic poetry: Milton Satirical poetry: Pope Satirical prose: Swift Social novels: Richardson, Fielding	Philosophic novels: Voltaire, Rousseau The French Encyclopedists German poetry and drama from "storm and stress" to idealism: Lessing, Schiller, Herder, Goethe	Incident and character novels: Hugo, Balzac, Flaubert, Scott, Manzoni, Dickens Poetry of man and nature: Wordsworth Victorian idyls: Tennyson Realistic and impressionistic novels: Tolstoi, James, France, Hardy, Conrad *Gesamtkunstwerk*: Wagner	Prose experimentalists: Gide, Proust, Joyce, Faulkner, Hemingway, Mann
PHILOSOPHIC	Divine ethics: Jerome, Augustine, Boethius, Isidore of Seville, Alcuin, Erigena	Scholasticism: Aquinas Humanism: Erasmus Politics: Machiavelli	Scientific method: Bacon Rationalism: Descartes Political liberalism: Locke Scientific synthesis: Newton	Empiricism: Hume Critical idealism: Kant	Idealism: Hegel Liberalism: Mill Evolution: Darwin Communism: Marx Anti-intellectualism: Nietzsche Instrumentalism: Dewey	Logical analysis: Russell Psychoanalysis: Freud
ARCHITECTURAL	Functional arches in baptisteries	Basilican churches; vaulted, cruciform Romanesque abbeys with round arched openings; complex Gothic cathedrals with ribbed vaulting, pointed arches, and integral sculpture Palaces: back to classic Greek symmetry as found in Roman orders and arches	Churches and royal palaces: asymmetry and freedom within organized line and space, using orders in classic proportions	Government buildings: literal return to classic Roman, then Greek styles; with emphasis more on abstract form than function	Theaters, opera houses, colleges: revivals of Roman, Gothic, and later styles and forms in spirit of historical and national eclecticism	Industrial buildings (including factories and skyscrapers): functionalism, absence of ornament, new materials (F. L. Wright)

Trends in Other Fields

MUSIC ERAS (for comparison)	(Early Christian)	(Medieval-and-Renaissance)	(Baroque)	(Classic) (Rococo)	(Romantic) (Early Romantic)	(Modern) (Nationalistic and Impressionistic)
YEAR (A.D.)	350	850|1000	1580|1600	1730|1750	1790|1830	1890|1910 ?

PAINTING, SCULPTURE, AND MINOR ARTS

	(Early Christian)	(Medieval-and-Renaissance)	(Baroque)	(Classic/Rococo)	(Romantic)	(Modern)
	Biblical figures and stories: frescoes and mosaics on church walls, painted chapel panels, book miniatures; Byzantine decorative detail; absence of perspective. Sculpture: chiefly figurines, carvings, reliefs on sarcophagi, and architectural ornament (portals, columns, pulpits)	Stained glass windows; naturalistic frescoes: Giotto; rich painting sculpture; marble inlays—in Romanesque churches or Gothic cathedrals. Sacred and secular subjects: figures, landscapes, genres, portraits, pageants; virtuosic mastery of oils, colors, texture, chiaroscuro, anatomy, detail, design in murals and pictures (Masaccio, Raphael, da Vinci, Michelangelo, Tintoretto; H. and J. Van Eyck, Breughel, Rubens, Rembrandt, Vermeer; Dürer, Grünewald, Holbein; El Greco, Velázquez, Poussin) Sculpture in church portals, monuments, and statues (Ghiberti, Donatello, Michelangelo, Bernini) Gobelin tapestries	Chiefly secular Landscapes (Lorrain) French court life (Watteau) Portraits, aristocratic (Boucher) and middle class (Hogarth)	subjects by modern Bourgeois life (Fragonard) Romantic ruins (H. Robert) Still life (Chardin) Aristocratic portraits (Reynolds, Gainsborough) Fading Spanish aristocracy (Goya) Byzantine mysticism (Blake) French grace in sculpture (Houdon) Ancient classics and revolution scenes (David)	schools: Majestic nature (Turner) Dramatic sweep (Delacroix) Sentimental landscapes (Corot)	Abstractionism: Cézanne, Picasso Expressionism, primitive and oriental influence: Van Gogh, Matisse Sculpture: abstractionism, exotic influences, return to architectural uses, particularized materials (Moore, Calder) Everyday life, influence of photography (Manet, Degas) Impressionism (Monet, Renoir) Sculpture, realistic (Rodin) and simple (Saint-Gaudens)

GENERAL WESTERN HISTORY

	(Early Christian)	(Medieval-and-Renaissance)	(Baroque)	(Classic/Rococo)	(Romantic)	(Modern)
	Changes leading to new European states: first general council of Christian Church and Nicene Creed (325); barbarian and Mohammedan ascendancy; civil law developed by Justinian's and Germanic codes; Merovingian and Carolingian dynasties, partition into Italian, German, and French feudal states; Crusades, religious zeal, towns and commerce, conflict of princes and popes; peak of feudalism; Hundred Years' War; peak of Ottoman conquests	Growth of modern thought, government, society, and religion: Age of discoveries, worldwide colonization by Spain (world power), France, England (under Elizabeth), Holland; printing and spread of learning; aids to astronomy, navigation, and medicine Protestant Reformation Rise of capitalism	Peace of Westphalia (1648), ending Thirty Years' War and setting "balance of power" English Commonwealth and Restoration, stronger parliament Louis XIV and French power Russian contact with Europe under Peter the Great	Frederick the Great and Prussian power Seven Years' War, loss in French power and prestige Era of revolution in America, France Washington, first U.S. President, inaugurated 1789	Napoleonic empire Congress of Vienna (1815), setting many boundaries Revolutionary movements; imperial, economic, and capital-labor conflicts; military rivalry Industry and commerce expanded by advances in transportation, communication, machinery, new products U.S. Civil War, ending 1865	Expansion, nationalism, material progress: Strong national states Colonial and economic rivalry leading to world-wide wars New era of science and technology Efforts toward world federation

19

three successive eras that contributed most to the standard repertoire of our concert world.

THE STYLE PENDULUM IN ART HISTORY

Further consideration of our historical charts leads to some
provocative generalizations about the broad cycles of art history
and of music history in particular. Especially interesting are the
ways in which certain styles and tastes seem to have oscillated
from era to era with almost the regularity of a pendulum.

First, consider the contrast of ethos and pathos styles. *Ethos*
and *pathos* are terms preferred here (thanks to *The Commonwealth of Art* by Curt Sachs, listed at the end of the chapter)
to denote that opposition more familiarly if less adequately expressed by antitheses like classic and romantic, or static and
dynamic. Ethos art is objective art; it seeks to get at one ideal, perfect representation of its subject through laws that are perma-
nent, absolute, and rational. It avoids extremes and it remains
pure, unconfused by any disconcerting mixture of other arts.
Pathos art is subjective art; it appeals more to the emotions than
to the intellect by revealing its subject as it has happened to appear in actual living, no matter how distorted, extreme, or illogical. It seeks out the personal and colorful as influenced by the
time and the locale.

An example in painting and then one in music may help to
make this basic opposition clearer. Painting offers many analogies
that promote an understanding of music. Here are two pictures
(see Plate 7a, 7b), one showing a lane of chestnut trees as they
happened to appear when the photographer came upon them,
the other showing an idealized composition of this very scene by
the artist Cézanne. The painting evinces strong ethos tendencies.
It shows the trees in their "ideal" form, with leaves. It eliminates
extrinsic matter such as the marble railing at the back right of the
photograph. And it further "purifies" the scene by regularizing
the rows of trees and their branches, by reducing the design to

fewer trees and fewer significant directions of line, and by modifying the perspective so as to keep the picture nearly on one plane. (See the more detailed analysis on p. 50 in Erle Loran, *Cézanne's Composition*, Los Angeles, 1943.) Another painter might have preferred to develop the pathos qualities in this same scene, perhaps exaggerating its accidents of nature and other irregularities.

To point to a similar process in music one might show how the sounds of nature in a thunderstorm are neatly organized in Rossini's "ideal" thunderstorm that occurs during the "Overture" to his opera *William Tell*. But since most music is idealized sound, anyway—that is, since it is usually removed from the literal sounds of nature—let us be more to the point by finding the pathos as well as the ethos style in composed music. Sharply contrasted ethos and pathos styles are found, for instance, among the *Preludes* of Chopin (Appendix II, No. 1). If we list certain of the antitheses by which Curt Sachs develops these terms (*The Commonwealth of Art*) we can illustrate those distinctions with at least the following specific traits in *Preludes* nos. 7 and 18:

Ethos: *Prelude in A Major,* no. 7	Pathos: *Prelude in F Minor,* no. 18
"perfection"	"imperfection"
regular phrases	irregular phrases
symmetrical design	asymmetrical design
"impersonality"	"personality"
plain harmony	colorful harmony
regular rhythmic patterns	irregular rhythmic patterns
"limitation"	"boundlessness"
narrow pitch range	extreme pitch range
moderate dynamics	extreme dynamics
"beauty"	"character"
smooth contour of line	jagged contour of line
"serenity"	"passion"
untroubled harmony	sharply dissonant harmony

Curiously, the distinction between ethos and pathos styles usually underlies the pairings of composers or other artists that are made to sum up an artistic generation. Mozart and Haydn, Keats and Shelley, Monet and Renoir are examples of such pairings. The mature works of Mozart and Haydn may sound very similar on first hearing, for they do have certain broad features in common, especially the forms and idioms that were the common currency of the Classic Era. But more specific and penetrating comparisons show these works to be complementary, or rather, mutually exclusive in many respects. Within the predominantly ethos style of the whole Classic Era, Mozart often is to Haydn as ethos is to pathos. In other words, these men describe the extremes, not simply the middle of their generation's road. Much the same can be said, respectively, for such familiar pairings as Palestrina and Lassus, Handel and Bach, Schubert and Schumann, Brahms and Wagner, or Ravel and Debussy. (In fact, in this book some of our best opportunities to know the great masters grow out of this sort of comparison—comparison and synthesis being prime means of converting factual information into knowledge and understanding.)

So far, we have only considered ethos and pathos styles as being coexistent, whether in the same generation or even in the same composer. In an increasingly broad and general sense there are oscillations between these styles in successive phases of an era, in successive eras themselves (as noted on the charts), or even in successive civilizations—wheels within wheels, again. It is interesting to note how a new era first reveals itself not so much through positive traits of its own as through an intense desire to negate the styles that had just prevailed. We live in a predominantly ethos era. Our present-day composers can no more feel at home in what they regard as sentimental effusion in a Romantic, pathos piece like *Hearts and Flowers* (or much worthier examples) than our present-day authors could feel right if they were to revert to the style of Horatio Alger (or much worthier examples).

If anything, the artists of one era are more likely to feel in tune with the still previous era in a sort of grandparent relationship. The extraordinary interest in Mozart today, one aspect of neo-classicism in the Modern Era, may be partly explained by the fact that Mozart's music is the very heart of another ethos era.

At a still broader level in the style pendulum one may regard the period around 1600 (or 1500 in the opinion of others) as a grand dividing line between two groups of eras making up one giant cycle. Even at this level of generalization, where many exceptions must be disregarded, certain large trends can be discerned. To begin with, pre-1600 art is predominantly ethos in quality; post-1600 art is predominantly pathos. Second, pre-1600 art is predominantly *additive* and *open* in form, its components being strung together without planned interrelations or limits; post-1600 art is predominantly *integrated* and *closed* in form, everything conspiring toward one organized whole. Third, pre-1600 art finds its most original and significant expression in architecture and architectural ornament; post-1600 art in music and music drama. Fourth, pre-1600 art centers primarily around sacred interests; post-1600 art around secular interests. And fifth, pre-1600 music is influenced more by vocal, post-1600 music more by instrumental, considerations. The limit for these sweeping generalizations must be fixed early in the Modern Era, for with such evidences as our great new forces in society and the completely new styles in architecture one may suppose that we are entering a new giant cycle with its own grand dividing line among groups of eras yet to come.

As for the nature of any one era, the arcs are appropriate symbols at the head of the charts. Each era has its own rise, peak, and decline—its youth in which spontaneous enthusiasm and emotion prevail, its maturity in which intellect and emotion or form and content counterbalance, and its old age in which finical theory seems to supplant emotionally inspired creation. Thus, the sudden, somewhat haphazard rise of opera in northern

Italy, its mastery in the noble style of Alessandro Scarlatti, and the stereotyping of it by his Neapolitan successors illustrate these three phases in the Baroque Era.

The overlap of the arcs on the charts is significant, too. That the successive eras overlap is simply another way of saying that one era dies while the next begins. In our own day we have witnessed the death only two years apart of Richard Strauss, one of the last great Romantics, and Arnold Schoenberg, one of the first great Modernists. Occasionally a great composer has lived during the overlap and kept pace with the times. The foremost example was Beethoven, who began as a Classicist and ended as a Romantic, though a thoroughly special and individual Romantic.

The overlaps themselves, however, have mostly been peopled by lesser men, albeit men individual enough to give the period a name all its own (as Rococo, Early Romantic, Impressionistic). Such brief periods are transitions—decompression chambers, so to speak—between the extremes of the main eras. However, art is always changing. One must not think of the main eras as being any more static than the periods of overlap.

The overlapping of eras also points up the fact that each era, though it turns away, has roots in the one before. Or, conversely, each era contains some seeds of the next. Observe the dashes from column to column on Chart I. Sometimes only the name of a musical form, with but little of its same meaning, survives in the next era. For instance, "sonata" as used in the Baroque Era came to imply some very different traits in the Classic Era.

Finally, although the era designations do not necessarily correspond in the several arts, profound interrelations between music, the other arts, and world events cannot escape notice. These are but hinted in the summaries beside Plates 1-6 of each era. As suggested earlier, such interrelations are likely to exist not so much between specific facts as between general style trends. The coincidence of domestic discord in Mozart's real life and a particular sharp dissonance in his opera *Don Giovanni* can hardly be more than coincidence. On the other hand, there is a very perceivable relationship in the Rococo period between the elegant, bejeweled court life of Louis XIV and the elegant, highly ornamental harpsichord music of his chief court composer Couperin.

SELECTED READINGS

Warren D. Allen, *Philosophies of Music History*. New York: American Book Company, 1939.

Glen Haydon, *Introduction to Musicology*. Chapel Hill: University of North Carolina Press, 1959 [1941], Chapter VIII.

Curt Sachs, *The Commonwealth of Art*. New York: W. W. Norton, 1946.

An Introduction to Literature and the Fine Arts ("a collaborative study of the arts of literature, of music, and of architecture, sculpture, and painting in the development of the Western tradition"). East Lansing: Michigan State College Press, 1950.

Cannon, Johnson, and Waite, *The Art of Music*. New York: Thomas Y. Crowell, 1960.

Paul Lang, *Music in Western Civilization*. New York: W. W. Norton, 1941.

Curt Sachs, *Our Musical Heritage*. Englewood Cliffs (N.J.): Prentice-Hall, 1955.

Peter Garvie (ed.), *Music and Western Man*. New York: Philosophical Library, 1958.

Donald Jay Grout, *A History of Western Music*. New York: W. W. Norton, 1960.

W. W. Norton has projected separate histories of six eras in Western music as follows:

Gustave Reese, *Music in the Middle Ages* (including the Early Christian Era), 1940.

Gustave Reese, *Music in the Renaissance Era*, 1959.

Manfred Bukofzer, *Music in the Baroque Era*, 1947.

Paul Lang, *Music in the Classic Era,* in preparation.
Alfred Einstein, *Music in the Romantic Era,* 1947.
Adolfo Salazar, *Music in Our Time,* 1946.
Oxford University Press has projected a similar series in eleven volumes, *The New Oxford History of Music,* now in progress.

Part II

The Elements and Styles of Music

Chapter 3

The Nature and Instruments of Musical Sound

SOME ELEMENTARY ACOUSTICS—PITCH, INTENSITY, TIMBRE

Music is an organization of sounds in time (the longs and shorts of rhythm) and in aural "space" (the highs and lows of melody). In this chapter we look into the nature and production of musical sound itself, saving rhythm and melody for Chapters 4 and 5, respectively. First come certain elements of *acoustics,* the science of sound.

Musical *sound* is made by regular vibrations, as distinguished from the irregular vibrations of a mere noise. There are four usual agents of regular vibrations in musical sounds. One is a string stretched between two fixed points, as on a violin or harp. Another is an air column enclosed in a stationary pipe, such as a trumpet. A third is a membrane stretched across a hoop, as on a kettle drum. And a fourth is a resonant solid, such as a wooden bar of a xylophone. In Modern times a fifth agent is found in an alternating electrical current when its oscillations are amplified by a loud-speaker. The vibrations go through the air as waves of density and rarefaction, causing sympathetic vibrations in the eardrum. (The air itself travels no more than does the water in a choppy sea, the flag that flutters, or the stationary freight car that jerks when another is coupled to it.)

Whether the *pitch* that results is high or low depends on the frequency of the vibrations (or the length of the sound waves, if you prefer). The faster the vibrations (or shorter the waves), the higher the pitch. Vibrations can be received by the ear in any amount from a low of about 20 to a high of about 20,000 per second, the extremes depending on aural differences from one individual to another. Their frequency in turn depends on five possible attributes in one or another of the four vibrating agents: length, slackness, density, diameter, and area. Increasing any of

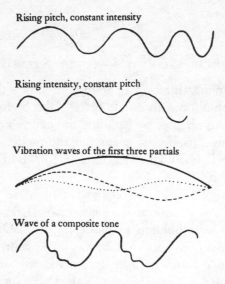

Rising pitch, constant intensity

Rising intensity, constant pitch

Vibration waves of the first three partials

Wave of a composite tone

these lowers the pitch; decreasing raises it. The performer most often controls the length during performance—for example, when he shortens the effective length of a violin string by stopping it with his finger. Note that the extent (amplitude) of the vibrations affects *intensity* or volume, not pitch. The greater the extent—that is, the greater the crests and valleys of the sound waves—the louder the tone.

Now comes a phenomenon under the heading of *timbre*, which is of the greatest importance to tone quality, sonority, instrument design, hearing, and harmony. Every musical tone has an individual timbre (color or quality) owing to the fact that it is actually not one simple tone but a composite of various *partials* derived by natural laws from the fundamental (lowest) tone that you hear (Fig. 13, p. 79). In accordance with the mathematical series known as a harmonic progression, a string or a column of air vibrates not only as a whole, but in halves, thirds, fourths, fifths, and so on, all at the same time. The whole gives the fundamental partial, the halves give a higher tone with twice as many vibrations, the thirds a still higher tone with three times as many vibrations as the whole, and so on, though at constantly diminishing intervals of pitch and intensity. A membrane or solid may

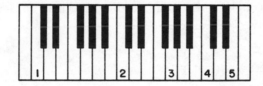

vibrate in accordance with this same or some other mathematical series.

The presence of upper partials is readily shown at the piano. With the right hand gently depress the keys corresponding to the second, third, fourth, and fifth partials of a tone (as numbered on the adjoining keyboard) so as to raise the dampers without making the strings sound. Now if you strike the first partial or fundamental forcefully you will cause the other, higher four tones to be excited into sound by sympathetic vibration with the partials of the fundamental. But if you silently depress any other tones—some black keys, for example—there will be no response when the same fundamental is struck.

Differences in timbre itself are determined primarily by the relative weakness or strength, or the actual absence or presence, of partials in the composite tone. Instrument construction, the acoustics of the hall, any bunching of successive "cycles" of waves in the air, the range of a loud-speaker, or the manner of performance—any or all of these may tend to inhibit or reinforce certain partials. If there were not these differences, all instruments would sound alike. Orchestras would be made up of only one kind of instrument, with variations only in size so as to produce a full range of pitches and intensities. As it is, we can speak of the "nasal-sounding" oboe, the "silvery" flute, the "mellow-sounding" trombone, and many other qualities (Appendix II, No. 2). Timbre is also affected by the nature of the ear—so much so, for example, that we are even made to hear low "resultant" tones on the pipe organ that do not exist in reality. Reverberations, temperature, and extraneous noises, from bow squeaks and horn gurgles to coughs and program rattling, also may be factors in the total quality of a musical sound.

ORCHESTRAL INSTRUMENTS CLASSIFIED

Although there are more scientific bases for classifying instruments, we usually distinguish between *strings, winds,* and *percussion* among standard orchestral instruments because of obvious differences not only in physical make-up but in timbre, vibrating agent, and function. With regard to function, the strings have been called the chief instruments of melody, the winds of harmony, and the percussion instruments of rhythm, though the exceptions surely must be as numerous as instances that follow the rule.

By distinguishing the means of activating the vibrating agents we arrive at useful subclassifications in each of these three main groups. Thus, the strings on stringed instruments may be bowed, as on the violin; plucked, as on the harp; or struck, as on the piano. The air column in wind instruments may be activated by blowing past a single or through a double artificial reed, as in the "woodwinds"; or by blowing through a cupped mouthpiece, with the lips serving as a double reed, as in the "brasses"; or by blowing across a sharp-edged hole, as in the flute. (But observe that the terms "woodwinds" and "brasses" are not wholly reliable sub-classifications as such, except by tradition; for the instruments with artificial reeds are often made of metal, the instruments with cupped mouthpieces might be made of other metals than brass, and in the manner of blowing as well as certain peculiarities of timbre the flute must fall somewhere between the two categories.) Percussion instruments may be struck, shaken, plucked, or rubbed. However, a more useful distinction here is that between instruments with definite pitch, such as the timpani, and those without, such as the bass drum. While the piano and organ may be classified as stringed and wind instruments, respectively, the special nature of the keyboard earns them separate treatment in a later section.

Finally, a basis for sub-subclassifications is range. Almost every stringed or wind instrument (and many a percussion instrument, too) belongs to a family of its type. In other words, it has once appeared or still exists in a variety of sizes and ranges all the way from a large instrument in the bass range to a small one in the soprano range. (See the average voice ranges in Fig. 1, p. 47.) Thus, the relatively new saxophone belongs to a complete family of six ranges, all members of which remain in use. On the other hand, the flute, which stems from antiquity, is only rarely heard now in its bass and alto forms, being chiefly known as a high or soprano instrument, with a still higher member of the family in the piccolo. Whereas the piano, harp, and organ embrace the orchestra's entire range of some seven octaves, the bowed or human-blown instruments rarely exceed the two to three octaves that the trained singer of corresponding range can manage. Actually, many instruments originally came into importance, during the Medieval-and-Renaissance Era, as reinforcements or replacements of particular voices in choral singing. This historical fact is still recalled in such terms as tenor trombone or the French word "alto" for viola.

Here follows a classification of standard orchestral instruments,

General Range ↓	STRINGS		WINDS			
	Bowed	Plucked	Reed		Sharp-Edged Hole	Cupped Mouthpiece
			Single	*Double*		
high soprano			E♭ clarinet		piccolo	
soprano	violin		B♭ or A clarinet	oboe	flute	trumpet (B♭)
alto	viola	harp	E♭ clarinet and basset horn alto saxophone (E♭)	English horn (F)		French horn (F)
tenor	cello			bassoon		tenor trombone
bass	double bass		bass clarinet (B♭)	contrabassoon		bass trombone tuba

PERCUSSION	
definite pitch	kettle drums, bells, chimes, celesta, xylophone
indefinite pitch	snare drum, bass drum, cymbals, tambourine, triangle, gong

first by general make-up and timbre, then by vibrating agent, and finally by principal range, except for the classification of percussion instruments just mentioned. Note that the piano and organ are not "standard" orchestral instruments. Pitch names are used in identifying certain "transposing" instruments, as explained on page 38. The illustrations of instruments being performed singly, in small ensembles, and in full orchestra and band that apply to the present chapter and Chapter 7 will help you to visualize this classification and the descriptions of instruments that follow

(Plates 8-15). How the various instruments are combined in the standard instrumental groupings will come up as an aspect of texture and sonority in Chapter 7. As for the sounds of the individual instruments, listen to Benjamin Britten's *Variations and Fugue on a Theme of Purcell* (Appendix II, No. 3), a lively work deliberately composed to display each main instrument at its idiomatic best in both solo and ensemble passages. There are also several recorded anthologies of similar purpose that depend for illustrations on a variety of quotations from the standard literature, sometimes prefaced by verbal commentaries and enhanced by illustrated booklets. Representative of these anthologies are *The Complete Orchestra* (issued by the Music Education Record Corporation) and the more comprehensive Vox *Spotlight* series in five albums (brass, keyboard, percussion, strings, and woodwinds).

STRINGED INSTRUMENTS

The *violin* family is the chief among numerous families of stringed instruments (Plate 9). It includes the violin (or fiddle, colloquially) and the slightly larger viola, both held under the chin; the cello (short for violoncello), which rests between the knees; and the bass (short for string-, double-, or contrabass, or bass viol), played from a standing position. This family came into lasting importance in Italy during the Baroque Era, not only in chamber and solo music but as the heart of the orchestra. Some of its most characteristic music was written by Corelli and Vivaldi and some of its finest instruments were made in Cremona by Amati, Stradivari, and Guarneri. (However, the fabulous prices that these "name" instruments command do not necessarily prove them to be superior to the best present-day makes.)

The essential parts of the violin are its body, fingerboard, tailpiece, and bridge, as well as the sound post and bass-bar within the body. The four strings, made of wire, gut, wire-wound gut, or nylon, are fastened between the tailpiece and the pegs in the pegbox at the scroll end of the fingerboard. But their effective length is shorter, being that between the bridge and a "nut" or ridge just short of the pegbox. Here is how the performer controls the pitch when the strings are not merely played "open"—that is, when they must be stopped by the fingers. (The thumb is not used to stop violin or viola strings.) By shifting to positions successively closer to the bridge, where the string must be stopped at ever smaller intervals, higher and higher tones can be produced. Conversely, the spacings between stops become wider on the lower, deeper instruments, since the strings become longer (and somewhat thicker, too). Thus, a mere leaning of the finger may

(scroll end of the violin)

open:	G string		D string		A string		E string
1st finger:	A	same	E	same	B	same	F(#)
2d finger:	B	pitch	F(#)	pitch	C(#)	pitch	G(#)
3d finger:	C	as	G	as	D	as	A
(4th finger):	(D)✓		(A)✓		(E)✓		(B)

be enough to advance one tone near the top of the violin range, whereas the whole span of the hand is needed to advance one tone in the lower range of the double bass.

Rolling the finger to and fro produces a pitch *vibrato*, a warm effect when not overdone. Lightly touching a string at any of its divisions ("nodes") in the harmonic series produces an appealing whistling sound known as "harmonics." When a mute is placed on the bridge a hushed, sweet sound results. Occasionally the string is plucked ("pizzicato") by either hand, but mostly it is bowed by a springy concave stick strung with horse hair. When the bow is drawn, the violin string moves with it slightly before snapping back, which act repeats fast enough to produce the vibrations necessary to sound. The right-hand control of the bow is as much of a skill as the left-hand control of pitch, not to mention the coordination of the two hands. (If you have the opportunity, try simply to pull the bow evenly and slowly across one string of a violin, staying midway between bridge and fingerboard.) An extraordinary variety of bowings is available to the player—short, broad, crisp, staccato, bounced, "hammered," and many more. Some bowings strongly affect timbre, such as those that get near the fingerboard or near the bridge, resulting in flute-like or glassy sounds. To shift from one string to any other, the player rotates his bow arm in a vertical arc, the strings being set apart by notches on the arched bridge. Double- or triple-stops occur when two or three strings are sounded simultaneously. With all these and numerous other possibilities, is it any wonder that the stringed instruments are commonly rated second only to the voice in their expressive capabilities?

The older *viol* family, popular in the Renaissance and Baroque Eras, went out after the violin family came in, although its members have been revived of late for the performance of older music. Viols have flat backs, sloped shoulders, fretted fingerboards, and a much thinner, gentler tone, produced by a curved-out bow. Still older is the Medieval *vielle* family, which has also been revived (Plate 8).

The *lute,* a plucked instrument that flourished at the same time, was the domestic instrument then as the piano is today. It has a fretted fingerboard, a body shaped like half of a pear, and usually about six pairs (courses) of strings along with up to six more bass strings that simply resonate without pitch alteration by the performer. The lute, too, comes in a variety of sizes. Its nearest relative still in common use in various regions today is the mandolin. A successor to the lute, especially in eighteenth- and nineteenth-century Italy and Spain, was the guitar, which has an extensive and not undistinguished literature of its own and still can claim exponents of the highest artistry in men like Andrés Segovia.

The *harp* is now the only standard plucked stringed instrument in the orchestra. It is usually a "double-action" harp, meaning that by a system of seven pedals each string is capable of two half-step changes in pitch other than its original tuning.

WIND INSTRUMENTS

In *wind instruments* (Plate 10) the tension on the reed and the length (if not the diameter) of the resonating air column determine the pitch cooperatively, the phenomenon of partials playing an important part. By regulating the tension of his lips and hence that of the separate reed where one is used, the performer selects approximately the partial that will stand out and thus the general region of his pitch. By regulating the exact length of the pipe, he selects a specific tone to be resonated within that region by the air column. The pipe's length may be shortened by uncovering successive holes so that the air comes out sooner, as on the clarinet. Or it may be lengthened by extending an inner slide, as on the trombone; or by opening valves that cause the air to detour through crooks of various lengths, as on the French horn or trumpet. Since the lips can choose among several partials from each length of pipe by "overblowing," it should be clear how an instrument like the trumpet, with but three piston valves, has not only enough fingerings for the thirty-odd tones in its range but optional fingerings in several instances.

Rotary valves on the horn, piston valves on the trumpet, and keys on the woodwinds were not perfected until the early nineteenth century. Therefore the use of such instruments was more limited in the art music of previous centuries. The continuing use today of *transposing instruments*—for instance, a horn *in F* —dates back to a time when an instrument had to be built in the key of the piece in question because it lacked the mechanical devices needed to play in more than one or two keys. Then a performer either had to have instruments of more than one size on hand, just as most clarinetists still keep both B-flat and A clarinets, or he required some expedient means of changing the length of his instrument, such as the different sized crooks that a horn player could exchange as necessary.

Present-day connoisseurs of wind instruments sometimes argue that timbres have depreciated in artistic quality in the process of being "mechanized." However, the prime determinants in wind timbres are shape and size rather than mechanics. Whether the bore of the pipe or the mouthpiece is long, short, wide, narrow, conical, cylindrical; whether it flares out in a bell or bulb; whether the reed is stiff or soft, large or small, thick or thin—any of these factors must affect the timbre in the various ranges of the instrument, producing brilliant or shrill or weak high tones, sinister or mellow or thick low tones, and all the other distinctive sounds that you hear.

The chief problems in the performance of wind instruments are proper breath support, sensitive control of *embouchure* or lip position, finger or slide agility, and the niceties of attack and release. To appreciate the problem of embouchure recall how the lips must be set for whistling. Anyone trying a wind instrument for the first time will not even produce a tone until he manages to make some such setting. A wind instrument tone may be perfectly smooth or it may be enhanced by a slight "natural" vibrato, though only a slight one if it is in good taste. The usual problem in "attacking" a tone is to start it cleanly, with much the same T sound that might be made if a piece of thread were ejected from the tip of the tongue. The usual problem in releasing it is to let it come to rest smoothly, without a parting gasp or last-minute distortion, much as a motorist tries to come to a smooth stop without a final jerk of the brakes.

The modern *flute* is called transverse because it is held laterally like a fife while the air is blown across a hole in its side. Another ancestor is the Medieval-and-Renaissance recorder, blown through one end like a flageolet or whistle. The recorder in various sizes has become very popular again today as a pleasant, easy-to-learn instrument for amateurs, playing alone or in groups. The flute timbres are among the most valuable in the orchestral palette, from a soft yet penetrating and full tone in the low register to a rather flat, glassy tone in the middle, and a shrill, clear tone in the high register. Still shriller and higher is the "little flute" or (*flauto*) *piccolo,* actually the highest-pitched instrument of the orchestra.

The standard soprano *clarinet* in B-flat, chief among the single-reed winds, has been in general use only since Mozart's time. Lower, deeper, more portentous sounding members of the clarinet family won more and more use in the nineteenth century, as in the many outstanding examples afforded by Wagner. Like most of the other larger winds the larger clarinets are bent to avoid unwieldy length. This convenience is not possible, obviously, on stringed and percussion instruments. The low, cavernous-sounding, "chalumeau" register and the high, brilliant-sounding, "clarino" register provide two strongly contrasted timbres on the clarinet. In the related saxophone family, which has been made known chiefly in jazz and recent French symphonic music, the timbres are even more variable and not simply coarser and stronger as commonly supposed.

Whereas the clarinets are cylindrical, the less closely related members of the double-reed *oboe* family are conical in shape. The *English horn* flares out into a bulb, and the *oboe, bassoon,* and *contrabassoon* into a bell. Pungent and nasal at their harshest, these instruments more often convey a bittersweet melancholy (Fig. 43, p. 243), a plaintive nostalgia, or even a grotesqueness, especially in the bassoon, that no other instrument can duplicate. With only the double reed as the mouthpiece between his lips the player can achieve extremely fine shadings of intensity and *intonation.* (Intonation refers here to minute adjustments of pitch by which a player can favor certain gravitational pushes and pulls within the underlying harmony.) The deepest relative in the oboe family, the *contrabassoon,* is at the same time one of the deepest instruments of the orchestra.

The *brasses* blend remarkably well as a choir, although almost every one is the sole survivor of a different family. This blending results from the adaptability of the human lips and the wealth of both high and low partials that are favored by cup mouthpieces.

In spite of notable uses by Bach and others the *trumpet* did not become a universally standard orchestral instrument until it became "mechanized" early in the nineteenth century. The peculiarly high tones that Bach scored for trumpet sorely tax today's trumpeter who has not developed the unusual lip control by which they were largely achieved. An important advantage of playing in the highest range of any of the brasses was the fact that nearly every tone in the scale could be found among the higher partials through lip control alone and without mechanical aids or the cumbersome exchange of crooks. A quick, precise technique is possible on the trumpet. Ranging in its fullest uses from gentle and sweet to martial and penetrating tones, this instrument is marked by unusual brightness and clarity, qualifying as one of the most telling members of the orchestra.

The *French horn,* alto of the brasses, has won many solos in orchestral music by virtue of its full, round, mellow tone. Most of its higher tones are managed largely by lip control, making accuracy a real problem. Its long pipe winds in circular coils and flares out in a bell. Like the trumpet and trombone, it can produce eerie muted sounds. But the horn player often inserts his hand into the bell rather than an artificial stopper when he mutes his instrument. Sometimes in emphatic passages he is called on to hold his instrument up and deliberately produce a harsh, hard tone ("cuivré").

The *tenor* and *bass trombones,* oldest of the brasses in their present state, produce a commanding, stentorian tone that can dominate the orchestra in their ranges. Efforts to replace the slide system with valves have never succeeded for long. The agility that can be achieved with the slide is astonishing. An upright *tuba,* remotely like a giant trumpet, has served the nineteenth century to reinforce the orchestra bass, though not as often as it and the circular tuba, remotely like a giant French horn, have been used in the band.

PERCUSSION INSTRUMENTS

Besides adding life and definition to the rhythm, *percussion instruments* (Plates 13, 14) point up crescendos, top climaxes, lend a sustaining effect somewhat like the right pedal of a piano, and contribute a variety of colors. They participate, of course, not only in loud music but in some very subtle effects. Just how subtle they can be is well known to anyone who has been able to hear authentic performances of primitive and oriental music in which percussion instruments predominate.

Most important of the percussion instruments with pitch are the *timpani* or *kettledrums,* used in pairs, threes, or even fours. The pitch is regulated by equal adjustments of about eight screws located around the drumhead rim, or by a recent mechanical pedal device. Absolute pitch (the ability to remember an exact pitch) helps the performer, who must often tune while the music is going on. Alternating his two sticks with their felt balls, he sometimes crosses them in tricky passages, produces a faint or thunderous roll, electrifies the music with resounding strokes, all with the greatest finesse.

The *snare* or *side drum* and the *bass drum* have no fixed pitch but add color with their ra-ta-ta-tat or dull thud.

Among other percussion instruments with definite pitch are two designed like a keyboard but played with hammers—the *glockenspiel* or *bells,* with its clear, bright sounds, and the *xylophone,* with its brittle sounds. There are also the *chimes,* consisting of about eighteen hollow tubes that are graduated in size and struck by a hammer. Their effect usually recalls the clamor of church bells. Actually the chimes are diffuse enough in pitch to be heard in combination with any other pitches, harmonious or not.

Illustrations

EARLY CHRISTIAN ERA (350-1000)

The more than six centuries included under "Early Christian Era" saw the virtual end of Roman civilization and the feudal beginnings of the Italian, French, and German nations to be. During these centuries classic Greek and Roman culture was kept alive by a comparatively few "transmitters" like Boethius, while Byzantine and Moslem (Mohammedan) influences pervaded the sphere of the Western Church at Rome by way of broad commerce, the Eastern Church at Constantinople (Byzantium), and the Arabian movements in Spain. Persistent invasions, wars, and economic disintegration underlay extreme pessimism and ascetic philosophies in this "vale of wickedness," as Saint Augustine called it.

The prime security and binding force was the Church, around which virtually all living centered. It is no wonder, then, that Early Christian art existed only to express and enhance devotion. Music's function was to enhance the Divine Office and the Mass. Its patron saints were Ambrose of Milan and Gregory of Rome, who superintended its organization in the liturgies. Significantly, secular music of the era has left almost no traces except as the Church proscribed it.

Known chiefly now as plainchant or Gregorian chant (Ex. 47), this music consisted in wonderfully free, proselike melodies, unaccompanied and therefore lacking harmonic "perspective" much as frescoes and mosaics of the time lacked depth perspective. It shared with most other Early Christian art its additive forms (strung together rather than integrated), its strict economy of means, and an ornamental complexity of Byzantine and North European origin. This last, as evident in melodic flights as in the profuse decorations of Early Christian churches (Ill. 1), contributes to the mystic, otherworldly quality of Gregorian chant and calls up the sweet, unquestioning rigors of monastic life.

PLATE 1. An Early Christian church under Byzantine influence (*S. Vitale* in Ravenna, early sixth century)

MEDIEVAL-AND-RENAISSANCE ERA (850-1600)

The compounding of two eras into one Medieval-and-Renaissance Era of more than seven centuries is justified by historians who regard the Renaissance as the final phase of the Middle Ages. Certainly in Italian art a continuity is implied by tracing most Renaissance trends back to a pre- or proto-Renaissance, even to predecessors of Giotto and Dante in the early fourteenth century. In music this compound era embraced hard-won solutions culminating in classic peaks of balance and clarity during the sixteenth century (Ill. 8).

The Middle Ages had reached its cultural peak in the thirteenth century. A sense of security and unity was imparted by the catholic (universal) Church militant and by Saint Thomas Aquinas' neat synthesis of Christian faith and Aristotelian reason. Yet underneath, the conflicts of popes and kings, the Inquisitions, even the edicts against newer art styles, signaled a disturbing dualism. This dualism is a clue to the emotionalism of Medieval art. We sense it when secular subjects appear in liturgical drama, and in sculpture and stained glass of ethereal Gothic cathedrals, and in chivalric songs of knightly Crusaders and later poet-musicians, and in "superstructure" motets with their juxtaposition of polyglot texts both sacred and profane.

Gradually, certain rousing forces—the Crusades, town commerce, the founding of universities, shifts from feudalism to nationalism, a flood of geographic and scientific discoveries, and enough church corruption to provoke Luther and a Protestant Reformation—led to the Renaissance ideal of a worldly, free man, an ideal revived, by Humanists, from classic arts and letters. Then man turned to himself for security. He learned to master the secrets of individuality, whatever the field or style. Artful, balanced integration of lines, colors, and depths was as evident in polyphonic motets (Ex. 26) and Masses as in their textile counterpart, Flemish tapestries, or in the anatomic perfections of Michelangelo, or the classic symmetry of an Italian palace (Ill. 2). The new attention to man and nature was revealed as truly in the poetry and music of "merry" English madrigals or programmatic French chansons as in Dutch genres or landscapes.

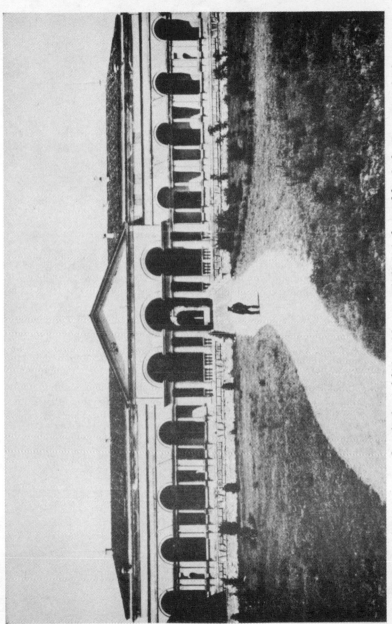

PLATE 2. A Renaissance palace (*Palazzo del Te* in Mantua, 1525-1535, designed by Giulio Romano and others)

BAROQUE ERA (1580-1750)

The Baroque Era, lasting some 170 years, witnessed much of historical importance, including severe conflicts of faith and reason, remarkable advances of learning, and the important reign of the "Sun King," Louis XIV. Faith was argued more ardently than ever by Catholics and Protestants alike after the Reformation and Counter Reformation had left an irreparable schism. Reason was argued optimistically on behalf of science, philosophy, politics, and a changing economy, by such men as Bacon, Galileo, Descartes, Locke, Newton, and Hobbes.

Like the term Gothic, "baroque" was first applied to the arts in disparagement. It meant a degenerate excess of Renaissance styles. Much Baroque art was in fact rooted in Renaissance art. But even where this art did represent exaggeration, the qualities of brilliance, grandeur, unrest, theatrical virtuosity, and rich, colorful ornateness that especially distinguish the earliest and latest Baroque products justified themselves in some of the world's greatest monuments to art (Ill. 3).

Nowhere more than in music were these qualities responsible for new styles and forms, among them a more compelling organization of melody, rhythm, and harmony; a new, Protestant source of melody (the chorale); a new, independent use of instruments; new vocal forms like the opera and oratorio; and new instrumental forms like the fugue, suite, and concerto grosso. Opera, itself a conscious attempt at a classic revival, actually became the foremost innovation in Baroque music. It started early in Italy but its spread was delayed more than a half century by disruptive religious conflicts in other countries. Note the coincidence in Baroque art of opera and the golden age of English, Spanish, and French drama; of instrumental dance or occasional music (Ex. 36) and lustrous court life; of intellectual, recherché polyphony (Ex. 28) and scientific speculation or experimentation; of a violinist like Corelli (Ex. 37) and a craftsman like Stradivari; of sublime sacred choral works by Bach or Handel and the epic creations of Rubens or Milton.

PLATE 3. A Baroque church (S. *Maria della Salute* in Venice, 1631-1656, designed by Baldassare Longhena)

CLASSIC ERA (1730-1830)

The mere century spanned by the Classic Era began with the gradual decay of the French monarchy under the ever weaker successors to Louis XIV. This decay, the philosophical fermentation of the Enlightenment, and repercussions of the American Revolutionary spirit were vital factors in the French Revolution, which implanted the idea of a republic in spite of the Napoleonic empire and later monarchic revivals. Among the arts, the most significant changes took place in music, literature, French ballet, and costume. Architecture turned chiefly to past styles (Ill. 4), painting flourished mainly as an elegance, and sculpture suffered a general decline.

Music made a radical shift in the masterworks of Haydn, Mozart, and Beethoven from "wig and bustle" to simplicity, directness, ideal proportions, and perfect union of form and content. It thus reflected Rousseau's cry "Back to nature!" or at least the popular belief in "nature enslaved by reason." As in the Baroque Era, Italian opera took the lead, French music served as a sort of catalytic agent, and Austro-German music attained the peak. And as before, one of music's best hosts was England. The most conspicuous changes appeared in instrumental music, where the Classic sonata idea, including the highly integrated, cumulative "sonata-allegro" form, became the essence of the symphony, solo concerto, string quartet, and piano sonata.

The transitional period between the peaks of Baroque and Classic maturity is called Rococo after the Louis Quinze decorative style of extravagant shellwork and endless irregular curves. It led to the international light "gallant style" in music, especially harpsichord music (Ex. 29). In the North Germany of Frederick the Great this style deepened into introspective emotional fantasy not long before the novels, poetry, and drama of the Storm-and-Stress movement turned against superficiality and frivolity.

PLATE 4. A Classic ("late French Renaissance") government building (*Petit Trianon* in Versailles, 1762-1764, designed by Ange Jacques Gabriel)

ROMANTIC ERA (1790-1910)

The century and a quarter that comprised the Romantic Era reached from the French Revolution to World War I. Not liberalism but a disheartening wave of reaction and suppression followed the Napoleonic wars, leading to further widespread revolts in the Europe of 1830 and 1848. Here was one explanation for some remarkable contrasts and contradictions in this era, chiefly those of individualism versus mass organization and integration. On the one hand the watchword was freedom—freedom of thought, of trade, of religion, of art styles. On the other, the guiding force was such as led not only to vast networks of communication, huge factory production systems, world-embracing philosophies, societies of brotherly love, or a resurgence of Catholicism, but to complex syntheses of the arts (Wagner's *Gesamtkunstwerk*), broad versatility in their mastery (Blake, E. T. A. Hoffmann, the Rossettis), and complete integration within any one art form (Ill. 5).

Romantic music has its own sharp contrasts, as between the intimacy of a Schumann art-song and the grandiloquence of a Verdi opera aria; the brevity of a Chopin prelude and the magnitude of a Bruckner symphony; the conservative, objective style of a Mendelssohn fugue and the subjective, radical style of a Berlioz tone poem.

The Romantic movement traces back to the anti-Classicism and pre-Romantic spirit of the German Storm-and-Stress movement, and to German authors who found new promise in the Romanesque culture of the Middle Ages. The spirit of musical Romanticism was at first the sweet, insatiable yearning of enraptured youth (Chopin, Ex. 30; Schumann), and then, in its second bloom, an adult mastery of idea and passion (Brahms, Wagner). Thereafter, only exhaustion, sentimentality, formalism, harsh realism, or excursion into nationalistic color (Mus. 12) was left to it. The Romantics did not create any wholly new forms; rather they Romanticized the Classic ones, chiefly by preoccupation with the harmonic content (Ex. 18). Their first interest was often instrumental music (even in vocal accompaniments). Hence the unprecedented developments in piano literature, in virtuosity (Liszt, Paganini—Exs. 42, 34), in orchestral size and colors, and in instrument construction.

PLATE 5. A Romantic opera house (*L'Opéra* in Paris, 1861-1874, designed by Charles Garnier)

MODERN ERA (1890–?)

The Modern Era in which we live must be described by only half an arc on our Historical Charts, for it is perhaps but half spanned by now. We are too close to judge it in perspective, but we can recognize the birth pangs of a new age in the convulsive world-wide wars, in the extreme "isms" that have grown out of nationalism and other expansive forces of the Romantic Era, in unprecedented scientific achievements that may serve us well or become Frankenstein monsters. Today's art lovers, if they live in the present, must certainly react feelingly to today's art, for they can find in it all the frenzied pressures, neuroses, regimentation, and theorizing that surround them.

In this new age the three-dimensional arts—architecture, sculpture, furniture—with their simple, functional lines, have clearly found themselves already (Ill. 6). The "later" arts—literature, painting, and music—still show traces of the dying Romanticism or of floundering in arbitrary theories. Modern music continues to make at least a token use of Classic and Baroque forms, especially in deliberate neoclassic trends. But it so transforms them by intensifying their rhythmic and harmonic drive, by smoothing over their divisions, and by pruning decorative matter that they almost lose their original identity. The point of departure for these changes, and a transitional stage between eras, was the musical Impressionism of Debussy, closely allied to the visual Impressionism of painting. Then followed some other isms of music such as the Expressionism of Schönberg, similarly allied to that of Viennese painting.

As in the other arts, the means and methods have been expanded enormously. Brilliance, precise and startling colors, melodic projection in bold relief, phenomenal technique, are the assumed stock in trade of today's musician (Ex. 19). Psychology, youngest of the sciences, is even suggesting ways to systemize musical aesthetics. Whether the content has kept up with these means is not unlike the serious question of whether society has kept up with its startling scientific advances.

PLATE 6.   A Modern industrial building (*S. C. Johnson Administration Building* in Racine, Wisconsin, 1937, designed by Frank Lloyd Wright; photograph, courtesy of Johnson's Wax)

PLATE 7. (a) Pathos: The actual photograph of a motif (from Erle Loran, *Cézanne's Composition*, Los Angeles, 1943, by permission)

(b) Ethos: The same scene idealized in a painting (*Cézanne, Aisle of Trees*)

PLATE 8.   A concert of Medieval-and-Renaissance music (two alto vielles, tenor singer, and tenor vielle; the Vielle Trio; photograph, courtesy of Werner Landshoff [right], manager; Ben Greenhaus photograph)

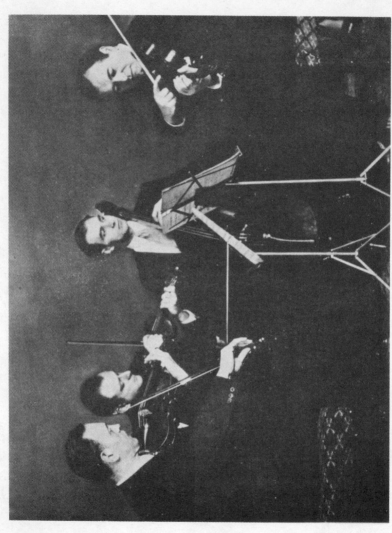

PLATE 9. A string quartet (first and second violins, cello, and viola; the Kroll Quartet; photograph, courtesy of Wilfred L. Davis, Concert and Artist Management)

PLATE 10. A "woodwind" quintet (flute, clarinet, French horn, bassoon, and oboe; the New Art Wind Quintet; photograph, courtesy of Norma Waldon Associates, Inc.)

PLATE 11. A "unit" pipe organ with two manuals and a pedal keyboard (New England Conservatory of Music; photograph, courtesy of Aeolian-Skinner Organ Company)

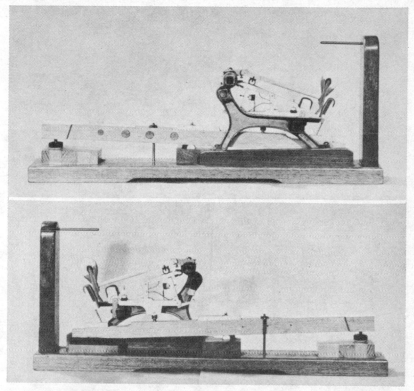

PLATE 12. A cutaway model of the action on a grand piano (by permission of Steinway & Sons)

PLATE 13. A full symphony orchestra (The New York Philharmonic-Symphony Orchestra; photograph, courtesy of The Philharmonic-Symphony Society of New York)

PLATE 14. A concert band (The United States Marine Band; official U.S. Marine Corps photograph)

PLATE 15.   A performance of Baroque chamber music (Louis Michel Vanloo, *The Sextet*, 1768; Palace of the Hermitage, St. Petersburg)

PLATE 16.   Opera in a Baroque theater (Giovanni Paolo Panini, *Concert Given in Rome, November 27, 1729, on the Occasion of the Birth of the Dauphin, Son of Louis XV*; Louvre, Paris; photograph, courtesy of Archives Photographiques, Paris)

PLATE 17. Impressionism in painting (Claude Monet, *Waterloo Bridge*; photograph, courtesy of Worcester Art Museum)

PLATE 18. Expressionism in painting (Oskar Kokoschka, *Caricature, the Red Egg*, 1940-1941; photograph, courtesy of publishers of *The Studio,* January, 1942)

Among the other instruments without pitch are the *cymbals,* which may be crashed, rolled, or struck; the *tambourine,* which may be rapped, shaken, or rubbed; the *triangle,* usually rolled; and the *gong,* usually struck.

PIANO, ORGAN, AND OTHER KEYBOARD TYPES

Keyboard instruments have one main disadvantage. The mechanical keys and other levers that are interposed between the performer and the vibrating agent materially limit his control over his instrument. For example, he cannot ordinarily produce a vibrato or swell the tone. Nor can adjustments of intonation be made, since the pitches of all tones are regulated only prior to performance. In fact, a consistently pure tuning is impossible and must necessarily be sacrificed on keyboard instruments to an all-purpose *equal-tempered tuning,* as it is called. Stated briefly, a small but fundamental discrepancy that arises when perfectly tuned octaves and fifths are compared must be dispelled on keyboard instruments by compromises—that is, by dividing it equally among all the tones. Otherwise, a few keys would be well in tune and all the rest hopelessly out of tune.

But keyboard instruments have compensating advantages. The very absence of these controls permits a beginner to make fairly rapid strides into actual music. And what is more important, keyboard instruments provide a means of playing several notes at once, which is not possible on most other instruments and much less convenient on most stringed instruments. This means that keyboard performers are not only self-sufficient in solo playing but can play any music literature, orchestral or whatever, in arrangements and reductions for keyboard.

The *pipe organ,* which stems from antiquity, has been more and more mechanized over the centuries until the more recent consoles of four to seven manuals look as complex as the panel of a manned space ship. Indeed, there has been a movement to restore essentially the instrument with two manuals and pedal key-board (Plate 11) that was used by Bach, composer of some of the most important literature for organ. Four main components figure in the complete pipe organ. First, there are the one or more sets of pipes of different sizes, each with its valve that opens by me-chanical, pneumatic, or electrical means to admit air past a sharp-edged hole or a metal reed of fixed pitch. Second, there is the wind chest with its supply of air. Third, there must be some means of feeding this air very steadily, whether by a bellows that is operated manually or hydraulically or electrically, or by a reser-voir under a constant pressure, which is in turn fed by a rotary electric blower. And fourth, there is the console containing the keyboards as well as all other controls that the performer oper-ates. The controls include the "stops" that govern the varied timbres produced by the row upon row of pipes in many sizes and shapes. Each manual operates an entire, separate division of pipes, known successively as the "great organ," the "swell organ," the "choir organ," the "solo organ," the "echo organ," depending on the number of manuals. Intensity can only be varied by adding or subtracting stops, or by opening and closing "shutters" on the "swell box." Tastefully played in a good location, such as a recital hall of moderate size and satisfactory acoustics but unfortunately not often a huge cathedral, the pipe organ becomes one of music's most telling and versatile instruments.

An approximation of the pipe organ is achieved more or less satisfactorily on present-day electric organs such as the Allen, Baldwin, or Hammond. These are but one species of a variety of new electrophonic instruments that are being developed in this Modern Era (including the space-controlled Theremin!). A more modest sort of organ music is possible on the domestic *reed organ,* which in smaller types like the harmonium or melodeon is still a familiar and favorite domestic instrument in many homes. Of course, as with the guitar, the final significance of any of these instruments must also take into account the player and what he plays. Even the lowly *mouth organ* or *harmonica* is raised to a high position when a top artist and virtuoso like Larry Adler uses it to play music by Bach that he has transcribed for it.

The *harpsichord* and *clavichord* are keyboard instruments that were developed in the Renaissance and especially the Baroque Eras. However, a revival of interest in their use for the performance of old music has brought them into service and manufacture again today. The harpsichord was the concert instrument (Plate 15). It was usually equipped with two manuals that enabled abrupt contrasts of intensity, particularly those echo effects and "terrace dynamics" so essential to Baroque musical thought. A surprising variety of timbres and of tone couplings in octaves and even double octaves is made available through the use of several pedals. But a graduated control of intensity is scarcely possible on this instrument. Whereas the keyboard action of the harpsichord causes the strings to be twanged more or less brightly by a plectrum, that of the clavichord permits the constant thrust of a bridge on the strings, producing only a very soft tone not suitable for concert use, but extremely expressive. A limited control of intensity and even a sort of vibrato are possible on the delicate clavichord. Which of the two instruments was intended when the mere word "clavier" (keyboard) appears in the title of Baroque music is not always known.

The *pianoforte* (literally, "softloud") supplanted the harpsichord and clavichord in the Classic Era chiefly because it was capable of the dynamic graduations that were lacking on the harpsichord and a degree of intensity not possible on the clavichord. But these gains, which may be credited to the piano's controlled hammer action, were at the expense of the varied timbres and the delicately expressive tones of its predecessors. Notwithstanding popular notions, piano timbres are largely "neutral" and cannot be varied by any method of touch on the keys. When a piano key is depressed a felt hammer strikes one or more strings, simultaneously causing a damper to draw away from the strings until the key is released. The action has become much more complicated than it sounds, however, for several reasons (Plate

12). The hammer must release instantly, even though the key is held, so as not to dampen the tone just struck. It must spring back quickly for the same reason even when a soft, gentle tone is played. And it must spring back immediately in case the key is to be repeated rapidly.

"Scale drawing" is the piano designer's highly skilled art of balancing the requirements of density, length, thickness, and tension in his choice of strings and other components. A nine-foot concert grand piano has the advantage over smaller pianos of a larger, resonating sounding board and longer, thinner strings for its bass tones, though all pianos necessarily have equally short strings for the highest tones. Another advantage of larger pianos lies in the action, which permits the hammers to be flung at the strings rather than drawn up to them as on some present-day spinet pianos. There are 88 keys, yet about 230 strings, on today's pianos with 7⅓ octaves. The additional strings are used to reinforce the higher tones at the unison so as to counterbalance the great intensity of the large, single, lowest strings, some hammers striking two, and most striking three, strings. The right pedal on the piano enriches the total sound. It releases all the dampers (none being needed near the top) so that tones can be sustained while the same chord prevails, and so that the maximum number of partials can be reinforced by sympathetic vibration. The left pedal reduces the intensity either by moving the hammers closer to the strings on upright pianos or by shifting them so that they strike one or two less unison strings on grand pianos. The center pedal, when it is not just a dummy, holds only the tones that are sounding at the moment it is depressed, thus freeing the fingers to go on to other keys without a steadily accumulated blurring of sound.

THE HUMAN VOICE

Finally, we come to the instrument that ranks first in importance in the total literature of music, the human voice. The voice may be classified loosely as a double-reed wind instrument, albeit an extraordinarily complex, sensitive, and supple one. Its "double-reed" is the pair of "true" vocal cords, which function much as the lips do in the playing of a cupped-mouthpiece instrument. However, its "pipe" is not really a stationary pipe of fixed length and fundamental pitch. Rather it is a highly flexible combination of resonating cavities that include the nasal, oral, and laryngeal pharynges. Primarily, the vocal cords initiate the sound and determine its pitch. The singer forces air through them from the lungs while tensing them appropriately by means of two sets of muscles, one for a low and the other for a high register. The cavities act as resonators and qualifiers of the sound in accordance

Fig. 1. Ranges of women's and men's voices

with the way the singer controls his jaw, throat, lips, tongue, diaphragm, ribs, and all else that affects the vocal apparatus. Thus, for example, are formed the distinctive timbres that we differentiate as the several vowel sounds.

There are six main ranges of the voice (Fig. 1). As illustrated here, they are the ranges of average chorus singers. Trained concert singers can go several tones lower and as much as an octave higher.

The teaching of singing is somewhat elusive, since the vocal cords and cavities cannot be seen. Mental or psychological images of proper voice production must usually be invoked, such as the idea of "throwing the voice" here or there. The singer must learn how to distinguish, develop, and coordinate the high and low ranges (sometimes called "head" and "chest" tones) so that all tones are properly "placed" and the passing from one range to the other is imperceptible. He must master the proper enunciation of consonants and especially vowels, which carry the large burden of actual sound. He must cultivate, or rather avoid inhibiting, a natural vibrato. He must learn to sing in at least English, French, German, and Italian, and in the styles peculiar to each of these languages. And he must learn to project himself, if not actually to act, as he sings!

SELECTED READINGS (ALL CONTAINING ILLUSTRATIONS)

James Jeans, Science and Music. New York: Macmillan, 1937.

Curt Sachs, The History of Musical Instruments. New York: W. W. Norton, 1940.

Karl Geiringer, Musical Instruments. New York: Oxford University Press, 1946.

Robert Donington, The Instruments of Music. London: Methuen, 1951.

Cecil Forsyth, Orchestration. New York: Macmillan, 1941.

Laurence McKinney, People of Note. New York: E. P. Dutton, 1940. (These clever verses about orchestral musicians, delightfully illustrated by Gluyas Williams, are more than amusing, for they evince a very knowing acquaintance with what goes on backstage in a major symphony orchestra.)

Anthony Baines, Woodwind Instruments and Their History. New York: W. W. Norton, 1957.

William Leslie Sumner, The Organ. New York: Philosophical Library, 1952.

Eta Harich-Schneider, The Harpsichord. St. Louis: Concordia, 1954.

Arthur Loesser, Men, Women and Pianos; A Social History. New York: Simon and Schuster, 1954.

Chapter 4

Rhythm: Its Notation, Patterns, and Tempos

NOTE VALUES

Rhythm means periodicity or the persistent recurrence of something, whether it is a pattern in wallpaper, an ornament in architecture, a peak in a chain of mountain peaks, an idea in an essay, or a section in a musical composition. In this chapter we are concerned especially with that more local application of rhythm known in verse and music as *meter*. The recurring element in meter is a pulsation or series of strong and weak beats that is muscular in origin. Actually, as we shall see, even at this level musical rhythm is something more than the organization of constant pulses implied by meter. It is a combination of two factors: first, the underlying pulsation, and second, whatever pattern of long and short tones is superimposed on that pulsation.

(To appreciate this distinction try tapping one foot to something like the refrain from *Stars and Stripes Forever*. At a band concert or other strongly rhythmic performance one's first instinct is nearly always to tap the pulse. Now stop your foot and let one hand tap the long and short note values of the melody itself. If, finally, you can do both pulse and pattern together in this manner there will be no question about your perceiving both the distinction and the musician's problem of combining these two essentials of Western rhythm.)

The durations of the steady pulses or beats and of the longer or shorter tones are expressed by a system of *note values* in musical notation. The explanation of this system is simplicity itself, although while it was being evolved, during the Medieval-and-Renaissance Era, the problem of how to notate rhythm occasioned some of Western music's worst growing pains. The eventual solution was based on relative rather than absolute values. Just as in the measurement of distance you can tell how long a foot will be once an inch is established, so in the measurement of musical time you can tell how long, say, a whole-note will be once a quarter-note is established. One need only remember that the successively shorter note values decrease by one half from each one to the next (Fig. 2).

Fig. 2. Note values from whole- to 16th-note

The direction of the stem is merely a matter of eye appeal, usually being down when the note head is above the third line of the staff, and up when it is below. However, when two melodies are placed on a single staff they are distinguished by stems laid in contrary directions no matter where the note heads lie (Fig. 26, p. 158). With regard to the use of beams or separate flags, ordinarily at least a quarter-note's worth of 8th-notes or lesser values are put on the same beam or beams (ⲭⲭⲭⲭ). But when there is only one note per syllable in vocal music (Fig. 46a, p. 258), separate flags are used (ⲭⲭⲭⲭ). Occasionally as many as six flags or beams occur in the standard literature, but only in slow music where there is time enough to get in such short values.

"Simple" Meters

The basic meters in music are groupings of two or three beats comparable to poetic feet like the trochee (- ◡) and the dactyl (- ◡ ◡), and to bodily rhythms like those of walking and the heart beat. It is interesting that our psychological tendency to organize whatever we notice virtually compels us to hear one or the other of these groupings, even in the absolutely steady beats of a metronome. One or more of either grouping constitutes a *measure*. In other words, the definition for *meter* may be restated as the grouping of strong and weak beats into measures. Measures are marked off in musical notation by vertical bars.

Before a meter can be established in notation its underlying pulse or unit beat must be assigned a note value. The value most frequently used to represent the unit beat since the late Baroque Era has been the quarter-note. Once, a much longer value was used for the unit beat, but this value has grown smaller and smaller ever since the introduction of Western rhythmic notation. The decrease is explained partly by the quicker notes of gradually increasing virtuosity, although we shall see that the absolute time value of the unit beat has probably remained fairly constant in all music.

At the start of a piece and at every change of the established meter a "fraction" called the *time signature* is placed (a fraction, that is, in terms of the whole note). The numerator of this fraction tells how many unit beats are grouped in each measure, and the denominator tells what value is assigned to each unit beat. In other words, learn to read the time signatures of "simple" meters (as distinguished presently from compound meters) by saying, "There are

          this many (numerator)
        of these units (denominator)

in a measure." For example, the time signature $\frac{3}{4}$ means that there are

three

quarter-note units

in a measure, and $\frac{2}{8}$ means that there are

two

eighth-note units

in a measure.

The meter expressed by the time signature $\frac{4}{4}$ combines two two-unit groups, ♩♩♩♩ (using the accent sign ► to indicate the strong beat or stress in each group). This meter is so prevalent that it is called "common time." For historical reasons it is often indicated simply by the sign C. This is not "C" for "common" but a broken circle, as compared with the complete or perfect circle that was reserved in the Medieval-and-Renaissance Era for

Fig. 3. A rhythmic pattern in simple meter (*Frère Jacques*)

three-unit groupings, probably in ideal association with the Trinity.

Try performing the $\frac{4}{4}$ meter of *Frère Jacques* (Fig. 3) by counting aloud the underlying pulses or unit beats—"one, two, three, four (without 'ands,' please)"—while clapping the superimposed pattern of long and short note values that you read. Notice that the pulse and the pattern coincide for two whole measures and wherever else there are quarter-notes. Accent the strong beats. (The final double bar is a sign used to indicate the end of a piece or section.) One such experience in clapping and counting can hardly make you a professional musician but it can certainly give you a better feeling for the kind of material with which the professional musician works.

FURTHER VALUES AND METERS

So far, our note values have been limited to whole-, half-, quarter-, 8th-, and such notes; that is, one and the powers of one half. To write any other possible value, three devices are added in the notation of rhythm—the dot, the tie, and the irregular cluster.

1. A *dot* placed on the space nearest to the right of the note head increases the value of that note by one half. Thus, ♩. lasts the equivalent of three rather than two quarter-notes, ♪. equals three 8th-notes, ○· equals three half-notes. Observe, therefore, that dotted notes have a triple rather than a duple subdivision. When a dotted note is used as a unit beat the meter is called *compound,* as distinguished from *simple* meter with the duple subdivision such as you found in the unit beats of *Frère Jacques.* In other words, the difference between compound and simple meter shows up not in the pulse itself but in the way the pulse subdivides; three quarter-notes in a measure will sound just like three dotted quarter-notes until you hear how these pulses subdivide. You can recognize compound meter visually by the fact that the numerator of its time signature is always a multiple of three (for example, $\frac{6}{4}$, $\frac{9}{16}$, or $\frac{12}{8}$). One more step than was used in reading simple time signatures is required to read compound time signatures. First, divide the numerator by three and multiply the denominator by three before reading "this many (numerator) of these units (denominator) in a measure." Thus, $\frac{9 \div 3}{16 \times 3} = \frac{3}{♪\cdot}$. (Of course, remember that the denominator in the metric "fraction" will be not 16 but a 16th.) The result, incidentally, makes a much more sensible and meaningful sort of time signature for compound meter, and one being used by some present-day composers.

For a further distinction between compound and simple meter, compare the meters $\frac{6}{8}$ and $\frac{3}{4}$, respectively, which represent measures of equal length because they are equal fractions, but which call for different groupings and subdivisions of the unit beat within the measure. Applying the rule,

$$\frac{6}{8} + \frac{3}{8} \times \frac{3}{8} = \frac{2}{4} \cdot = \quad \text{♩. ♩.} = \text{♫♫ ♫♫,} \quad \text{whereas } \frac{3}{4} = \text{♩ ♩ ♩} = \text{♫♫♫,}$$

which is a quite different rhythm, as Bach, Brahms, and many other masters have delighted in showing us by alternating these two meters or even opposing them in simultaneous combinations. (It is fun trying this opposition by tapping one of the two meters while another person or group taps the other. The 8th-notes will coincide, of course, but the normal metric accents will conflict.)

2. A *tie,* which is one use of the curved line known as a slur in music notation, produces any desired value simply by binding any two notes that will add up to that value. The tied note values may be plain or dotted but must occur on the same pitch, of course, if they are to be bound into one. If it is desired to notate a tone that will last through the total value of, say, thirteen 16th-notes, one tie will suffice, as in ♩♪, or several ties can be used, as in ♩♩♩♪ (which may or may not read more awkwardly, depending on the meter and the musical context). The tie can replace the dot (♩. or ♩♩) and usually does replace it if the total desired value will cross the bar ($\frac{4}{4}$ ○♩♩).

3. The irregular cluster crowds more notes within the space of one or more unit beats than would be arithmetically correct. It may contain any number of notes (Fig. 34b, p. 197) but occurs most commonly as a *triplet* used in the course of a simple meter (Fig. 22b, p. 114). The irregular cluster is marked off by a slur and an italicized number indicating how many notes are crowded in the total value:

$$\frac{4}{4} \quad \text{♩} \quad \overset{3}{\overbrace{\text{♫♫}}} \text{♫} \quad \overset{5}{\overbrace{\text{♫♫♫}}}|$$

One other essential in the notation of rhythm is the set of symbols called *rests.* A rest is used to fill up any silent portion of a measure, whether it is simply a "breathing" place in the flow of the music or one of those more dramatic pauses that have expressive meaning in their own right. The values of the rests correspond to those of the notes. But the whole rest is often used loosely to fill out any sized measure that is completely silent. Rests are occasionally dotted but never connected by ties or beams. To notate the value of any silence that is not a power of

Fig. 4. Rests in a rhythmic pattern

one half, it is only necessary to group together whatever rests total that value. The principal rests may be illustrated as they might occur in an actual rhythmic pattern (Fig. 4).

RHYTHMIC PATTERNS, NEW AND FAMILIAR

With the devices presented so far, any rhythm of Western music can be notated. Here is a rhythm for you to practice by simultaneous counting and clapping (Fig. 5). (Remember that

Fig. 5. A rhythmic pattern to clap and count

inserting "ands" on the 8th-notes, except for clarifying the arithmetic, only defeats the object of opposing pulse and pattern.) Actually this rhythm contains a much wider variety of patterns than could ordinarily be assimilated in one short composition. The measures are numbered in parentheses for discussion in succeeding paragraphs.

Measure 1 is preceded by an incomplete measure called an *upbeat,* which is similar to an anacrusis in verse meter. Count and clap the upbeat as if it were the end of a measure filled out by rests, ♩♪♫ —that is, so that the two 16th-notes are clapped in the latter half of the fourth count.

Syncopations occur in the first two beats of measure 5 and in the third beat of measure 6. A syncopation is a displaced accent. In measure 5, for example, the first quarter-note does not coincide with the regular metrical pulse of quarter-notes but straddles half of each of the first two beats, making a strong or long tone land on a weak beat and no tone where one is expected on the normally strong beat. The remarkable effect of a syncopation is to make the hearer as well as the performer almost reach out physically (kinesthetically) to replace the wayward beat himself. Think of the first syncopation in equivalent notation as ♫♫ and the second one as ♫♫♫, counting and clapping each first without, and then with, the tie.

Alternative notations with ties will also help you to do the dotted rhythms in measures 4 and 6, which may be read as ♩♫ and ♫♫♫ and again practiced first without, then with, the ties. Feeling instead of clapping the tied notes is something like supplying gestures instead of words when you recite "John Brown's _____ had a _____ upon his _____." To steady the counting and clapping try doing them as you walk in step to the pulse.

Fig. 6 gives you a compound meter to try, that of *Sailing, Sailing, Over the Bounding Main.* Remember that the real meaning of $^6_8$ is $^2_{\,\bullet\!\cdot}$, so that you will be counting two dotted quarter-notes, not six 8th-notes, per measure. The frequent division of a com-

$^6_8$ ♩. ♩. | ♩. ♩. | ♫♫♩ ♪ | ♩ ♪♪ ♪ | ♫♫♩ ♪ | ♩ ♪♩ ♪ |

| ♫♫♩ ♪ | ♩. ♩ ♪ | etc.

Fig. 6. A rhythmic pattern in compound meter (*Sailing*)

pound unit into ♩♪ may be thought of as ♫♩ for purposes of practice. This pattern gives the sense of galloping by which the listener can readily identify moderately fast compound meter. You will be hearing the same meter in the Baroque gigue (Fig. 36, p. 207) and you can hear it often in poetry, as in Browning's spirited lines telling *How They Brought the Good*

Fig. 7. The rhythmic patterns of nine dance types, chiefly Romantic and Modern

News From Ghent to Aix ("I sprang to the stirrup, and Joris, and he; I galloped, Dirck galloped, we galloped all three;" etc.) But can you hear the difference between the 2:1 relationship of ♩♪ in this compound meter and the even sprightlier "dotted" 3:1 relationship of ♪.♪ that often enlivens simple meters (as in the mazurka pattern that heads Fig. 7 or the equivalent pattern of ♫ in Dvořák's familiar *Humoresque*)? Inverting either relationship so that it is 1:2 or 1:3 results in the "Scotch snap," so-called because of its characteristic use in the strathspey dance and other Scottish tunes (recall each word "body" in *Comin' thro' the Rye*), although it is actually used much more widely.

Certain rhythmic patterns are identified with particular kinds of music, especially with dances. Some of the most familiar of these, chiefly Romantic and Modern dances, are notated here (Fig. 7). Other, Baroque dance patterns are given in Fig. 36 (p. 207). You will help yourself to *feel* musical rhythm from the inside if you practice counting and clapping each pattern, then listen to an actual composition in which it prevails (Appendix II, Nos. 4 and 28).

Modern composers have experimented extensively with rhythm. In general they seek to avoid the confining regularity of "square" phrases and "the tyranny of the bar line," against which Beethoven had already rebelled, though not altogether successfully in his own opinion. Many have tried to recapture the freer, proselike flow of such music as Gregorian chant. Two almost contradictory methods have been tried. One is to do away with time signatures and measure bars, retaining only a unit beat. The other is to change meters constantly in the interest of deliberate irregularity. The latter method is one characteristically employed by Aaron Copland, whose "Dance" from *Music for the Theatre* is listed in Appendix II (No. 5). This movement begins in $\frac{5}{8}$ meter (made up of a quarter- plus a dotted quarter-note), then quickly shifts to $\frac{2}{4}, \frac{3}{4}, \frac{5}{8}, \frac{2}{4}, \frac{3}{4}, \frac{2}{4}, \frac{5}{8}$, and so on. Throughout this and other movements of the same suite are those quasi-jazz syncopations that figured in so much sophisticated art music of Europe and America earlier in the Modern Era (including the ragtime in Debussy's well-known *Golliwogg's Cake Walk*).

Before going on you may enjoy trying your own hand at notating the rhythm, from time signature to double bar, of some of the familiar community songs that you recall (as was done in

Figs. 3 and 6). First, determine the meter by counting the pulses from one strong beat to the next as you sing. Then observe on what syllables the strong beats occur, after which the weaker, intervening beats are likely to fall into place. Counting and clapping will help you to figure out specific patterns within the beats.

TIME AND TEMPO

The conductor of an orchestra, chorus, or other large musical organization holds his group to a uniform pulse by beating time. He waves his baton according to certain conventional patterns, of which those for the three most common meters are shown in the accompanying diagram. In all meters his first beat is down and his

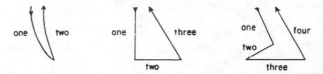

last beat is up. Certain intricate movements that give flow and resiliency to the beat are not shown in the diagram. In slow music and choral music many conductors find the hand itself to be more expressive than the baton.

Of course, beating time is only one, and not the most important, of the conductor's functions. In fact, if this were all he did, a veteran organization could manage fairly well without him, even in the starts and stops. Mainly, he is needed so that one experienced concept will prevail of tempo, dynamics, phrasing, balance, tone quality, and all else that goes into style and interpretation. Only the tempo concerns us in this chapter.

Tempo is the musician's word for rate of speed. Like so many other musical terms it is an Italian word, for Italian is the musician's Esperanto (a fact that rightly suggests how much past music owes to Italy). One of the conductor's or any performer's chief responsibilities is to arrive at the best tempo for a particular work or section. His principal guide has been the Italian tempo indications used since the early Baroque Era and still in general use in spite of a preference for the vernacular on the part of many Nationalistic and Modern composers. These numerous indications, such as adagio, allegro, and so on, center around five basic tempos—very slow, slow, moderate, fast, and very fast—aptly suggesting varying qualities of physical movement appropriate to each tempo. Since rhythm is fundamentally muscular in nature,

Term	Meaning	Approximate tempo
adagio	slowly, gracefully, and easily	very slow
lento	slowly, seriously	very slow
largo	broadly, sweepingly	slow
andante	at a walking pace, flowingly	moderate
allegro	gaily, cheerfully	fast
vivace	in a lively manner, vivaciously	very fast
presto	nimbly, immediately	very fast

it is this suggestion of movement that makes the tempo indications so meaningful. In addition, a number of modifiers are often used—for example, *piu, meno, molto, poco,* and suffixes like *-etto, -ino,* and *-issimo*—as a means of indicating intermediate or extreme tempos. One does have to recognize some inconsistent uses of the tempo terms by different composers in different eras, and even some absurdities such as "più moderato" (about like saying "more medium") or Schumann's instruction near the end of his *Piano Sonata in G Minor,* "Prestissimo" (as fast as possible) followed a few measures later by "sempre più presto" (constantly faster)!

The choice of tempo invariably has a profound effect on the meaning of the music. For example, think how it affects music in compound meters. A slow compound meter may produce the gentle lilt you can hear in the "Andante" of Mozart's *Concerto in A,* K. 488 (Appendix II, No. 34,II) or in the aria "He Shall Feed His Flock" from Handel's *Messiah* (Appendix II, No. 44e). This

lilt associates with the *siciliano* dance (as in the tender movement by that name from Bach's *Sonata in E-flat*, S. 1031, for flute
and harpsichord). A moderately fast compound meter associates
with the lively gigue dance previously mentioned (such as the
Irish Washerwoman's Jig or *Funiculi, Funicula*). And a very fast
compound meter is likely to suggest the swift tarantella dance
(originally supposed to cure the poisonous bite of the tarantula
spider), which you can hear early in the ending or coda of
Tchaikovsky's *Capriccio italien* (Appendix II, No. 12) and in
the finale of Schubert's *String Quartet in D Minor* (Appendix II,
No. 32,IV).

Conversely, the nature of the music can do much to determine
the tempo. Thus, a practical limit to its speed is fixed by the physical difficulty of playing it, by the thickness of its texture (a light
textured angel-food cake can be devoured in quick gulps whereas
a heavy fruit cake must be nibbled a bit at a time), and by the
rate of its harmonic rhythm (chord change, p. 87), among other
factors.

Since Beethoven's time the metronome has often been used to
indicate an exact tempo in number of beats per minute. However, tempo cannot be pinned down quite so precisely, for it varies
somewhat with the time, place, and style of performance. Nor
does the metronome convey the idea of a particular quality of
physical movement in the way that the Italian words do. Beethoven himself resorted to the metronome as a means of specifying
tempos in his later years, eventually decided that his markings
had been too fast, and ultimately abandoned the device. Brahms
preferred to use only sparing verbal indications, remarking that
"the right tempo is what the musician feels." The report goes,
however, that Brahms generally felt his music was played too
fast, perhaps too fast for the rich content of the harmony to be
digested.

All this much about tempo is included primarily to focus attention on one of the chief and most contentious problems of musi-

cal performance. It is hard to say whether the error is more often in the direction of a tempo so slow that the flow cannot be felt or so fast that the meaning is lost. Perhaps in the high pressure of our Modern Era the latter is the worse danger.

An important side light on this matter of tempo is the question of whether all tempos do not resolve into one fairly standard, absolute tempo of from 60 to 80 beats per minute. In other words, whether the metronome calls for 80 or 40 or 160 beats per minute, the performer and the listener may still feel an underlying pulse of 80. This rather well-demonstrated theory is based on the argument that there are physiological bases for the sense of pulse, perhaps the heart beat or accompanying chemical changes.

Now, to return briefly to the functions of the conductor, certain liberties in the regularity of the metric pulse must be under constant control. *Accelerando* and *ritardando* are the terms for a graduated increase or decrease of tempo. *Fermata* refers to the prolonging of a particular tone or chord. *Rubato* is the much-belabored term for a general elasticity of the pulse, preferably a subtle give-and-take in the tempo. Performance in rubato style tends to dwell on significant changes in the melody or harmony and to pass that much more quickly over less important tones. Rubato is associated above all with the music of Chopin but is generally more appropriate in any music of a pathos character. To sense the spirit of rubato, try beating three-part time with a recording of any Chopin mazurka (for example, Appendix II, No. 4a), and see if you can stay with it as the performer slows down and speeds up.

SELECTED READINGS

Howard Boatwright, *Introduction to the Theory of Music,* Chapters 2, 4, 5, and 7. New York: W. W. Norton, 1956.
E. A. Sonnenschein, *What Is Rhythm?* Oxford: Blackwell, 1925.
Mathis Lussy, *Musical Expression.* London: Novello, 1895 (and later editions).

William J. Finn, *The Conductor Raises His Baton*, Chapters I, II, and III. New York: Harper, 1944.

William S. Newman, *The Pianist's Problems*, pp. 81-91. New York: Harper, 1956.

Curt Sachs, *Rhythm and Tempo*. New York: W. W. Norton, 1953.

R. E. M. Harding, *Origins of Musical Time and Expression*. New York: Oxford University Press, 1938.

Chapter 5

Melody: Its Notation and Pitch Organization

KEYBOARD CONCEPTS OF PITCH AND SCALES

In the previous chapter the duration of tones, long and short, was our starting point. In this chapter the pitch level of tones, "high" and "low," is the starting point. ("High" and "low" are merely psychological associations with pitch. In ancient Greece, for example, writers called the tones "high" that we call "low," and conversely.) The concept of pitch in music is literally clarified in black and white by the keyboard. On the accompanying diagram (Fig. 8) you see the complete piano keyboard of seven-and-one-third octaves, aligned with the bass and treble staffs (to

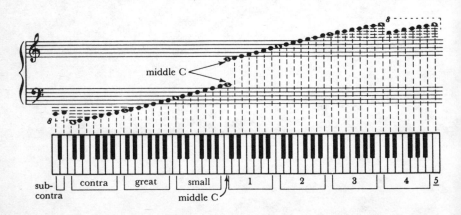

Fig. 8. Alignment of the keyboard and staff

be discussed in the next section). From the lowest key at the left to the highest at the right, the *white keys* pass through seven music alphabets, each A to G (or seven overlapping *octaves* if we think of the eight notes from A to A each time), plus three more letters, A to C, of an eighth alphabet. Note that all keys of the same letter name look alike and sound alike except for octave differences. Each D, for example, always falls in the middle of a two-black-key group, each B at the right of a three-black-key group. In a matter of minutes you can memorize the look of each of the seven different white key positions. Do this by picking out all the G's, all the E's, and so forth, at random. Also try picking out familiar tunes on the white keys, reciting the letter name of each key you play. *Middle C,* which is something of a dividing line in pitch because it lies near the center, is the fourth C from the bottom or the fifth from the top of the keyboard.

The *black keys* do not have letter names of their own but are named in relation to the nearest white keys. For instance, E-flat is the black key just to the left of E; F-sharp is the one just to the right of F. The black keys bring up the matter of *half* and *whole steps,* which are the most usual units for measuring pitch (much as the quarter note is the usual unit for measuring duration in rhythm). If all twelve white and black keys within each octave are included, the statement holds that *any two adjacent tones define a half step.* Usually this means a white and a black key, but there are two pairs of white keys that define half steps, B to C and E to F, because they are adjacent and have no black key between them. Remember that a *flat* lowers a tone by one half step and a *sharp* raises it by one half step. Usually a flat or sharp is a black key, but not always. B-sharp proves to be the same as the white key C. It is, in music jargon, the *enharmonic* (alternative spelling) of C.

A whole step is, of course, two half steps. Thus, any pair of white keys with a black key in between is a whole step apart. A double sharp or double flat is used to alter a tone one whole step up or down. Do you see why C-double-sharp and E-double-flat, for example, are both enharmonics of D? One enharmonic spelling is preferred to another in music for reasons of good spelling, somewhat as the spelling "cough" is preferred to "cawf," although the sound is the same. Thus, it proves easier to read C-flat, D-flat, E-flat in alphabetical order than B, D-flat, E-flat. Familiarize yourself with half and whole steps by reciting the two or three enharmonic spellings for each of the twelve white or black keys. You will find thirty-five spellings in all. Which is the one key that has only two spellings? Also, pick out any key, spell it with any one of its enharmonic spellings, and find the correct spelling for the half or whole step above or below it, using the next letter of the alphabet in each instance. For example, if B is spelled C-flat then the whole step below it will be B-double-flat.

A musical *scale* is sometimes called the alphabet of music. However, it is really much more. In the first place, a scale makes a good melody in its own right, but the order of letters in an alphabet yields no words or sentences. Secondly, a composer may choose from an extraordinary variety of scales, but a writer ordinarily draws upon only one alphabet. And third, the tones of most scales gravitate to the bottom or initial tone, called *tonic* or *keynote,* for which there is no counterpart in an alphabet. Scales differ in their mode or flavor according to how the whole and half steps are arranged. Sometimes there is even a step-and-a-half in the succession of tones. The *chromatic scale* consists only of half steps, the *whole-tone scale* only of whole steps. As a result, both scales lack any gravitation to a clear tonic, which seems to depend on more "organic" mixtures of different sized steps. Yet, perhaps for the very reason that they can break away from this gravitation into "free space," both the chromatic and the whole-tone scales have become important springboards of Modern music. Most important since the Baroque Era have been the *major* and *minor* scales, often associated, rightly or wrongly, with the qualities "happy" and "sad." In the Medieval-and-Renaissance

Era the ecclesiastical or *church modes* prevailed. Among them, the Dorian mode can be heard by playing the successive white keys from one D to the next, the Phrygian from one E to the next, the Lydian from one F to the next, and Mixolydian from one G to the next. Many other scales have been invented by individual composers. Here are the pitches of *Yankee Doodle* in its proper mode, major; then some slight alterations sufficient to suggest the flavor of other modes:

> C C D E C E D B C C D E C   B G,
> C C D E F E D C B G A B C   C.

To play this same tune in the "melodic minor" mode, simply flat every E.

To play it in the Dorian mode, flat every E and B.

To play it according to the whole-tone series, flat every G, A, and B, and sharp the F.

To play it according to a scale invented by the American Charles Tomlinson Griffes, flat the D, E, and A, and sharp the F.

Let us look more closely at the *major scale,* which comes the nearest to being a universal scale and can even be explained largely by natural laws (as existing in an alphabetical redistribution of a fundamental tone's partials). The major scale is what you sing when you go up on the syllables do, re, mi, fa, sol, la, ti, do. The pattern of whole and half steps in a major scale is always $1\text{-}1\text{-}\frac{1}{2}\text{-}1\text{-}1\text{-}1\text{-}\frac{1}{2}$. Memorize this pattern. It can be applied by starting on any white or black key. Only on C can it be played with white keys alone. That is why we tend to think of the music alphabet as going from C to B rather than A to G, as you can see from the way that the successive alphabets are designated on the foregoing keyboard (Fig. 8)—subcontra, contra, great, small, 1, 2, 3, 4, and 5. (Can you find great G at the keyboard, F^3, small E-flat, C^5, subcontra A-sharp?)

Try picking out the major scales on each of the other keys, reciting the letter names and whole or half steps as you go. For example, "Starting with E and applying the pattern that was given, the first whole step leads to F-sharp, the second whole step leads to G-sharp, and the half step leads to A; the first of the next three whole steps leads to B, the second to C-sharp, the third to D-sharp, and the final half step comes out on E again." When there is a question of which spelling to use, these two rules will help: (1) Always follow alphabetical order, neither repeating nor skipping a letter. (2) Do not mix flats and sharps in the same scale. Occasionally you may have to use a double-flat or double-sharp to follow these rules.

STAFF NOTATION

Notation is essential to the preservation and development of any art that occurs in time. Painting, which occurs in space, is its own notation. But the great riches of past music would not be ours were there no adequate system of music notation. Thus, the art of dancing, which also occurs in time, has been seriously underdeveloped until now for want of an adequate notation. Except as recent systems like the so-called "Labanotation" are helping, there has been no real library of choreography where a dancer might "read" and recapture creations of past choreographers. Like that of rhythm, the notation of pitch underwent severe growing pains (in still earlier centuries) before it evolved into the present relatively uncomplicated system. Besides the staff the most successful methods of indicating pitch have been pictorial systems in which the actual position on the keys, strings, or holes is illustrated in a simplified manner. Known as *tabulatures* in the fifteenth to seventeenth centuries, these systems may still be seen in the ukelele chord positions diagrammed above the voice part in jazz sheet music, and in the illustrations for those "short-cut" methods of playing the piano or other instruments.

Gregorian chant was originally notated by signs called *neumes*, related to accent signs of ancient literature and, for example, to the subsequent acute and grave accents used in written French. Neumes merely suggested the rise and fall of melody as a reminder to those who already knew it. A vital step toward specific notation was the introduction (notably by Guido d'Arezzo in the eleventh century) of the lines that were to make up the present staff (Fig. 8, p. 64). The number of lines in the staff was variable at first, depending on the range of the melody, but has come to be fixed at five (except for the four-line staff and "square" notation still used in writing Gregorian chant, Fig. 47, p. 267). Now, when the range exceeds five lines, little sections of additional lines, called *ledger lines,* are merely added above or below the staff as needed. When the range greatly exceeds the staff an *octave sign,* 8ve···, is used to avoid too many ledger lines, indicating that the tones are actually to be sounded an octave higher or lower than they appear.

The successive lines and spaces of the staff represent successive letters of the music alphabet, ascending as the alphabet and pitch ascend. Thus, the alphabet must be recited backwards or "down" when you "descend" on the staff or ledger lines to figure out a note. Just which letter of the alphabet the staff begins on depends upon the "key" to the staff, or *clef* sign that is provided. Since the origin of the staff three clef signs have been used, always on one of the lines, never on a space. These are G,

G or treble clef   F or bass clef   C or alto clef   C or tenor clef

Fig. 9. Middle C in four clef positions

written 𝄞 on the second line and used mostly for high ranges; F, written 𝄢 on the fourth line and used for low ranges; and C, written 𝄡 on the third or fourth line and used for middle ranges, especially viola, cello, trombone, and bassoon, when playing around middle C. In Fig. 9 see these three clefs in their most usual four positions along with a whole-note indicating where middle C would be written.

Piano scores generally use only the G or *treble* clef for the upper right-hand staff and the F or *bass* clef for the lower left-hand staff. Curiously, these clefs provide no place on either staff for the most central note of all, middle C, which must be written between them with a ledger line—that is, one ledger line below the right-hand staff or above the left-hand staff. Familiarize yourself with the staff and its relation to the keyboard, first by picking out white keys at the keyboard and writing them on the proper line or space of the proper staff; second, by writing notes on either staff or any ledger line, or space beyond a ledger line, then finding the note on the keyboard. Gauge the exact octave of the played or written note by its nearness to middle C. Thus, the E that is one ledger line below the bass staff proves to be the second E below middle C on the keyboard (or great E). A time-honored method of reading notes on the staff until they are remembered at sight is the use of separate aids for lines and spaces in each hand, reading bottom up.

> right-hand lines, *Every Good Boy Does Fine*
> right-hand spaces, *F-A-C-E*
> left-hand lines, *Get Busy, Don't Fall Asleep*
> left-hand spaces, *All Cows Eat Grass*

Memorize and apply these aids if you do not already read notes, but remember that they apply only to the staff itself. For ledger lines and spaces, use the appropriate aid to find the nearest staff line or space, and figure up or down the alphabet from there.

The lines and spaces of our present five-line staff represent only white keys. Six-line and other staffs have been suggested that provide for the black keys, too; eliminate the use of different clefs; and read the same in each octave range. But as with the allegedly more convenient keyboards that have been devised—

or, for that matter, recent typewriter keyboards that distribute the typing better between the hands—tradition dies hard. At present, black keys and enharmonic spellings for white keys must be indicated by symbols for the various *accidentals,* as they are called: the flat (♭), double flat (♭♭), sharp (♯), and double sharp (✗). A natural (♮) is an accidental used to cancel any other accidental at least for the remainder of the measure. With the aid of these accidentals you can now construct major scales on the staff as well as at the keyboard. Follow these steps: (1) Write the eight notes (as whole notes) from the desired tonic up to the tonic an octave higher, leaving room between for accidentals if needed. Put in only the accidental for the tonic now, provided, of course, you have selected a scale that starts on a flat or sharp. (Write large accidentals, clearly on a line or space and at the *left* of the note concerned.) (2) Between and well under each pair of notes (so as to be out of the way of accidentals) write the figures indicating the major scale pattern of whole and half steps. (3) On the basis of this pattern and the two rules given earlier (p. 68), insert any accidentals that are needed. Here in Fig. 10 are the three steps as used to work out the major scale on the second A-flat below middle C, or great A-flat:

Fig. 10. Three steps in building a major scale

With this much information, an interesting challenge for you would be to try notating on the treble staff any uncomplicated, familiar tunes that you can recall. Insofar as you can, select keys with few or no flats or sharps. Work at the piano or, if possible, "by ear." With regard to the note values, the earlier suggestions for notating a rhythm (p. 58) should prove helpful.

THE TANGIBLES AND INTANGIBLES OF MELODY

Melody is the very essence of forthright music whether it occurs as an obvious tune (p. 195) or a profound lyrical expression. It may be defined as the seemingly continuous line or contour made by a coherent succession of tones that vary in pitch and usually in duration. Beyond this fact the styles of melody vary in the extreme. Thus, the progress from tone to tone may be largely *diatonic* (confined to the tones of the prevailing scale, as in *Marines' Hymn*) or chromatic ("colored" by the half- or whole-step alterations of frequent accidentals, as in *St. Louis Blues*); it may be *conjunct* (stepwise, as in *Deck the Hall*) or *disjunct* (marked by leaps, as in *The Star-Spangled Banner*). The range of tones may be narrow (as in the main theme of Sibelius' *Finlandia*) or wide (as in Schumann's *Träumerei*). The general contour may be smooth (as in "Largo" from Handel's opera *Serse*) or angular (as in "Air" from Bach's orchestral *Suite in D Major*, no. 3, better known in the solo-violin arrangement called *Air for the G String*). Altogether, the contour may describe a few broad curves (as in *Danny Boy*, also called *Londonderry Air*) or many little waves (as in *Star Dust*). And the melody may divide into clearly defined phrases (as in the theme of the variations in Haydn's "Emperor" *String Quartet*, op. 76, no. 3, better known as Austria's national anthem) or spin endlessly out of an initial motive (as in "Prize Song" from Wagner's opera *The Mastersingers of Nuremberg*).

True to the nature of all art, there is no absolute basis for evaluating a melody as "good" or "bad." About sixty years ago the English theorist Ebenezer Prout tried at least to show what he thought was *not* good in a melody by devising the most unmelodic series of tones that he could imagine (Fig. 11). But tastes have changed radically from era to era. Recently the American theorist Karl Eschman (listed at the end of Chap. 8) showed how this same series might be construed as a melody well suited to later tastes. Compare, for that matter, the wide-ranged melody by Shostakovitch that is quoted in Chapter 6 (Fig. 19, p. 101). At most one can only generalize about the characteristics found in many successful melodies. (For the sake of analysis, a melody may be put in graph form, with the pitch intervals represented

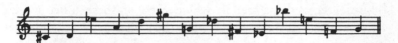

Fig. 11. Prout's example of an unmelodic series of tones

by a vertical coordinate and the duration intervals by a horizontal coordinate. It was with such a method that the Brazilian Villa-Lobos translated the skyline of New York into a melody!)

Here are four characteristic properties of melody:

1. Smaller pitch intervals preponderate over larger ones (Fig. 48, p. 270), chiefly because the ear relates tones most readily when they are near together, somewhat as the eye takes in objects close together easier than objects widely scattered.

2. When bigger intervals occur, they occur more often in the rise than the fall of melody (Fig. 19, p. 101), much as a person tends to climb with big steps, but to brake his descent with smaller, mincing steps.

3. The peak of interest usually occurs near the end (Figs. 18 and 21, pp. 97 and 112), ⟋‾‾╲ , just as it does in a novel or a sonnet, and not in the middle, ⟋‾‾╲ , as it often does in a space design such as a building with an elaborate central entrance (Plate 5).

4. A melody usually falls rather than rises to its final tone (Fig. 32, p. 192), somewhat as an activity tends to relax as it concludes.

All four traits happen to appear in the opening phrase of Mendelssohn's *Variations sérieuses*, op. 54 (Fig. 12). But which traits do not appear, for example, in the melodic line by Bach that is quoted in Fig. 32 (p. 192)?

Fig. 12. Typical traits of melody (Mendelssohn's *Variations sérieuses,* op. 54, for piano)

The degree and manner in which each of these traits applies help to explain distinctions between the melodic styles of different eras, cultures, social uses, composers, and musical designs. For example, wide leaps are the exception in Renaissance vocal music but abound in Romantic vocal music. The melodies of primitive tribes typically start on a high tone and descend, whereas those of our Western culture tend to do just the opposite. Later we shall see that the character of a melody can also be influenced by other elements of music, especially harmony, texture, timbre, and dynamics. The Englishman Donald Tovey went so far as to call melody merely "the surface of harmony," which description often does fit Romantic melodies—for instance, the melodies in such favorite piano pieces as Schubert's *Impromptu in G-flat Major,* op. 90, no. 3; or Liszt's *Liebesträume, No. 3;* or the second theme in Chopin's *Fantaisie in F Minor,* op. 49.

If we are still unable to categorize the "good" and "bad" of melody, we at least have some bases now for applying the broad criteria of any art, chiefly intelligibility, coherence, a firm skeleton or framework, and satisfying proportions. The intelligibility of a melody depends mainly on whether its pitch relationships, near or remote, are assimilable by the ear. Coherence depends on the perception of some internal, unifying pattern (for instance, the rhythm and pitch pattern that recurs in nearly every measure of *Home, Sweet Home*). A firm skeleton concerns the most essential tones, which themselves should make at least an acceptable if not an appealing outline. Thus, the chorus from *Keep the Home Fires Burning* is essentially a descending major scale. Satisfying proportions are as necessary to a melody as they are to the recipe for a cake. But they are certainly less predictable, notwith-standing the efforts of some aestheticians to find them in laws of mathematics such as the summation series 1, 2, 3, 5, 8, 13, and so on. Mozart achieved ideal balance with surprisingly regular struc-tures, Haydn with frequently irregular ones!

Of course, the evaluation of a melody may depend consider-ably on subjective reactions. Conditioning and experience matter a great deal. A lecture in Latin will hardly appeal to the man who knows no Latin. For example, one dare not condemn Modern music as being amelodic until he has become familiar with the idiom. One should strive to know some of the great melodies of every era, of which the following long-time favorites of the present author may be listed as representative:

Wipo, *Victimae paschali laudes,* about 1050, a late type of plain-chant known as a *sequence* (p. 266), syllabic style (one note to a syllable), concerned with the Christian sacrifice of the lamb at Easter time.

John Dowland, *Weep You No More, Sad Fountains,* 1603, ar-ranged both as a song with lute accompaniment and as a polyphonic madrigal in which the lowest three voices sing the parts given to the lute.

J. S. Bach, "Adagio" from *Violin Concerto in E Major,* about 1720. Note the contrast of the impassioned, free violin solo against the more even-tempered, steady accompaniment figure in the orchestra.

Mozart, "Andante" from *Piano Concerto in A Major,* K. 488, 1786 (Appendix II, No. 34,II). The carefully balanced phrases of this melody are defined with great clarity.

Beethoven, "Cavatina" from *String Quartet in B-flat Major,* op. 130, completed in 1826. Beethoven himself said this movement al-ways made him weep.

Schubert, "Adagio" from *String Quintet in C Major,* op. 163, 1828, a remarkably sustained, deeply serious melody, accompanied by delicate commentaries in the other instruments.

Chopin, opening section of *Ballade in F Minor* for piano, op. 52, 1842 (Fig. 30, p. 184; Appendix II, No. 22). It is interesting that even this intensely introspective line is accompanied by the characteristic um-pah-pah (p. 113) of the nineteenth century.

Mendelssohn, "Andante" from *Violin Concerto in E Minor,* op. 64, 1844, a model of a well-planned, unfolding line, complete with its telling climax near the end.

Wagner, the monolog of Hans Sachs in the second act of the opera *The Mastersingers of Nuremberg,* completed in 1868, a superb example of Wagner's "endless" melody, which flows on and on without ever quite being allowed to abate throughout this scene. Sachs philosophically resigns himself to the idea that a younger man deserves the young lady he himself loves.

Brahms, "Andante con moto" from *Piano Trio in C Major,* op. 87, completed in 1882, a set of variations in which the three instruments sing forth the melodic line, sometimes individually and sometimes together.

Puccini, the love duet that concludes the first act of *La Bohème,* 1896, a rapturous outpouring of melody characteristic of the best Italian opera.

Richard Strauss, the final scene from *Der Rosenkavalier* (*The Rose-Bearer*), completed in 1911, a luxurious trio of women's voices in which the Princess von Werdenberg expresses a philosophy akin to that of Hans Sachs in *The Mastersingers of Nuremberg.*

Roger Sessions, "Andante" from the first *Sonata for Piano,* 1931, a freely flowing melody that occurs before each of the three movements, though differently each time.

Ravel, "Adagio assai" from *Piano Concerto in G Major,* completed in 1931, a gentle, intensely expressive melody played first by the piano, then by the orchestra against an exquisite tracery in the piano part.

SELECTED READINGS

Karl Wilson Gehrkens, *Music Notation and Terminology.* River Forest (Ill.): Laidlaw, 1942.

Howard Boatwright, *Introduction to the Theory of Music,* Chapters 3 and 9-13. New York: W. W. Norton, 1956.

John L. Dunk, *The Structure of the Musical Scale.* London: J. Lane, 1940.

Ernest Toch, *The Shaping Forces of Music* (especially the second part, "Melody"). New York: Criterion, 1948.

Arthur C. Edwards, *The Art of Melody*. New York: Philosophical Library, 1956.

Deryck Cooke, *The Language of Music*. New York: Oxford University Press, 1959.

Arthur Lourié, "An Inquiry into Melody," *Modern Music*, VI-VII (1929-1930).

A. H. Fox Strangways, "Tune," *Music & Letters*, III (1922).

H. J. Watt, "Melody," *Music & Letters*, V (1924).

Chapter 6

Harmony and Tonality

INTERVALS, BOTH CONSONANT AND DISSONANT

Harmony in music concerns the sounding of more than one tone at a time. It is one of Western civilization's chief accomplishments in music. Around the ninth century there developed an artful, planned blending of tones whereby a new depth was imparted to music in a world that had probably known only single melodic lines (*monophony*) or accidental mixtures of sounds (*heterophony*). This blending began in a style of sacred vocal music called *organum* (pronounced or'ganum), which was little more than a note-for-note parallelism of two or more lines a fourth or fifth (four or five scale degrees or letters) apart.

Since the time of organum the art of combining tones has developed both "horizontally" and "vertically." In a horizontal sense, concurrent melodic lines have gained remarkable independence through contrary rather than parallel motion and dissimilar rather than coinciding note values. In a vertical sense, superimposed tones have been built up into such a variety of "chords" that the composer now has an almost limitless vocabulary of sonorities at his disposal. Both developments have been profoundly influenced by changing concepts of dissonance and consonance, or discord and concord (clash and blend of tones).

Dissonance and *consonance* help to create in music that polarity of tension and release, struggle and repose, rise and fall, variety within unity, that is essential to any dynamic art form.

There have been complete about-faces from era to era in the matter of what *intervals* (pairs of tones) or chords seem dissonant and what consonant. Since the Medieval-and-Renaissance Era consonance has gradually taken over more and more tone combinations formerly considered dissonant, while dissonance has explored still more biting combinations.

However, the polarity of dissonance and consonance is not determined solely by changing tastes as regards what intervals seem to disagree, like clashing gears, and what seem to blend, like well-meshed gears. A certain scientific basis for these distinctions is found in the theory of partials (p. 31), which has been the starting point for so much else in music theory, too. This basis may be seen in the first sixteen partials of a fundamental tone, great C (Fig. 13).

Fig. 13. The first sixteen partials of great C

In *traditional harmony*—that is, the harmony of the past three centuries, which still underlies much of the art and social music in our present experience—the intervals defined by various pairings of the first eight partials yield all the accepted consonances, while various pairings higher in the series produce the recognized dissonances. But music of more recent times has tended to find consonant as well as dissonant intervals among the higher partials of the series (Fig. 19, p. 101). Perhaps, as some argue, dissonance will not again forge ahead of consonance in the series until we break out of our present system of twelve half steps in the octave, introduce smaller steps corresponding to the still higher partials, and develop instruments that can play these intervals conveniently (of which, more on pp. 102–103). In any case, there are enough inconsistencies in this "scientific" distinction between consonance and dissonance—including the blacked-in notes, which do not correspond to our usual tunings of those tones—to remind us that music is still an art by no means wholly chained to mathematics.

Any further reference to dissonant and consonant intervals and to their remarkable range of expressive values would mean going further into the nature of the intervals themselves. Such technicalities are among the rudiments with which most courses in harmony are prefaced. They are offered in the next five paragraphs in answer to the marked curiosity about them often expressed by those newly confronted with music's inner workings. Other readers will find this material pertinent but not indispensable to the main progress of this book.

Every interval in traditional harmony occurs in three or four sizes, graduated by half steps. Thus, C-E♭♭, C-E♭, C-E♮, and C-E♯ all qualify as thirds since all are three letters apart, but from one to the next they differ in size by a half step. The unison, fourth, fifth, and octave occur in three sizes—diminished, perfect, and augmented. The others, the second, third, sixth, and seventh, occur in four sizes—diminished, minor, major, and augmented. Note that intervals that occur in perfect sizes do not occur in major or minor sizes, and vice versa.

Obviously, if you know one of the sizes of an interval you can determine any of the others simply by adding or subtracting half steps as necessary. For instance, the diminished fifth G-D♭ measures three whole steps, as a reference to the keyboard will show. Therefore, the perfect fifth will be G-D♮, a half step larger; and the augmented fifth will be G-D♯, another half step larger. To know some one size of each interval you need only remember this principle: Each perfect and each major size is precisely that formed by the keynote of any major scale and the corresponding scale degree above it. In other words, if you want to identify any interval you need simply think of its lower tone as the keynote of a major scale, then compare its upper tone with that of the corresponding perfect or major interval that will always occur in that scale. For example, by regarding the lower tone of C-F as a keynote, we know this fourth must be a perfect fourth because F, not F♭ or F♯, is the correct fourth tone in the C-major scale (and because, as indicated at the end of the previous paragraph, the fourth, like the unison and octave, is classified as perfect rather than major or minor).

Traditional harmony distinguishes two classes of consonant intervals, *perfect* and *imperfect,* and only one of dissonant intervals. The perfect intervals are the perfect sizes of the unison, fourth, fifth, and octave. With the possible exception of the perfect fourth, these intervals blend so completely that two voices repeating any one of them at different pitch levels tend to merge and lose their identity. Hence, one of the strictest rules of traditional harmony (and one of the first to be abolished in Modern music): "Avoid parallel octaves and fifths between any two voices or parts." The imperfect intervals, by which are meant the major or minor sizes of the third and sixth, blend fairly smoothly but with just enough conflict ("beats") between the sound waves of the two tones to give them a recognizable tang or character. Far from being ruled out, "parallel" thirds and sixths are frequently present in long chains in music of a rich texture (Fig. 22b, p. 114). These intervals are in fact the consonances one intuitively hits upon when he "harmonizes," as in a "barbershop quartet."

The dissonant intervals, while they are all classed under the one head of dissonance, do differ markedly in degree of clash (and can be codified on this basis, as noted under Hindemith, p. 103). Thus, the minor seventh (for example, C-B♭) has been on the borderline of consonance (measure 1 of Fig. 22a, p. 114) ever since the Baroque Era, whereas the major seventh, with its much harsher clash, has only been used as an independent sound in fairly recent music (as it often is by Ravel). In general, the intervals just on either side of the perfect unison and the perfect octave are the harshest or most unsettled, notably the minor second and major seventh. Since dissonances do not blend, the strongest tendencies of their tones are to contract or expand into intervals that do blend, especially into imperfect consonances (second measure of Fig. 27, p. 163).

Among all twenty-eight possible sizes of the eight intervals from unison to octave, only eight are perfect or imperfect consonances. And even among these the perfect fourth is only treated as a consonance when it is sounded along with a consonant third or fifth below its lower tone. The twenty dissonances, which account for all the remaining sizes, include some intervals that would not sound dissonant if heard alone. These are the ones that are enharmonic equivalents of consonances, and are only made to sound dissonant—for which read "active, tense, in need of resolution"—by the context in which they appear. For instance, the interval B♭-F♯ at the end of Fig. 22a (p. 114) is actually the enharmonic of the minor sixth B♭-G♭, an imperfect consonance. But it is made to sound dissonant here by its tendency to expand, or its need to resolve, into the same major third E♭-G (or major tenth, if you prefer) on which the example begins, E♭-G.

You can best be introduced to the expressive values of consonant and dissonant intervals by joining with someone else to sing them yourselves. Simply start up the major scale (from *do* to *do,* or on some neutral syllable like *la*) and let your partner do the same, first one note later so that you are singing seconds, then two notes later so that you are singing thirds, and so on. Besides the degree of clash or blend, the relative difficulty or ease with which you can hold to your own part (try stopping up one ear) will leave little doubt as to which intervals are dissonant and which are consonant. In the nature of the scale not all intervals in any one series will come out exactly "parallel" (exactly the same size). For example, can you hear and feel which fourth is the disturbing and vocally difficult one of three rather than two-and-one-half steps? (See the further mention of "tritone" on p. 100.)

CONSTRUCTING CHORDS FROM INTERVALS

A *chord* means a group of three or more tones sounded together. In traditional harmony chords are built up in superimposed thirds from a *root* or generating tone. Thus, to construct a four-tone chord on the root E you simply take every third letter, figuring up from E, until you have four tones in all: E-G-B-D. A chord of three tones is called a *triad*, whereas chords of four, five, six, and occasionally as many as seven tones are called seventh, ninth, eleventh, and thirteenth chords, respectively, according to the interval between the root and the highest tone (Fig. 14).

Chords have different forms or flavors just as scales and intervals do. Whether the superimposed thirds are major (two

triad   7th chord   9th chord   11th chord   13th chord

Fig. 14. From triad to thirteenth chord by adding thirds

steps in size) or minor (one-and-one-half steps) accounts for nearly all of the differences. The most common form, even before and since the centuries of traditional harmony, has been the *major triad*, made up of a major third topped by a minor third. In fact, the major triad is sometimes called "the chord of nature" because its three tones correspond with the first three tones of different letter names to be found in the series of partials. Next most common is the *minor triad*, made up in just the reverse order of a minor third topped by a major third. Although the minor triad has no equally simple explanation in nature, it and the major triad are the only two chord forms accepted as completely con-

sonant in traditional harmony. That is because they are the only
chord forms in which no traditional dissonances occur in any
possible pairing of their tones except as the perfect fourth in a
dissonance.

Fig. 15 shows the seven most common forms of traditional
harmony, all of them composed only of major (+) or minor (−)
thirds superimposed.

Familiarize yourself with chords (1) by constructing the seven
most common chords on any or all of the white and black keys in
turn, and (2) by searching out these chords in any book of hymns

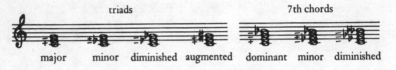

Fig. 15. The seven most common chord forms

or community songs. In the latter process you will want to know
that the bass or lowest tone of a chord will not always be its root,
but may be any one of its tones. The composer decides between
the root position and some *inversion* of the chord mainly according to which tone helps to make the most purposeful line out
of the successive bass tones. But you can always discover a traditional chord's root by finding which of its tones yields all the
others according to the principle of counting up every third letter
from that tone.

The prime directions of harmonic movement

An isolated chord is usually named according to its root and
form. This principle applies even when the order of its tones is
inverted. Thus, as just suggested, B-D-G is still a "G-major" triad.
However, when we wish to show the relationship of one chord to
another we usually give it a Roman numeral or a functional name
according to the degree of the scale tone that serves as its root.

Thus, G-B-D is a "V" or "dominant" chord in the key of C because its root is the fifth tone in the C scale and because the fifth tone of any major or minor scale is known as the dominant tone. The Roman numeral and the functional name for the triad on each of the seven degrees of any major scale are illustrated in Fig. 16. In this instance the C-major scale is used.

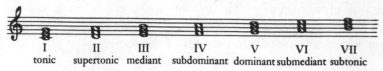

| I | II | III | IV | V | VI | VII |
| tonic | supertonic | mediant | subdominant | dominant | submediant | subtonic |

Fig. 16. A number and name for the triad on each scale degree

Notice that the triads on different scale degrees have different forms when only the tones of the one scale are drawn upon. If you were to compare these forms with those in Fig. 15, you would find that the triads on the first, fourth, and fifth degrees are major; those on the second, third, and sixth degrees are minor; and the one on the seventh degree is diminished. Lower-case Roman numerals are generally used for the nonmajor triads. The functional names are almost self-explanatory according to the position of the scale degree. *Tonic* means *the* tone or keynote. *Dominant* is named for the fifth step, which literally dominates, both in melody and harmony. The subdominant is so called less because it is next below the dominant than because the fourth step is five scale degrees *below* the tonic just as the fifth step is five above. In this latter sense, *mediant* and *submediant* lie halfway between the tonic and the two dominants. The *subtónic* is often called the leading-tone in the major and other scales where it leads by only a half step into the tonic.

To get better acquainted with chord designations, try yourself on drill questions like these, disregarding accidentals if necessary: What are the tones of the ii triad in the major scale on A? (Answer, B-D-F♯.) What are the tones of the dominant triad in the major scale on B♭? (Answer, F-A-C.)

The three major triads in the foregoing example—the I or tonic, IV or subdominant, and V or dominant—are called *primary triads,* as distinguished from the other four, subordinate triads. I, IV, and V define the prime directions of all movement in traditional harmony. They define the fundamental orbit of harmony. Or, to put it more in a functional sense, they establish a kind of balance in which the tonic serves as a fulcrum or point of repose between the counterbalanced dominants a fifth away on either side, which are chords of suspense:

I

C E G

F A C   G B D

IV   V

With regard to their main, more specific functions, the tonic chord begins and ends the music, the dominant chord marks halfway points, and the subdominant chord provides digressions counter to the pull of the dominant. In a psychological sense, the tonic has a neutral or final effect, the dominant gives the impression of being on the bright or joyous side of the tonic, and the subdominant on the dark or gloomier side. If you will try over the *The Whistler and His Dog,* Arthur Pryor's charming tune, you will hear these chord functions and effects in miniature. The first of the four phrases into which this tune divides ends on the tonic, the second on the dominant, the third on a variant of the subdominant, and the last on the tonic again. We shall have occasion later (as on p. 168) to see how typical is the same order of harmonic functions in the broader relationships of much larger pieces.

The three primary triads also provide the stock endings or *cadences* in music. One of these is the *final cadence* IV-I$_4^6$-V-I (end of Figs. 18 and 46c, pp. 97 and 258), which you can hear in your mind on the closing syllables,

"-ing, Old Black Joe."

IV   I$^6_4$ V   I

(I$^6_4$ designates a peculiarly compelling though unstable inversion of I in which the upper tones lie a fourth and a sixth above the temporary bass—for example, G-C-E.) Another common cadence is the less final *half cadence* I-V (middle of Fig. 46c, p. 258), as on the two accented syllables in the phrase,

"And I'll *nev*-er see my darling any *more*,"

I   V

from the chorus of *Darling Nelly Gray*. A half cadence is used at temporary halts in music and lets one feel that more must still be coming.

Since together they contain every note in the scale, the three primary triads alone can supply a purposeful, solid harmony to any melody that centers largely around the major or minor scale. Thus, if the melody is in the key of C, any use of B can be harmonized by the V chord, any E by the I chord, and so on. There is even a choice on the first or fifth scale degrees, which your ear will help you decide. The chord may be changed, as in most hymns, with almost every note of the melody (*fast harmonic rhythm*, Fig. 33, p. 195) or, as in most folk songs, only once every measure or so (*slow harmonic rhythm*, Appendix II, No. 6). Like tempo, harmonic rhythm strongly affects the sense of the music. In fact, we have seen that the faster the harmonic rhythm the slower the tempo is likely to be. Can you imagine *America* played first with a change of chord on every melody note, then with simply the tonic chord held from start to end? Especially in slow harmonic rhythm some of the melody notes may be *foreign tones* —that is, tones that do not belong to the chord but usually will be found to pass stepwise into some tone of that chord (measure 1 of Fig. 20b, p. 106).

You will enjoy trying to play familiar tunes by ear with your right hand, then adding the primary triads in the left hand as your ear dictates. This experience can do much to sharpen your harmonic awareness. Actually, "playing by ear" is often learned intuitively by enterprising persons who have never tried to play piano before. Your choice of chords for the start of *Old Folks at Home* might be as follows:

> Way down up-on de Swa-nee
> I - - - - - - - -
>
> River,
> IV -
>
> Far, far a-
> I - - -
>
> way;
> V -

and so on. As you progress, try counting the melody's pulse. Can you recognize the $\frac{4}{4}$ meter? In this experiment, for example, it would help you to know where the bars fall. Especially since the Baroque Era, meter has had a distinct influence on the timing of the chord changes. Thus, one rule-of-thumb calls for a change .of chord over the bar. The location of the bar also governs dissonance treatment and the use of foreign tones. For instance, a tone on the first beat that proceeds stepwise should ordinarily be treated as an *appoggiatura* (one kind of foreign tone) by choosing the chord that contains not it but the tone to which it goes. Thus, harmonize both syllables of "bon-nie" in the second measure of *Annie Laurie* with IV rather than V-IV.

The *subordinate triads* add variety, sometimes at the expense of solidity, by serving as substitutes for the primary triads. In *America* the third chord and sometimes the second one are of this sort as this piece is usually harmonized. When a subordinate triad replaces the last I triad in a final cadence, the result is a *deceptive cadence* that unexpectedly prolongs the flow (as hap-

pens near the end of Handel's familiar "Largo" from *Serse*).
The numerous chromatic chords are chords containing accidentals not in the scale (Figs. 18, 20b, 33, and 42, pp. 97, 106,
195, and 240). Their effect is most commonly to intensify the
pull of the dominant, sometimes to the point of sentimentality,
as in *Sweet Adeline*. One of these chords is actually called a
"secondary dominant," or "dominant of the dominant." You can
hear it, among countless instances, on the word "fruit-ed" that
precedes the middle cadence in *America, the Beautiful*.

KEYS AND KEY RELATIONSHIPS

A *key* is defined here as a family of tones centered around a
keynote, especially the tones of a major or minor scale. Such an
organization of tones occurs not only in an alphabetical arrangement of the scale but in the varied arrangements of tones in
melodies, and in the chords that define the I-IV-V-I harmonic
orbit.

To say that a piece is in the key of D major means that its
tones largely gravitate toward an end on D. A piece may be in the
key of any of the twelve tones in the octave, each involving a
different number of sharps or flats except the key of C-natural,
of course. A common device for learning the keys along with
their sharps or flats is the circle or "clock" of fifths. As the numbers on a clock face are separated by five-minute intervals, so the
key names are here separated by five-letter intervals. (But, of
course, there is one less letter than minute mark each time; since
the musical fifths overlap, the final letter of one fifth is the first
letter of the next.) At the zero or twelve-o'clock hour is C, the
major key of no flats or sharps. Progressing clockwise by fifths
lies the order of sharp keys, with G, the key of one sharp, being
at the one-o'clock position, D, the key of two sharps, at the two-
o'clock position, and so on. Progressing counterclockwise by fifths
lies the order of flat keys, with F, the key of one flat, being at the

eleven-o'clock position, B-flat, the key of two flats, at the ten-o'clock position, and so on. Since there are seven tones in a major (or minor) scale, keys up to seven sharps or seven flats are possible. Altogether, then, with C included there would seem to be fifteen possible keys. Actually there are only twelve keys with fifteen names—only twelve, that is, since there are only twelve different white or black keys to serve as keynotes. As indicated by the dotted line, the three keys of five to seven sharps are merely the enharmonic equivalents of the three keys of seven to five flats.

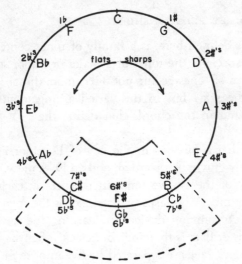

The interval of the fifth, the most perfect of consonances other than the octave itself, begins to seem like nature's own magic number in music, founded, as it is, early in the series of partials (Fig. 13, p. 79). It governs not only the circle of keys, the distance from a tonic to either dominant, and the outer dimensions of major and minor triads, but such matters as the interval between strings on most bowed stringed instruments, the timbre and the fingering on the clarinet, and the distance between the ranges of the F and C or the C and G clefs. Now we find one more application of the fifth in the *order of accidentals* for any key. To illustrate, the key of one sharp is G and the one sharp itself is F-sharp, which fact you can verify by building on G the major scale pattern 1-1-$\frac{1}{2}$-1-1-1-$\frac{1}{2}$ that you worked with in the previous chapter. Counting up five letters from this F-sharp yields C-sharp, the additional sharp needed for the next key (D, two sharps), and so on. Similarly, by counting *down* five letters at a time from B-flat, which is the one flat in the key of F, each additional flat may be found. Here is the complete order of seven accidentals. From left to right it becomes the order of sharps; from right to left, the order of flats.

order of sharps ⟶

F C G D A E B

⟵ order of flats

As with the lines and spaces on the staff (p. 70), one can use the time-honored sentences or invent new ones to help recall these relationships of keys and accidentals, such as *Fat Cows Go Down Alleys Eating Bumpkins* for the order of sharps, or perhaps *For Bold Effects Apply Dark Green Colors* for the order of flat keys. One trouble with such memory devices is that one must finally devise a sentence with which to remember the sentences! In any case, with the circle of fifths and the order of accidentals, the make-up of any key is quickly discovered. Thus, if we want to know how many and what accidentals occur in the key of A, a look at A's position on the circle shows that it has three sharps, and a look at the order of accidentals, reading from left to right for sharps, shows that those three sharps are F, C, and G. Or if we want to know what key uses the first four flats (B, E, A, D, reading right to left), the circle shows that key to be A-flat.

In a music score the accidentals for the prevailing key are shown at the left of each staff in what is known as the *key signature* (placed between the clef sign and the time signature). Com-

pare the signatures for each of the sharp and flat keys with the
order of accidentals (Fig. 17).

Minor keys could be shown on a similar circle. They relate to
major keys in two distinct ways. The closest relationship is that
of the *tonic* minor (or "parallel" minor as it is often called), which
has the same keynote but a key signature that differs by three
accidentals in a counterclockwise direction around the circle of

Fig. 17. The fourteen standard key signatures

fifths. The other relationship is that of the *relative* minor, which
has the same signature but a different keynote one-and-one-half
steps below that of the related major key.

major:	C D E	F G A B C
parallel (natural) minor:	C D E♭	F G A♭ B♭ C
relative (natural) minor:	A B C	D E F G A

Actually, tonic minor and major became almost indistinguishable
with the trend toward highly chromatic harmony in the Romantic
Era. The major key incorporated foreign tones, including "borrowed tones" from the minor key, and vice versa, until one cannot say which mode prevails. Jazz often deliberately exploits this
confusion, an instance being the manner in which the third step

is alternately lowered and raised on the words "Got the blues" at the middle of *St. Louis Blues*.

TONALITY AS AN AGENT OF LARGER ORGANIZATION

Perhaps you have already concluded that harmony must exist on several levels. We have seen how tones combine into intervals, intervals into chords, and chords into the orbits of harmonic movement that outline keys. Now we come to one more, still broader, level, that at which several keys unite in a larger plan called tonality.

Tonality as defined here means the particular organization of keys around the home key in a musical work. Or more briefly, it is the key scheme of that work. In that capacity tonality vitally influences the total form and character of music. It represents, in fact, one main way of viewing musical form. Like the six blind men from Indostan who came to inspect and report on the elephant, various theorists have preferred various vantage points from which to view musical form. Rhythm in its largest sense of periodicity (peaks in a chain of mountain peaks) is another such vantage point. Melody as a network of motives or themes is another. Dynamics as an over-all design in intensity might be another. And the structural influence of certain melodic elements in musical texture is still another. In fact, as noted in Chapter 1, this last is the vantage point preferred in the present approach (Chap. 8). But there is no denying the significance of tonality as one main cohesive force in musical form, especially during the centuries of traditional harmony.

A tonal scheme has been regarded as a kind of grand, prolonged cadence in music. In this sense a composition that changes from key to key during its course—and there are very few compositions that do not exploit this basic means of musical variety—may be said to make its own particular tour around selected "high spots" in the circle of fifths. It might, for example, start in C

major, move on for a while to A minor, then F major, then D
minor, then G major, finally returning home to C major. Do you
see how this tour might be outlined as a broad emphasis of the
cadence I-vi-IV-ii-V-I?

Actually, a number of musicians, led by the late Viennese
theorist Heinrich Schenker, insist on that view and more when
they argue that a composition written in one unifying key cannot in the same sense be in several keys. Strictly speaking, this is
unassailable logic, somewhat equivalent to saying that a man does
not forsake his citizenship simply by making a grand tour of several foreign countries. An apparent change, then, from the home
key of C to the foreign key of G would in reality be only a prolonged emphasis on the dominant side of the one home key. Such
an analysis does promote a more panoramic, over-all view of the
tonality.

Certainly while we are still bound to the traditional terminology of music we ought to speak advisedly of key changes or
"modulations," as they are called. At best, there is always a question in the analysis of musical form as to when a modulation *is*
a *modulation*— a real shifting of the tonic or center of gravity, so
to speak. Is it one when the change is so transitory that it merely
colors the harmony of the moment? When it is sufficiently distinct and prolonged to mark off one section of the music? When
it is so extensive that it influences the broad tonal scheme? Does
our citizen change his residence when he makes a day visit without packing his bags? When he closes his home to get away for a
month's vacation? When he rents it to spend two years of study
abroad? There are many borderline cases that simply defy unequivocal pronouncements.

A brief explanation of how modulation takes place should further the understanding of these distinctions in tonal movement
that are of such importance to musical style and form. Modulations from key to key take place by way of fence, pivot, or common chords, as they are variously called—that is, by way of

chords that can be heard momentarily in both the old and the new key. Three steps are involved: (1) establishment of the old key, obviously necessary if we are to get any sense of leaving it; (2) one or more pivot chords; (3) establishment of the new key, equally necessary if the modulation is to sound complete. The process is somewhat like punning, but without ordinarily aiming at wit. Consider this absurd quip (in the manner popularized by Rube Goldberg).

Question:	Why is a cravat like a strictly educated suitor?	
Answer:	A cravat is a tie;	(old key)
	a tie is a draw;	(first pivot chord)
	draw is what one does to a rigidly taut bow;	(second pivot chord)
	and a rigidly taught beau is a strictly educated suitor.	(new key)

Now, we classify modulations as near, moderately distant, or remote. Roughly, these degrees of modulation correspond to the distance between the old and new key on the circle of fifths. But there are exceptions. For instance, we know that a change from major to tonic minor makes a difference of three accidentals but *no* change of tonic. A somewhat more reliable measure is the interval formed by the old and new tonic. The modulation goes to a nearly related key if the interval is a perfect consonance, to a moderately distant key if it is an imperfect consonance, and to a more or less remote key if it is a dissonance.

A modulation to a nearly related key can be made through a chord that is actually common to both keys (much as "tie" in the punning analogy relates to both cravat and draw without change of spelling). This sort of modulation (D minor to A minor) is what takes place tonally in the first, 22-measure section of the "Scherzo" from Schubert's *String Quartet in D Minor* (Appendix II, No. 32,III). A modulation to a moderately distant key usually requires that the common chord be heard first in one mode, major or minor, then the other (somewhat as "draw" must serve first as a noun, then as a verb). For an example of this type (F major to D major) listen to the second section (measures 17-62) in the finale of the same work. A modulation to a remote key is often made through a chord that must be respelled enharmonically to relate it to the new key (much as "taut bow" was respelled "taught beau"). An example of this type occurs in the wonderfully Schubertian passage shortly after the opening of this work (Fig. 18).

Nearly related modulations have occurred in general practice since the Baroque Era, moderately distant ones since the Classic and Early Romantic Eras, and more remote ones increasingly throughout the Romantic Era. The use of transitory modulations for purposes of harmonic color also became an increasingly important style trait during the Romantic Era. You can hear it to fine advantage in the passage just cited (Fig. 18), where the stepwise, generally chromatic line of each instrument makes the modulation a smoothly graded process. And you can hear it to equally good advantage in the "Prelude" to Wagner's opera *Parsifal* (Appendix II, No. 6), where the brasses in the middle section make stunning, abrupt modulations at each dramatic new entry.

What makes modulation in such examples recognizable by ear? Its general effect as a heightener of the tonal tension is undeniable. But specific recognition of modulation as such is often hard for the lay listener to achieve. The examples just cited do provide one clue, and a clue that is even more likely to serve in Baroque and Classic music. That clue is the use of *sequence*, or the reiteration of melodic and harmonic patterns at successively higher or lower pitch levels. Especially in Baroque music (Fig. 37, p. 208) a pattern simply may be repeated on each step of the ascending or descending scale until the desired new key is reached. The composer jumps on the moving stairway, so to speak, and gets off at his floor. You will have several chances to

Fig. 18. Modulation through remote keys for the sake of harmonic color (Schubert, *String Quartet in D Minor,* "Death and the Maiden," I)

hear such sequences in the fugues, dances, and other music of J. S. Bach.

New tonal vistas

Thus far in this chapter we have been concerned chiefly with traditional harmony and tonality, the sort that was identified with music of the past three centuries. *Modality* rather than tonality is the proper term for the organization of the Dorian, Phrygian, and other ecclesiastical modes that had been employed in the Medieval-and-Renaissance Era, as mentioned in Chapter 5 (Figs. 26 and 47, pp. 158 and 267). Compared with tonality, modality is more static and therefore less of an organizing agent in musical form. It is less a grand tour than it is a many-sided view of the same locale. Its static quality derives from the ecclesiastical modes themselves, whose tones reveal only a comparatively passive attraction to any tonal center.

If tonality in the Medieval-and-Renaissance Era was hardly operative yet in the traditional sense, it must be said to have become hardly operative again in the Modern Era. It is losing much of its significance because its very function is being undermined. When chromatic chords and remote modulations occur too often, the ear fails to assimilate them in one broad plan and tonality ceases to function as an agent of larger organization. Color interest soon overshadows structural value and eventually the colors themselves become excessive, fusing into a gray mass of sound. Wagner's great love opera *Tristan and Isolde* heralded this crisis in the later nineteenth century. Subsequent, forward-looking composers had no choice but to react, and react violently, in a different direction. It is no wonder that harmony and tonality undergo the most conspicuous changes in Modern music. The increased dissonance, or rather the wider latitude of consonance, and the seeming lawlessness of Modern harmony have certainly aroused more discussion and probably more resistance than other, perhaps more profound, trends such as the greater freedom of rhythm (Chap. 4), the wider scope of melody (Chap. 5), or certain modifications in texture and over-all form (Chap. 8).

One important Modern trend has been *atonality*, which very word implies the sharp negation of the past that is so characteristic of any young era. Associated especially with the late Viennese composer Arnold Schoenberg, atonality has been viewed as the means of releasing music into "free tonal space," chiefly by doing away with the gravitational pull of the I-IV-V-I orbit. In place of this binding influence Schoenberg introduces the *tone row,* which is an arrangement of all twelve tones of the chromatic scale in any order. An example is the tone row with which Schoenberg's *Quintet for Wind Instruments* begins (Appendix II, No. 7):

E♭	G	A	B	C♯	C♮	B♭	D♮	E	F♯	A♭	F
1	2	3	4	5	6	7	8	9	10	11	12

(Recall that Prout's "unmelodic" line, Fig. 11 (p. 73), was a remarkable if unwitting anticipation of the tone row.) The tone row usually repeats without interruption, like a continuous thread, although the fact that it may be built up vertically or spun out horizontally, written backward or upside down, divided into separate six-note "tropes" or smaller units, and expanded by octave skips makes this twelve-tone, dodecaphonic, or serial technique (as it is variously called) less a guide for the listener than a crutch for the composer. Supposedly, by continually reintroducing every tone it lets no one tone become a key center of attraction for all the others.

Some critics have objected to atonality as a defiance of harmonic laws inherent in the very nature of tone and its composite structure of partials, and also as a method more restrictive in its efforts to escape tonal gravitation than is tonality itself. Others have even charged that atonality has been a haven for composers who had previously failed in more traditional styles (but not including Schoenberg!), much as alleged "ink blots" have won prizes for painters whose more conventional efforts had never won more than a polite honorable mention. For some three decades atonality did flourish largely as the object of a cult. But each time its death knell was thought to have been sounded it has come back with renewed vigor, until today it must be recognized as the single most consistent and cultivated movement in Modern music. Almost every important Modern composer has paid homage to it to some extent or other, even including Stravinsky in recent years.

However, you will want to hear the atonal music of Schoenberg and his best-known disciples (especially Berg, Webern, and Křenek) many times before attempting to pass judgment one way or another on so new an art. Be sure not to fall into the frequent error of judging it in terms of what it is not meant to be. The listener who fidgets irritably during the performance of an atonal work may be straining to hear the very things the composer was trying to escape. Such a listener is likely to wait in vain for a familiar tune or merely that "singable melodic line" he insists all music must have before he can accept it. Just what can and does replace these traditional interests and means of musical security is the problem of atonality and at best hard to say in an art too new yet to permit of theorizing. But something there must be, however intuitive at this stage, if the art is really to survive. Thus, one new unifying principle has been seen in the symmetry and balance with which the tone rows themselves are disposed.

Another modern trend has been an effort to revitalize traditional harmony, especially through new scale patterns, a broader concept of consonance, and the construction of chords by other intervals than thirds. Some well-known examples may be cited. Thus, a prominent interval in the six-tone "mystic chord" of Scriabin, Russian of the early Modern Era, is the augmented fourth or *tritone,* which is a fourth three whole steps wide (as F-B). The tritone has the suspensive effect of a dominant chord, giving the music a permanently unsettled, troubled character and virtually eliminating the all-important reposeful tonic in tonality. The Frenchmen Debussy and Ravel often upset the tradition of contrary motion in harmonic movement by writing parallel strands of chords. The Hungarian Bartók frequently introduces the specially flavored scales of Hungarian folk music. The Frenchman Milhaud finds new resources in *polytonality*, the simultaneous combination of two and even three keys at once. For instance, near the middle in the second movement of his first *Sonate* for piano (Appendix II, No. 8), he sets up a swaying figure in C-sharp major in the right hand, against which the left hand enters on a songful melodic line in G major. Directly growing out of traditional harmony are the Modernisms in Fig. 19—the extraordinarily disjunct and wide-ranged melody, the added "consonances," the chords disposed in fourths, and the smooth yet remote modulation. This passage occurs near the opening of one of the most performed among present-day symphonies, *Symphony No. 5* by Shostakovitch.

Fig. 19. Extended horizons in Modern harmony (Shostakovitch, *Symphony No. 5*, I)

(The rhythm of the continuing accompaniment figure is reduced to whole-notes here, after the first measure, so that the
stepwise line of each part can be more readily observed.)

A few musicians have actually tried to alter the very matter of
music, chiefly by dividing our present half steps into smaller intervals called microtones—third or quarter tones, for example.
One theorist, Joseph Yasser, evolves a "scale of the future" based
on a system of nineteen tones to the octave, including twelve
white and seven black keys. He derives this purely speculative
scale largely from higher tones in that same series of partials to
which music theorists have returned time and time again. His
ingenious deductions are nothing if not a jolt to nearsighted
pessimists who think music has spent itself, leaving no further
roads to travel. In fact, he has even devised a keyboard and some
elementary rules of harmony to accommodate this "supradia-
tonic" scale.

Another theorist, the late Joseph Schillinger, has attempted to
find mathematical laws governing music (and all the other arts,
for that matter), and to codify these laws. Symptomatic of the
times, his object is to make available in a systematic manner
(largely through permutations) not some but *all* of the possibilities in any given situation. A composer is actually enabled to
"create" by mathematical operations. Schillinger offers suggestions for composing not only in traditional and earlier styles but
in any future style that employs our present tonal matter. His
formulas cover every aspect of composing, including dynamics,
orchestration, timbre, and even emotions! The system has become a must for harried jazz arrangers and composers of film
music. George Gershwin credited it with revitalizing his ideas
in his last years. Critics have charged that composing by mathematics is like putting a nickel in the slot and drawing out a
finished piece. But free choice is not eliminated by Schillinger.
An unimaginative composer will write just as dully in this way as
by any other instruction.

One other renowned musician who has sought to expand the horizons of tonality within our present system of twelve tones is the German Paul Hindemith. By looking for still more basic principles in the relationships of partials, Hindemith attempts to slough off the excess verbiage that has accumulated in traditional harmony. Two means of codifying harmonic tension and relaxation result, one covering all possible groupings of tones into chords, the other all possible tonal relationships in time. Especially interesting is his chart by which the graduation from consonant to dissonant chords is very precisely evaluated. Hindemith's own skillful compositions since about 1937 are the first examples that you will want to hear of his logical theories. Some musicians prefer his earlier music, regarding it as less artificial and intellectualized. But no one can deny the clarity and slick, well-oiled efficiency of the new style (Appendix II, No. 9).

Finally, there has been considerable interest among special groups of Modern composers in going quite beyond (or behind) the realm of organized harmony and tonality and into the realm of raw sound itself. Sirens, whistles, and all manner of percussion instruments not confined to fixed pitch schemes provide the main resources of these composers. Also characteristic are experiments with tape recorders combined in novel ways, with other electrophonic instruments (p. 44), and with structures derived arbitrarily from a variety of mathematical and other formulas. Among pioneer ventures were *Ionisation* and *Density 21.5* by the French-born American Edgar Varèse, and *Iron Foundry* by the Russian A. V. Mossolov. American experimenters have included Henry Cowell and John Cage, while in Germany Karl Heinz Stockhausen has been among the leaders.

SELECTED READINGS

Howard Boatwright, *Introduction to the Theory of Music,* Chapters 1 and 14. New York: W. W. Norton, 1956.

Howard A. Murphy and Edwin J. Stringham, *Creative Harmony and Musicianship.* Englewood Cliffs (N.J.): Prentice-Hall, 1951.

Felix Salzer, *Structural Hearing*, 2 vols. New York: Charles Boni, 1952. A pedagogic introduction to Schenker.

Allen Forte, "Schenker's Conception of Musical Structure," *Journal of Music Theory*, III (1959).

George Dyson, *The New Music*. New York: H. Milford, 1948.

Gerald Abraham, *This Modern Music*. New York: W. W. Norton, 1952.

Arnold Schoenberg, *Style and Idea*. New York: Philosophical Library, 1950.

Karl Eschman, *Changing Forms in Modern Music*, Chapter VI. Boston: E. C. Schirmer, 1945.

René Leibowitz, *Schoenberg and His School*. New York: Philosophical Library, 1949.

Rudolph Reti, *Tonality, Atonality, Pantonality*. New York: Macmillan, 1958.

Alan Walker, "Unconscious Motivation in the Composing Process," *Music Review*, XX (1959).

Joseph Yasser, *A Theory of Evolving Tonality*. New York: American Library of Musicology, 1932.

Harry Partch, *Genesis of a Music*. Madison: University of Wisconsin Press, 1949. An extraordinary defense of a new 43-tone scale and new instruments on which to play it.

Carlos Chávez, *Toward a New Music; music and electricity*. New York: W. W. Norton, 1937.

Chapter 7

Texture and Sonority as Style Clues

MONOPHONY IN EXOTIC AND WESTERN MUSIC

Texture is the manner of blending chords and lines. It is to music what the manner of joining yarn, say, is to fabrics, whether by knitting, crocheting, weaving, hooking, or darning. *Polyphony* is one sort of musical texture in which several melodic lines intertwine (Fig. 20a). *Homophony* is another sort in which one line projects against a chordal background (Fig. 20b). *Monophony*, strictly speaking, is no texture at all, since it involves no simultaneous combinations of tones, only a single line. But it may be considered here as the chief alternative to polyphony or homophony (Fig. 20c). (Accent the short vowel in the second syllable in all three terms.)

One tends to think of polyphony as emphasizing the horizontal, and homophony the vertical, aspect of texture, although a careful look at the first two passages in Fig. 20 will reveal elements of the opposite aspect in each, too. In any case, musical texture is an important clue to musical style. Polyphony is largely associated with the Medieval-and-Renaissance, the Baroque, and the Modern Eras; homophony with the Classic and Romantic Eras; and monophony with the Early Christian Era. These are only prevailing tendencies, however, and certainly not invariable traits. Since the advent of harmony, great composers have always drawn on any or all styles of texture as needed, often right in the same work, as Wagner does in "Prelude" to *Parsifal* (Appen-

* (shim - mers?)

Fig. 20. Styles of musical texture: (a) polyphony (Frescobaldi, *Canzon dopo l'Epistola*); (b) homophony (Chopin, *Nocturne in E Major,* op. 62, no. 2); (c) monophony (*In the Pines,* as sung by Willard Sellers, Wananish, N.C., May, 1952; recorded by Robert Gould, researcher in folk song, Music Department, The University of North Carolina)

dix II, No. 6). The density or complexity of the texture provides another clue to changing styles in successive eras, even in
different nations and within individual styles. For instance, the
many black notes, thick chords, and complex sounds of a Strauss
symphonic poem (Appendix II, No. 37) are in keeping with the
pathos quality of the Romantic Era, but far removed from the
thin clean scoring of a Mozart concerto (Appendix II, No. 34),
product of the ethos-minded Classic Era. Texture also concerns
something more than style. As noted earlier, it may have a profound bearing on musical form. But that aspect of texture must
be saved for the next chapter.

As Occidentals, we ordinarily have too little opportunity to
hear *monophony*. Yet monophony is the style of most of the
world's music, the chief exception being our own Western harmony since the start of the Medieval-and-Renaissance Era. No
one aspect of exotic (non-Western) music stands out more than
the fact of its monophony. If you can arrange to hear some representative recordings of Oriental and primitive music (now included under the term *ethnomusicology*) you will find yourself
being introduced to quite new musical experiences. The music
will mean all the more to you after you can learn to hear it without imagining a "sad" or "happy" harmonic accompaniment,
Western style, merely because the underlying scales may sound
minor or major. You will also be intrigued by the greater freedom
of this music both in rhythmic organization and variety of pitch
intervals. In fact, some of it defies notation in any system that we
now know for writing duration and pitch.

Prior to recent influences from the West, *Oriental music*, including ancient Greek music, had attained classic summits that
equal in their own terms any developments of Western music,
and in several instances are of much greater antiquity. Research-
ers can find extensive writings about the theories and instruments
of this music, but naturally its actual practice and sound are
harder to rediscover. As far back as records go, all main classes of

instruments—string, wind, and percussion—have been used. From the earliest times special emphasis seems to have been placed on the functions of music, whether ceremonial, sacred, dramatic, social, or folk. In fact, this music must be regarded as largely inseparable from dance or speech.

Insofar as any generalization can be ventured about so broad a subject, an Oriental melody—one from Japan, for example— often starts near its highest tone and descends or "glides" down, according to one of several stereotyped melodic outlines. While this outline repeats indefinitely, its recurrences may be infinitely varied by elaborate, unpredictable changes of detail—ecstatic ornamental flights, minute differences in intervals, intricate rhythmic complications (Appendix II, No. 10). To the Western temperament the effect is that of an almost hypnotically persistent idea, toyed with in a nervous manner. It almost suggests one's habit of "doodling" absently during earnest conversation, making endless embellishments of a simple, basic design. Many kinds of scales are used, from the five-tone or pentatonic scale (like the five black keys on the piano) to very complex scales with microtones. The nearest approaches to texture are drone effects, occasional approximations of organum, and especially *heterophony,* which is an accidental mixture of sounds resulting from loose or decorative unison singing. The forms are generally open and additive.

Gregorian chant is one main variety of *plainchant* (that is, unaccompanied chant), the sacred monophonic song in the West and Near East that flowered during the Early Christian Era (Fig. 47, p. 267). Its generally rhapsodic, mystical quality shows Gregorian chant to have been more exotic than Western in character. We shall return to it in Chapter 16 on sacred music.

Primitive music does not differ essentially from Oriental music at our present level of discussion, although by definition primitive societies lack the recorded history, theoretical writings, and formal classifications to be found in civilized societies. These lacks have not precluded remarkable developments among the African Negroes or American Indians, to mention two races closely investigated for their music. In those few remaining places where it is still possible to hear and record true primitive music, untouched by "civilizing" influences, we have a living demonstration of how music may have begun among ancient peoples who have since attained higher cultures and a developed musical tradition.

Most *folk song* is not now thought to be the spontaneous outpouring of the masses, as was once assumed, but rather the gist of texts, melodies, and styles that have seeped down from the prevailing culture. The process is one of simplification and individual adaptation. Only the elemental and tangible ideas, the clear rhythms, the singable melodic progressions are taken over during the oral rather than written transmittal from generation to generation and place to place. Reduced to such basic materials and touching on almost every conceivable subject, all folk song naturally has much in common. Yet there are distinguishable traits in different nations, such as the raised fourth step that still turns up in the very Polish mazurkas of Chopin (or the lowered second step, as in Appendix II, No. 4a). The English and Scottish ballads made so notable in the definitive collection of Francis Child have retained much of their identity when transplanted to Appalachian and other American regions (as shown in studies and collections by the Englishman Cecil Sharp).

Within this great wealth of folk song a significant representation can be found in this country (Fig. 20c, p. 106; Appendix II, No. 11), as collected by experts like the Lomaxes, father and son, and at centers like the Library of Congress. Its unspoiled charms are today nurtured in a very sophisticated environment by such sensitive artists as Burl Ives, Carl Sandburg, and John Jacob Niles. To be sure, these men usually strum appropriately simple harmonic accompaniments to this essentially monophonic music. In this book it is important to note how extensively folk song has been employed in art music of the past century. Fine starting points are the telling arrangements by musicians like the Hungarian Bartók and the Englishman Vaughan Williams, who have been almost as important to the study of folk song as to the art of composition. Many a composer has turned to folk song in the interest of steering between a Romantic type of melody that may now seem sentimental or a Modern type that may seem affected or freakish. Often the folk song becomes an integral part of the whole work. Refreshing and invigorating are Brahms' uses of German student songs in his *Academic Festival Overture* or the uses made of American songs by our own pioneer Modernist Charles Ives—for instance, his introduction of the revivalist tune *Bringing in the Sheaves* in the fourth movement of his *First Piano Sonata*. Folk music has indeed served as a fount of new ideas. On the other hand, folk music has hardly provided an answer to all the problems of art music, which depends as much on the *treatment* of musical ideas as on the ideas themselves (p. 287).

One other category of monophonic music to be mentioned here is the *minstrelsy of Medieval poet musicians*. This important body of songs began in the late eleventh century with the troubadours of southern (Provençal) France, then was furthered by the trouvères of northern France and the minnesingers of Germany during the next three centuries. The texts and melodies were of a warmer, freer character in the south, and were more reserved in the north, which fact is but a reminder of how often and greatly geography and climate have influenced the arts. Religion, love, the Crusades, epic historical adventures (*chansons de geste*), and many other topics made up the subject matter. From the various styles of versification employed, the melodies derived their forms. In fact, here was the origin of some of the first clear designs of music, including the "barform," whose sections occur in the order A-A-B, and the rondeau, which is based on the repeated alternation of two sections. A more pedantic, middle-class outgrowth of this aristocratic minstrelsy was the monophonic song of the German guildsmen of the fifteenth and sixteenth centuries known as "Meistersinger." In Wagner's great comic opera *The Mastersingers of Nuremberg,* the picturesqueness and ridiculously fussy musical standards of this group are skillfully restored, partly as a none-too-subtle reproach to his own critics.

HOMOPHONY, OR MELODY QUALIFIED BY ACCOMPANIMENT

Homophony is the style of much Western music since the advent of harmony. It is likely to predominate in opera, dances and marches, diversional pieces, accompanied community or folk songs, and any other music with clear, unobstructed melodies. From the standpoint of texture the main interest in homophony lies in the nature of the accompaniment rather than the melodic line. The important effect of the accompaniment is to qualify the melody in any of several ways, much as facial expressions and gestures may reinforce or perhaps even contradict the sense of speech; or much as spotlights may vary the appearance of an actor as they are played from different angles.

Several aspects of the accompaniment may have a qualifying effect on the melody. Foremost among these is usually the harmony. When the same melody is played with different harmonizations the changes in its meaning are pronounced. Very illuminating examples by Bach occur in that bible of the harmony student, *371 Harmonized Chorales* (Lutheran hymns; see p. 274), where a particular melody is sometimes adapted to several different texts and supplied with an even greater number of harmonizations. For instance, the familiar chorale melody best known as "O Head, Bloody and Wounded" appears with one or another of three texts in nine different harmonizations (Nos. 21, 74, 80, 89, 98, 270, 286, 345, 367), some of them altering its character radically. (Compare Nos. 21 and 98. The same melody is further qualified by still other texts and harmonizations in other works by Bach, especially his *St. Matthew Passion.*)

For a briefer illustration of the same principle, a passage may be quoted from Mendelssohn's *Songs Without Words* for piano (Fig. 21). Here a melodic phrase reaches what is at once its climax and its dissolution, through a change of harmony on its third statement. This process of melodic culmination by means of *the one* climactic chord that tops all else became almost a law in

Fig. 21. Harmony as a qualifier of melody—the climactic chord (Mendelssohn, *Songs Without Words,* op. 67, no. 5)

the highly integrated works of the later Romanticists (do you recall *The Lost Chord* by Sullivan?). A striking example occurs in the second and biggest statement of the "love theme" in Tchaikovsky's *Fantasy Overture, Romeo and Juliet.* A quite unparalleled example occurs at the end of *Tristan and Isolde* when Wagner at last supplies the climax and release that had been more and more imperative during nearly five hours of impassioned music.

Rhythm is another important qualifier of melody in homophony. By varying the rhythmic pattern of the accompaniment a sense of anxiety, or calm, or monotonous plodding, or other effect is aroused. Listen to the growing intensity of the theme in Mendelssohn's *Variations sérieuses* for piano (Fig. 12, p. 74) when the note values of the accompaniment change to 16thnotes in "Variation I" and 16th-note triplets in "Variation II" (Appendix II, No. 26).

Finally, the very manner in which the supporting harmony is disposed exercises a marked effect on the melody. Block chords produce a static or punctuating effect (Fig. 45b, p. 251). *Arpeggiated* chords, in which the tones are sounded successively, as on a harp, tend to make the melody flow. So do the other ways of breaking up chords that figure so often in the thoroughly pianistic writing of Chopin and Liszt (Figs. 30 and 42, pp. 184 and 240). The *Alberti bass* (named after an obscure pre-Classicist) sets off a songful melody by alternating the accompaniment's chord tones in relatively slow harmonic rhythm (p. 87), yet in a busy, light, and remarkably unobtrusive manner (Fig. 22a). Indeed, what results is the fluent *singing-allegro* style associated above all with Mozart and his fellow Classicists.

Among further methods of disposing the harmony, the alternation of a bass tone and higher groups of tones in the chord produces the um-pah-pah of the waltz, the um-pah-um-pah of the march, and similar patterns that abound in Romantic music from Schubert and Chopin (Figs. 20b and 30, pp. 106 and 184) to Johann Strauss (Appendix II, No. 4c) and Sousa. The device of *two-against-three*—that is, a triplet against a duple subdivision of the beat 🎵, or vice versa—often occurs between accompaniment and melody as a means of enriching the texture (Fig. 22b). (Try tapping this out, making the groups coincide on their first notes, and making the second of the two 8th-notes in one hand come exactly between the second and third notes of the triplet in the other hand.) As a means of enriching orchestral textures that lack polyphonic interest, the skillful orchestrator often scores not one but a whole variety of accompaniment styles, combining them so as to fill out the background without challenging the predominance of the melody. Thus, at least six different styles occur simultaneously during a climax (beginning at measure

Fig. 22. Two styles of accompaniment in homophony: (a) Alberti bass (Mozart, *Sonata in C Minor* for piano, K. 457); (b) two-against-three (Brahms, *Intermezzo,* op. 116, no. 2)

588) in "Festival at Bagdad" from Rimsky-Korsakov's popular symphonic suite *Scheherazade.*

But the fact should be recalled that any homophonic texture will have at least a slight horizontal or polyphonic interest if the *voice-leading* is well managed—that is, if each strand of the harmonic support moves by readily perceivable intervals. The masters have always attached much importance to careful voice-leading. See again, for instance, how precisely Shostakovitch conducts each "voice" line in Fig. 19 (p. 101).

Homophony actually does approach polyphony in an important variety of texture called *monody,* used in all opera and nearly all ensemble music of any sort throughout the Baroque Era (Plates 15, 16). To musicians monody does not mean the same thing as monophony. In monody the melody is accompanied by a *thorough-bass,* which means a through or continuous bass line of more or less melodic significance. This bass can often be recognized as a steady patter of detached 8th- or quarter-notes, which are likely to be bowed separately when a stringed instrument plays them. Together the melody and the thorough-bass establish a continuing polarity of high and low, between which the harmony is filled out extemporaneously by the harpsichordist, organist, or lutist who reads the thorough-bass part. This performer's guide for "realizing" the bass is a kind of shorthand—a system of figures that indicate the chords in terms of intervals above the bass (Figs. 46c and 37, pp. 258 and 208; recall the $^6_4$ chord, p. 87). The disposition of these chords, the rhythmic patterns in which they are cast, the introduction of related melodic bits, and all else pertaining to actual performance are left to on-the-spot ingenuity. Realization of a thorough-bass is almost a lost art today, most performers simply relying on the realizations worked out by the editor who prepares new editions of Baroque music.

In Chapter 2, "age of thorough-bass" and "age of the Alberti bass" were suggested as possible style designations for the Baroque and Classic Eras. We can now see that two main distinctions in texture are intended. First, the thorough-bass has much greater melodic weight than the Alberti bass, even to the point of competing with the interest of the principal melody. Second, the figures written or understood with each thorough-bass tone point to a quicker harmonic rhythm (more chord changes per measure; recall p. 87) than is usual in the Alberti bass. Both distinctions help to explain the heavy, ponderous style of much Baroque music as compared with the light, fluent style of most Classic music. The thorough-bass, Alberti bass, and um-pah-pah accompaniment may be regarded as among the most characteristic earmarks of their respective eras, Baroque, Classic, and Romantic.

POLYPHONY AND ITS APPEAL TO THE INTELLECT

Polyphony, also known by the more academic term *counterpoint,* is primarily the product of advanced musical cultures. Its mastery is as stimulating to the composer as is the solution of a refined problem in chess or mathematics, for it appeals aesthetically more to the intellect than to the emotions. No wonder, then, that it has predominated in ethos eras, although it is capable of great expressive warmth.

Surprisingly, the inexperienced listener responds readily to polyphony because it provides him, in a rather literal sense, with the most tangible threads to follow. For much the same reason, Medieval-and-Renaissance composers found in it the most tangible medium for giving form to early harmony. Among the earlier vehicles of harmony were the canon and the round of the fourteenth and fifteenth centuries. The *canon* is a follow-the-leader process in which one line strictly imitates the other, one or more beats later and at the same or different pitch levels. The *round* is a similar process, with the added fact that the parts keep coming "around" to the beginning again (as in *Three Blind Mice*). Perhaps the most famous of all rounds is that robust, pre-Chaucerian landmark of English music history, *Sumer is icumen in,* dating probably from the late thirteenth century and still performed often.

This *imitation* of one voice by another, which underlies not only the canon and the round but much other polyphony, demonstrates what has been called the "diagonal," as distinguished from the horizontal, aspect of polyphonic texture (Fig. 26, p. 158). It is interesting to observe that the listener can never hear all the melodic lines at once as separate lines. He may concentrate on one of the lines, with the others catching only his peripheral attention. Or he may shift his attention from line to line, as he would in following imitations. Or he may hear all the lines in a harmonic synthesis. (Ideal experience in the hearing of two and three melodic lines, including frequent imitations of ideas passed between them, can be had by listening to Bach's fifteen two-part *Inventions* and fifteen three-part *Sinfonias,* two highly artistic, concentrated collections now known to every budding pianist.)

These possibilities suggest a basic axiom of polyphony: The separate lines must differ enough to be clearly distinguishable, and at the same time blend enough to be accepted side-by-side. How may they differ? To differ melodically they may have quite different contours or at least must go off in different directions as much as possible. To differ rhythmically they may contrast in note values and perhaps even in meter. To differ in phrasing they must divide into phrases of varying lengths that overlap rather than coincide, resulting in a braidlike texture uninterrupted until all lines converge at a cadence. To differ in timbre the lines may be performed by instruments or voices of contrasting tone colors. And to differ in range the lines may, of course, be written in different registers of the total pitch compass. However, observe that when all other things are equal, the outer (highest and lowest) lines are more readily distinguishable than the inner lines.

How may the lines blend? Prevailing concepts of consonance and dissonance have always determined the "vertical" blending of the lines. Palestrina, in the sixteenth century, wrote some of music's purest polyphony by placing a maximum of restrictions on the conduct of consonant tones and the use of dissonance. His melodic lines interweave like the perfectly synchronized parts in a complex, well-oiled machine. He sanctions two types of dissonance: (1) a dissonant tone *suspended* on a strong beat, *prepared* by being heard first as a consonant tone, and *resolved* by being lowered one step into a consonant tone; (2) foreign tones on weak beats, almost always approached and quitted stepwise. (The tied D and the first E in the alto line of Fig. 20a (p. 106) illustrate these two types, respectively.) Bach's, Mozart's, Wagner's, and Stravinsky's polyphonic styles sound progressively harsher, by comparison, because of increased latitude in both types of dissonance treatment. Ever more compelling harmonies and rhythms have helped to keep this increasing dissonance within the hearer's comprehension, much as the outline of an

Impressionistic oil painting gives meaning to the rough brush strokes (Plate 17). (For illustrations of progressively freer treatment of dissonance, see Figs. 26, 35, 21, 44d, and 19, pp. 158, 201, 112, 245, and 101.) Extreme license is exhibited in a Modern polyphonic style known as *linear counterpoint,* in which the melodic value of each line is the sole concern and vertical blending is disregarded if not actually avoided.

The force of dissonance in polyphony is often enhanced by the *ornaments* that Bach and other Baroque composers used so profusely. These ornaments make for a more florid style, too, but serve first of all as spicy dissonance in the texture. They occur chiefly on strong beats, effecting an accent in the rhythmic drive that, in the nature of the organ and harpsichord, cannot be achieved by sudden finger pressure. In general, ornaments were not written out but were indicated by signs—another kind of Baroque shorthand, largely of French origin. Such were tr. or ⵒ for trill (a rapid alternation of adjacent tones), ⵒⵗ for mordent (a brief dip in the melodic line), ⵒ for turn (an embellishment from above and below), and special small notes for appoggiaturas (p. 88; Figs. 23 and 36, pp. 142 and 207; Appendix II, No. 18). The use of these ornaments reached its peak in French Rococo music and continued into the "gallant" style of the mid-eighteenth century, when polyphony in its way began to border on homophony. In the Classic and Early Romantic Eras only a few conventional ornament signs remained, after which composers generally preferred to write out the ornaments.

Vocal groupings

Since the human voice and most other instruments except keyboard types can carry only one line at a time, or are at their best in doing so (strings), their only means of sharing in polyphonic or homophonic music is through ensembles of various sorts and sizes. Scoring for these ensembles raises questions important to texture and to *sonority* in general (which may be defined as the total effect or quality of the sound, especially its resonance and balance).

Thus, the composer or arranger of vocal ensembles in two or more parts must decide matters such as these:

Does he prefer the clarity and more precise intonation of a *soli* ensemble with one singer to a part, or the wide dynamic range of a *choral* ensemble with multiple singing of parts?

Does he prefer the rich though limited timbres of a homogeneous group, men alone or women alone, or the wider range of pitches and timbres in the numerous kinds of mixed groups, for which most great choral music is written?

Does he want the purity of *a cappella* (unaccompanied) singing, such as was led by Palestrina in important Italian chapels of the later sixteenth century, or the support and enrichment of an accompaniment, which may be anything from piano to full orchestra?

These matters were often optional in earlier music but have come to be very precisely indicated, sometimes even to the number of singers on a part, in keeping with the present-day emphasis on highly specialized sonorities. The nature of the vocal grouping is bound to influence the character and even the form of the music. Thus, in a chorus of men alone the voices lie so close together that polyphonic texture is almost ruled out. Narrow chromatic movement is an all-too-tempting solution, partly explaining why the overlush "barbershop quartet" style is associated with men's voices. Women's voices alone lack the foundation of a bass part, which must then be supplied in an accompaniment if there is to be a bass part. Because of such limitations the compositions for either group tend to be short so as to avoid monotony. (All of which is not to say that singers and audiences do not enjoy the homogeneous groupings—no doubt, for social as well as musical reasons. Witness the glee clubs for men or women alone that are standard in almost every college.)

The variety of vocal groupings has been very great and very changeable throughout music history. For present purposes the most useful information should be a brief list of representative scorings in some representative vocal works of different eras. As you would suppose, the basic ranges of the human voice (Fig. 1, p. 47) and the advantages of the mixed chorus have made the combination of soprano, alto, tenor, and bass (commonly abbreviated S.A.T.B.) the most frequent combination by far in all the main flowerings of choral music (Appendix II, No. 15).

Soli ensembles permit of no broad generalization since they occur primarily in operas and oratorios where their make-up is determined by dramatic considerations. Here are a few well-known examples:

Duet for tenor and baritone, "In un coupé," from Act IV of Puccini's opera, *La Bohème* (compare Appendix II, No. 39e).

Duet for soprano and alto, "Et in unum Deum," from Bach's *Mass in B Minor* (Appendix II, No. 43e).

Duet for soprano and baritone, "Dite alla giovine," from Act II of Verdi's opera *La Traviata* (compare the duet for soprano and tenor, Appendix II, No. 39b).

Trio for tenor, baritone, and bass, "La mia Dorabella," from Act I of Mozart's opera *Cosi fan tutte*.

Trio for two sopranos and an alto, opening of Wagner's opera *Das Rheingold*.

Trio for soprano, baritone, and bass, "Ah, taci, ingiusto core!" from Act II of Mozart's opera *Don Giovanni*.

Quartet for tenor, baritone, soprano, and alto, "Un dì, se ben rammentomi," from Act III of Verdi's opera *Rigoletto* (compare Appendix II, No. 39d).

Quintet for soprano, mezzo-soprano, alto, tenor, and baritone, "Nous avons en tête une affaire," from Act II of Bizet's opera *Carmen*.

Sextet for soprano, mezzo-soprano, two tenors, baritone, and bass, plus mixed chorus, "Chi raffre a il mio furore," from Act II of Donizetti's opera *Lucia di Lammermoor*.

With regard to choral ensembles, the great bulk of scorings range from three to six parts. On the other hand, Lassus left some remarkably satisfying motets for two voices and there are on record freakish works scored for as many as forty different voice parts. Representative of the average and of combinations encountered most often are these:

Women's three-part chorus (two soprano parts and one alto part), "Lift thine eyes," from Part II of Mendelssohn's oratorio *Elijah.*

Men's four-part chorus (two tenor and two bass parts), "Pilgrim's Chorus," from Act III of Wagner's opera *Tannhäuser.*

Mixed chorus, *a cappella* (soprano, alto, tenor, and bass part), "Kyrie eleison," from Palestrina's *Missa brevis.*

Mixed chorus, accompanied (soprano, alto, tenor, and bass part), "Selig sind," from the opening of Brahms' *German Requiem.*

Mixed double chorus, accompanied (soprano, alto, tenor, and bass part in each chorus), "Wir setzen uns" from the close of Bach's *St. Matthew Passion.*

INSTRUMENTAL GROUPINGS

Among instrumental groupings the various "soli ensembles" are known as *chamber music,* since the latter generally calls for one player to a part and presupposes all the delicate refinements of intonation and ensemble that are made possible by that disposition. However, in the Baroque Era, single or multiple performance of each part and the use of one or another kind of instrument in each range were options often assumed or explicitly offered. (A typical title reads, *Twelve Sonatas for Two Violins and a Bass, or an Orchestra.*) Baroque chamber music, employing monodic texture, is scored for one or more high melody instruments, a harpsichord or other keyboard instrument on which the thorough-bass is played by the left hand while its figures are "realized" by the right, and one or more bass instruments such as a cello to reinforce that thorough-bass (Fig. 37, p. 208; Plate 15).

Since the Classic Era, with its gradual discard of the thorough-bass practice and replacement of the harpsichord by the piano, chamber music has divided into types with and types without piano. Those with piano stem largely from curious early Classic compositions scored for piano with optional (*ad libitum*) accompaniments for a violin and often a cello. In other words, this was a reversal of the usual duo or trio, since the piano now took the lead while the violin and cello did the filling in and doubling. By the time of late Mozart and Beethoven the violin and cello became independent and important enough to be labeled obligatory (*obbligato*). Chamber music groups without piano stem largely from Baroque groups in which the thorough-bass came to be played and realized by cello and viola instead of harpsichord. Here is a list of the most common chamber groupings, the parentheses in the two Baroque groupings indicating instruments that ordinarily participate even when they are not specified:

	Harpsichord	Piano	Violin	2d Violin	Viola	Cello
Baroque duo	x		x			(x)
Baroque trio (Appendix II, No. 29)	x		x	x		(x)
Later duos (Appendix II, No. 9)		x	x			
			x		x	
		x				x
Piano trio		x	x			x
Piano quartet		x	x		x	x
Piano quintet		x	x	x	x	x
String trio			x		x	x
String quartet (Appendix II, No. 32; Plate 9)			x	x	x	x
String quintet (1st type)			x	x	x	xx
(2d type)			x	x	xx	x
String sextet			x	x	xx	xx

"Woodwind" quintet (Appendix II, No. 7; Plate 10) flute, oboe, clarinet, French horn, bassoon

Various other combinations of keyboard, strings, and winds have been used, too. There are also many arrangements and a small but distinguished original literature for ensembles of two pianists, whether at one or two pianos. Furthermore, thanks partly to the use of double- or triple-stops (p. 37), a small but distinguished original literature exists for a single, unaccompanied cello, and a not so small but equally distinguished literature for a single unaccompanied violin. To each of these, and to flute alone, Bach has been the foremost contributor.

As suggested earlier, some Baroque *orchestra* music was simply chamber music with multiple performance of the parts. Pertinent is the fact that the strings, especially the string quartet, became the nucleus of the orchestra in the Baroque Era. Yet the indeterminate body of instruments that reinforced and realized the ever-present thorough-bass, the higher wind instruments that played as many as four to a part, and the polyphonic or at least monodic texture usually resulted in a certain heaviness, stridency, and unbalance by Classic standards. The string quartet is almost always the nucleus of the Classic and later orchestra, to which wind instruments were gradually added singly and in pairs. The size began to spiral as more strings were added to counterbalance more winds. Often the first violins or other groups of strings were themselves subdivided into two or more parts, while the double basses were frequently given a part of their own instead of the traditional doubling of the cellos an octave lower. By the end of the nineteenth century the grandiose orchestra had reached its largest size (Appendix II, No. 37). Since then many Modern composers have often preferred to return to something like the Classic "symphony orchestra" or to even smaller groups called "chamber orchestras" (Appendix II, No. 5).

On the next page is the instrumentation of four favorite orchestra works, spanning two centuries. The instruments are listed from top to bottom as they appear in the conductor's full score. Besides the instruments listed in the Beethoven and Mahler

Early 18th Century	Late 18th Century	Early 19th Century	Late 19th Century
Bach's (French) Overture (or 3d Suite) in D Major, S. 1068	Mozart's "Jupiter" Symphony in C Major, K. 551	Beethoven's Ninth Symphony	Mahler's Second Symphony
	flute	2 flutes	2 flutes and
		1 piccolo	2 flutes or piccolos
2 oboes	2 oboes	2 oboes	2 oboes
			2 oboes or English horns
		2 B♭ or A clarinets	2 B♭ clarinets
			3d B♭ clarinet or bass clarinet
			2 E♭ clarinets
	2 bassoons	2 bassoons	3 bassoons
		1 contrabassoon	4th bassoon or contra-bassoon
	2 C horns	4 D or B♭ horns	10 F horns
3 trumpets	2 C trumpets	2 D trumpets	6 F trumpets
		2 tenor and 1 bass trombones	4 trombones
			1 contrabass tuba
		triangle	triangle
			large gong
			small gong
		cymbals	cymbals
2 kettle drums	2 kettle drums	2 kettle drums	6 kettle drums (2 players)
			glockenspiel
		bass drum	bass drum
			side drum
			3 bells
			organ
			2 harps
first violins	first violins	first violins	first violins
second violins	second violins	second violins	second violins
violas	violas	violas	violas
thorough-bass (cello and harpsichord)	cellos basses	cellos basses	cellos basses

symphonies, a mixed chorus, a soli ensemble, and vocal soloists take part in the final movements. Also, the strings are often divided in the Mahler work. The number of string players on a part averaged—in the usual order of first violins, second violins, violas, cellos, and basses—4/4/2/2/2 in the Baroque orchestra, 5/5/3/3/2 in the Classic, 10/10/6/5/5 in the early Romantic, and 12/18/14/12/8 in the late Romantic. Today the major symphony orchestras still have about the same numbers of strings, bringing their total sizes to an average of 100 players, and even more when extra players have to be imported to play the largest scores or on gala festival occasions.

The wind band has made its way into the field of large-scale concert music only since the nineteenth century, although a substantial literature of art music for wind instruments alone can be found from the sixteenth century on. Before the nineteenth century the band was chiefly important on military and festive occasions. Trumpet-and-drum signals were used as early as the thirteenth century to summon soldiers to battle, and there are still older records of town brotherhoods of bandsmen. To these early resources flutes, oboes, bassoons, horns, clarinets, trombones, saxophones, and other instruments were added, in some instances filling out complete families. Today's symphonic band even uses a harp or two, string basses, and sometimes cellos. By comparison with the orchestra's original literature of symphonic proportions, that of the symphonic band is naturally very small. Yet it is worth noting that such composers in the last two centuries as Mozart, Beethoven, Weber, Rossini, Berlioz, Mendelssohn, Wagner, Saint-Saëns, Tchaikovsky, Vaughan Williams, Holst, Stravinsky, Prokofiev, Milhaud, and Hindemith have written original works ranging from marches to symphonies for bands of varying sizes.

Careful examination of the symphony orchestra and the concert band reproduced in Plates 13 and 14 will show you the seating arrangements of two major groups in this country. The concertmaster and first violins sit immediately to the left in this and most orchestras. The presence of tuba, contrabassoon, full percussion "battery," and six horns suggest the performance of a large Romantic orchestral score.

Scoring effectively for instruments is an art in itself. In chamber music with piano, the piano is often used in opposition to the strings, one accompanying the other in homophony, or interchanging with the other in a sort of dialog, or "competing" with the other in a polyphonic texture. In chamber music without piano the texture is even more favorable to polyphony. Each instrument gets about equal responsibilities, although since the first violin usually plays above the other parts in a string quartet it tends to stand out.

Orchestration is often handled by *choirs,* the strings alternating with the woodwinds, for example, or carrying the melody and bass while the brasses furnish a rich harmonic middle (Appendix II, No. 12). Balance of tone is always a problem, as in the scoring of a chord for full orchestra. Then the instruments are usually piled up with wide intervals at the bottom, getting narrower at the top like the series of partials, although very soft chords invite many other solutions. Pairs of instruments adjacent on the score may be arranged so that, for example, the two flutes are above the oboes, or encompass them, or double them, or are staggered with them. A complete, seemingly unbroken, seven-octave scale can be played in the orchestra by letting one instrument carry on from another, and by choosing instruments to do this that have similar timbres at the point of transfer. A flute in its lower register sounds like a French horn softly played in *its* medium register, for example. Ravel was a past master at such tonal sleight-of-hand, as in his *Bolero,* where the instruments seem to be piled on endlessly. Actually he keeps withdrawing some while the ear is being attracted by the others as they enter or re-enter on the main theme (Appendix II, No. 2).

The *band* has a completely idiomatic scoring of its own. If only because it divides less tangibly into choirs, it uses the choir principle much less. However, one may say very loosely that the clarinets are the "violins" of the band, the saxophones are its "violas," and the baritone horns its "cellos."

The problems of idiomatic scoring in any form are highlighted by the frequent practice throughout music history of making *transcriptions* from one medium to another. Mention has already been made (p. 43) of the many reductions of instrumental and even vocal ensemble scores to keyboard solos or duets. Such arrangements have been made mostly as a convenience to amateur enthusiasts and classroom teachers. But "concert transcriptions," like Liszt's from the Wagner and Verdi operas or numerous elaborations of the Johann Strauss waltzes, are still often heard in recital. More to the point here is the reverse problem of arranging solo music for ensembles from chamber to full orchestra. A very expert knowledge of the orchestra is required to transcribe something so idiomatic as a Chopin nocturne or mazurka without severe loss to the original. There simply is no adequate equivalent for some of the effects achievable on the piano. On the other hand, conductor-arrangers like Leopold Stokowski have preferred to present Bach's organ works in orchestral transcriptions, feeling that much color, clarity, and even dynamic interest are to be gained. Of course, each such transcription must be valued on its own merits, especially its good taste. But purists who disavow transcriptions on general principle have only to recall how freely and extensively Bach himself transcribed his own and others' works, in both reductions and expansions.

SONORITY PER SE IN RECENT MUSIC

A remarkable development in the expressive value of sound itself may be charted from the Medieval-and-Renaissance Era, when pieces were merely scored for voices and/or "any sorts of instruments" of appropriate range (Plate 8). In the Baroque Era the options were narrowed and orchestration became fairly specific, especially that of opera music. In the Classic Era clarity and balance were stressed, and new attention was paid to quality and contrast in solo passages. In the Romantic Era a growing interest in harmonic color for its own sake, such as can be heard in a Schubert modulation (Fig. 18, p. 97) or a Chopin chromatic figuration, was followed by a growing interest in tone color, as in the sensitive orchestral scoring of Berlioz, Bizet, and Rimsky-Korsakov. Now, in the works of Debussy (Appendix II, No. 36), Stravinsky (Appendix II, No. 13), Bloch, Bartók, and other Moderns, there are passages in which almost nothing happens of consequence to melody, rhythm, harmony, tonality, or even dynamics. Everything becomes mood and atmosphere as evoked by sonorities alone. Sonority then becomes an aesthetic fact in itself. And even where sonority is not the reigning factor, the orchestration of today's music is clear, telling, varied, and precise to a degree never attained before.

A perhaps alarming sidelight of the new interest in sonority is a pronounced trend toward hard, shiny, even raucous sonorities. If the offender is not the saxophone or the accordion or the electric guitar, it is one of the more respected instruments used in a raucous manner—a violin made to talk, a clarinet to squeal, a trumpet to flutter like a nervous parrot. Maybe this trend plus the glamor of a uniform, a deceptively "easy-to-play" metal instrument, and a football marching position explain the edge that the band has had lately over the orchestra in schools. Strings, for example, being gentler and more subtly expressive instruments, harder to start on, have become much scarcer. Fortunately, the best concert bands do not neglect the more delicate sonorities; and fortunately, widespread concern over the fate of school and community orchestras has been bringing about a healthy re-emphasis on the gentler instruments.

SELECTED READINGS

Curt Sachs, *The Rise of Music in the Ancient World* (on primitive, Oriental, Near Eastern, and Greek music). New York: W. W. Norton, 1943.

Jaap Kunst, *Ethnomusicology*. The Hague: Martinus Nijhoff, 1959.

Maynard Owen Williams, "Bali and Points East," *The National Geographic Magazine*, LXXV (1939). Cited as representative of many interesting articles in this periodical that have touched on exotic music.

"Folk Music," a 240-page article, country by country, in *Grove's Dictionary of Music and Musicians*, 5th ed. New York: St. Martin's Press, 1954.

The following five listings all include collections of the folk songs themselves:

Carl Sandburg, *The American Songbag*. New York: Harcourt, Brace, 1950.

Alan and John Lomax, *Folk Song U.S.A.* New York: Duell, Sloan and Pearce, 1947.

Cecil James Sharp, *English Folk Songs From the Southern Appalachians*, 2 vols. New York: Oxford University Press, 1952.

Evelyn Kendrick Wells, *The Ballad Tree*. New York: Ronald Press, 1950.

Bertrand Harris Bronson, *The Traditional Tunes of the Child Ballads*. Princeton: Princeton University Press, 1959.

Robert Erickson, *The Structure of Music: A Listener's Guide;* a study in terms of melody and counterpoint. New York: Noonday Press, 1955.

Archibald Davison, *The Technique of Choral Composition*. Cambridge: Harvard University Press, 1945.

Ruth Halle Rowen, *Early Chamber Music*. New York: King's Crown Press, 1949.

William S. Newman, "Concerning the Accompanied Clavier Sonata," *The Musical Quarterly*, XXXIII (1947).

Alexander Hyatt King, *Chamber Music*. New York: Chanticleer Press, 1948.

Adam Carse, *The Orchestra*. New York: Chanticleer Press, 1949.

Richard Franko Goldman, *The Concert Band*. New York: Rinehart, 1946.

Part III

Forms Based on Inner Laws of Music

Chapter 8

What Is Musical Form? (A Problem in Aesthetics)

"VARIETY WITHIN UNITY" AS THE STARTING POINT

So far, we have concentrated on the elements or building blocks of music—on sound itself, rhythm, melody, and harmony—and on the styles of texture into which these elements are blended. Now, in our broad inductive approach, we have reached the point where we can explore the essential problem of all art, the problem of how such elements and styles organize into over-all forms. Just as a painting grows out of the inherent behavior of line and color, so music grows out of the ways in which *its* elements tend to behave. The object of this chapter is to supply an intelligible answer to the rather elusive question, What is musical form?—elusive, you will recall, because the form has to be perceived aurally rather than in the more familiar visual manner. The answer to this question then becomes the basis for the discussions of specific form types in succeeding chapters. And, incidentally, it becomes our chief occasion (along with Chap. 17) for a dip into the *aesthetics* (artistic philosophy and rationale) of music.

A brief, obvious answer is that musical form is architecture in sound; it is the end product when the elements and the intangibles of the musical experience are coordinated in a particular fashion and within perceivable limits. But this really answers nothing. To get nearer the truth we do best to close in on the problem from more than one angle, then consider the nature of form in two distinct yet related senses. More explicitly, in the present section, a first angle of approach is provided by the familiar prescript for any art form: "variety within unity." In the next section, another grows out of the equally familiar distinction between "space" and "time" arts. Applying these general principles to music, the next three sections take up musical form first as a structural result, whether of "motivic play" or "phrase grouping," and second as a series of standardized designs. Finally, certain trends in Modern musical form are noted.

The one principle that underlies all art forms is that of *variety within unity*. Something must persist sufficiently to hold the form together (unity), yet something must differ sufficiently to give it interest (variety). Like hot and cold, positive and negative, east and west, variety and unity are interdependent concepts. Theoretically neither is any more possible by itself than is an absolute vacuum. A painting so unified that it is nothing but one solid mass must still impart a certain variety by contrast with its frame, or the wall, or the room where it is hung. A painting so varied that no color or line repeats must still reveal a certain unity in the very persistence with which its elements disagree. But we can acknowledge at once that either extreme leads to monotony. What is wanting is that all-important sense of proportion between variety and unity by which any art work must stand or fall.

The polarity of variety and unity can be expressed by numerous corollaries that are more specifically applicable within the arts. Among these are tension and relaxation, subordinacy and primacy, contrast and repetition. How do tension and relaxation figure in Longfellow's *Evangeline,* or subordinacy and primacy in da Vinci's *Last Supper,* or contrast and repetition in the Capitol at Washington? This seemingly obvious sort of questioning actually will provide you with an ever-richer means of penetrating significant works of art. For example, one critic used it to justify his opinion that too much emphasis was placed on the scene between Hamlet and his mother in the English film version of *Hamlet*. He started by asking what provides the main unity. In other words, what is this powerful drama about? "In essence, how a prince came to kill his king," he answered. By this criterion the variety provided in the other theme seemed to this critic to be predominant rather than subordinate.

Each of these corollaries has its applications in musical form. We have already seen that tension and relaxation can be created by dissonance and consonance (pp. 78–81; 117–118). Subordinacy and primacy may be readily shown in the use of a main theme, which is a unifying element, and one or more subordinate themes, which are elements of variety. As for contrast and repetition, the fact that so many of music's standardized designs are based on the alternation and recurrence of ideas makes this one of the most generally applicable corollaries. In the A-B-A design, for example, the B section affords contrast and the return to A affords repetition. We shall make a special use of this last corollary in the section on standardized designs (pp. 150–152).

STRUCTURAL ASPECTS OF A "TIME" ART

As we begin to narrow the problem of form down to music, the distinction between *space* and *time* arts becomes helpful. Among the "seven classic arts" painting takes place unequivocally in space, since it occupies a flat surface and can be perceived, or at least looked at, without significant lapse of time. Music takes place most completely in time, since it lasts through several minutes or even hours but cannot be seen in space. Again, neither extreme is possible. To the physicist, "time is space and space is time." Receding perspective gives a sense of time to painting, and the "high" or "low" of pitch a sense of space to music. The other arts intercross even more.

SPACE	TIME
painting	music
sculpture	poetry
architecture	drama

dancing

It literally takes time to walk around sculpture, and more time to explore both inside and outside of architecture. On the other hand, poetry conjures up visions of space, and drama actually takes place in space. Dancing occurs as much in one medium as the other.

The fact that music occurs in time is of real significance to musical form. First of all, whereas the form of a painting or other space art is perceived initially as a whole and only afterward in more detail, the form of music is perceived bit by bit during performance and only afterward as a whole. Some hearers even report a kind of flashback of the whole musical form during the moment after its completion (an interesting phenomenon that is usually blocked in public concerts by the customary immediate applause).

Second, the perception of such a form must depend on *memory,* without which there could be no interrelation of beginning, middle, and end. This rightly suggests that a poor or inexperienced memory for tunes can be a handicap to the enjoyment of music. But more to the point of the present discussion, one may say that the less the musical ideas stick in the memory, the less the form will be perceived. If they do not stick, perhaps the composer himself is at fault. He may be responsible for excessive variety—too many ideas, like too many names in an overinvolved novel. Or the fault may be insufficient interest, either because the ideas are inconsequential or because they are not stated emphatically enough. To stick in the memory, a musical idea must have some distinctive trait of rhythm, melody, harmony, or other element that makes it stand out from its context; it must occur where it will attract most attention, as at the beginning, end, or any climactic spot; and it must occur often enough to be recognized as a recurring element. In other words, the idea must benefit from those four memory aids so neatly classified by the psychologist—intensity, primacy, recency, and frequency.

Third, the *climax* of an art form in time is more likely to occur near the end than the middle for much the same reason that a melody is likely to climax near the end (p. 73). It is development and anticipation that maintain suspense. Following the climax the conclusion ordinarily will be short and to the point, like the brief denouement in a Mary Roberts Rinehart mystery story or the quick curtain after Mimi's touching death in Puccini's *La Bohème*. Otherwise this conclusion becomes an *anti*climax in the least complimentary sense. (Compare the protasis, epitasis with its catastasis or climax, and catastrophe in classic Greek drama.) Clearly, the location of the climax must be a fundamental determinant in the layout of a highly integrated musical form.

Fourth, there is the psychological consideration of *interest and boredom* in a work that occurs in time. The listener's interest is most likely to continue unabated when the music is intelligible, sufficiently varied, well planned, and not too long. An orchestral concert, with its much greater variety of timbres and intensities, can go on considerably longer than a piano recital without overtaxing the listener. Even so, with a maximum of variety, the hour-and-a-half symphonies of Mahler and the five-hour operas of Wagner overtax the endurance of many a listener. On the other hand, it is surprising how far and successfully the most experienced composers can carry the principle of economy of material, learning to do more and more with less and less, yet without tiring the listener. We shall see in Chapters 12 and 13 how the movements in a sonata or other extended, "cyclic" work are usually arranged to suit the normal increase and decline of the listener's attention.

Finally, the performance of a time art cannot be hung on a wall like a painting that can be viewed at will, but must be *re-created in time* on every occasion that it is to be enjoyed. This re-creation requires, first, a performer or middleman, so to speak, to bring the composer's product to the consumer; and second, a fresh interpretation by each performer. At best, the dynamic and tempo marks that composers have left, more and more in detail after Bach's time, can never do more than hint the interpretation. It is true that recordings eliminate the performer and take care of both the re-creation and interpretation after they are once made. But a recording played over and over sacrifices that very variety of interpretation that a composition seems to need if it is not to grow stale. The reason a person goes to hear the same composition over and over again is like his reason for going to see *Hamlet* again and again, surely not to find how it "comes out" each time but rather to get that fresh interpretation. In this sense and at best, a time art may be claimed to have an advantage over a space art—over a painting, for example, that must always look the same once it is created, framed, and hung.

One remarkable consequence of a sufficiently different interpretation is to alter the effect of the form, sometimes drastically. For example, as suggested in our discussion of tempo (p. 62), a miscalculation on the side of too slow a tempo may disrupt the flow of thought by separating the ideas too widely for the memory to relate them.

PROGRESSION BY MOTIVIC PLAY

It was stated earlier that the broad term "musical form" is best considered in two related senses, as a structural result and as a standardized design. To understand this distinction consider the analogy of the engine or power plant first in one sense and then the other. The engine is a *structural result* in the sense that the nature of its fuel ultimately determines its particular structure. If gasoline is used then there must be a carburetor, if there is a carburetor there must be compression, and so on; whereas, if electricity is used then very different components must lead to very different structures. On the other hand, the engine is a *standardized design* when it generally conforms to any typical structural result. Thus, the V-eight engine in any of its varieties is a standardized design because it represents one kind of structure that frequently results when gasoline is transformed into power.

Similarly, musical form is a structural result in the sense that its "fuel," whether that be a rhythmic pattern, harmonic pattern, or other musical idea, ultimately influences its particular form. And it is a standardized design such as A-B-A when that design is recognizable as the frequent result, say, of starting with clear phrases.

What, actually, are the "fuels" of musical form? In something so finite as an engine such a question raises no problems. In the much less tangible art of music a choice must be made between several possibilities, all of which are likely to apply and each of which has its champions (pp. 93–94). Two types of melodic ideas are preferred in this book as basic generators of form, partly because they seem to permit of the most concrete descriptions and partly because they seem to find the most universal application in the wide scope of musical form.

One of these melodic types is known as a motive and the other as a phrase. A *motive* is defined here as an idea that is incomplete, yet of primary interest by virtue of a characteristic pitch contour, rhythmic pattern, or harmonic implication. Motives often consist of no more than four notes, two of the most used examples being the "how-dry-I-am" fragment (p. 223) and the dot-dot-dot-dash or "V-for-Victory" that is so familiar in Beethoven's *Fifth Symphony*. A *phrase* is defined as an idea that is more or less complete melodically, rhythmically, and perhaps harmonically, yet one that does not necessarily stand out from its melodic context. A clear example is the opening phrase, ending on the word "grow," in *Carry Me Back to Old Virginny*. In this and the next section we shall see how these simple distinctions give rise to two very different styles of continuation, or what is here called *progression,* in music. Out of the very nature of the motive comes "progression by motivic play"; out of the very nature of the phrase comes "progression by phrase grouping." In short, we shall see how these two elements can exercise very different influences on musical form as it unfolds in time, bit by bit, to become a "structural result." After reading about these two processes you may want to refer to the chart (p. 290) that summarizes them briefly.

Let us take first the motive as a basic generator. For those who are curious about the why as well as the how of music's basic operations, here follows a number of reasons why the motive may *tend* to govern the style of progression and ultimately the form (although, of course, there are no invariable laws in art!):

1. Being "of primary interest" the motive tends to be the chief means of unity.

2. As the chief means of unity it must make a greater impression on the memory than any other element, which means that it tends to require more repetition than any other element.

3. Furthermore, being incomplete, the motive tends to renew itself in an unbroken flow of repetitions and imitations, which often are overlapped so as to avoid gaps.

4. In the motive's many repetitions there lies a need for contrast or variety, which may be achieved by changes (a) of range, (b) of scale degree, (c) of metric position, (d) of timbre, (e) of intensity, (f) of tempo, and (g) of the motive's very structure, provided the motive remains recognizable.

These structural tendencies give rise, in turn, to broader tendencies:

5. Repetitions, imitations, and overlappings of the motive in various ranges make a polyphonic texture preferable if not imperative.

6. Therefore, music generated from a motive ordinarily requires a medium capable of polyphonic performance such as a keyboard

instrument or an ensemble. An ensemble becomes especially desirable when a contrast of intensities or timbres between the voices is needed.

7. In the interest of the unbroken flow, suspensive or deceptive cadences (p. 88) become ideal progressions by which to harmonize the motive.

8. Both the use of suspensive or deceptive cadences and the repetitions of the motive on different scale degrees—in fact, on more degrees than any one key can provide—favor rapid harmonic rhythm and tonality in a constant state of flux (like the butterfly in its ever-changing flight).

9. The tendency of the motive to repeat in a continuous braidlike texture results in conflicting metric accents, and hence in a rhythmic flow more like that of free than of metrical verse.

10. Since the repetitions of the motive provide both unity and variety, there is no compelling need, and often no place, for distinctive contrasting ideas, either in the free voices of the texture or in the sense of clear departure and returns.

In summary, we reach a general description of progression by motivic play and of the kind of form to which it gives rise (insofar as any form may grow entirely out of one consistent process):

11. A motive tends to engage in *motivic play,* which means repetitions and imitations of the motive at different pitch levels either by exchanges between several voices in a polyphonic texture or by shifts of range in a single voice. Motivic play is further characterized by rapid harmonic rhythm, irregular metric grouping, and constant tonal flux. Finally, motivic play generates a structural result that is *monothematic* and *cursive* (running on without the return of any larger section).

Motivic play is illustrated in Fig. 23, from a Bach keyboard fugue. The four "voices" are labeled S.A.T.B. and the recurring motive is marked by a bracket. Motivic play is often described as imitative writing. It may also be thought of as a kind of mosaic work in music.

From a historical standpoint composers have handled the mo-

tive very differently from one era to the next. One of its generative traits or tendencies (4g, p. 140) provides an especially interesting clue to changing styles. That is the extent to which the
motive itself is altered as one means of variety during its repeti-

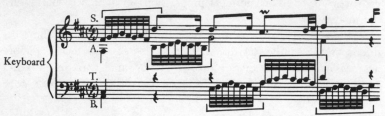

Fig. 23. Motivic play (Bach, four-voice "Fugue in D Major" from *Well-
Tempered Clavier, I*)

tions—for example, turned upside down, expanded in length, or
transformed in expressive character.

In the Gregorian chant of the Early Christian Era the question of
motivic play can hardly be raised, since even the nearly exact repetition of a motive in sequence is employed only infrequently.

In Medieval-and-Renaissance music motivic play often occurs,
most clearly in instrumental music free of a text. But the motive
itself may not retain its identity clearly (Fig. 26, p. 158), for several
reasons. First, polyphonic music of the Medieval-and-Renaissance
Era ordinarily lacks the strong tonal and metric drive needed to give
the motive a striking character of its own. Second, the motive freely
undergoes slight alterations as it repeats, in the interest of pliable
polyphony. Third, the motive usually trails off into a free melodic
line, with the result that its limits are not well defined. Fourth, the
frequent intellectual stunt of inverting, reversing, or augmenting and
diminishing (doubling or halving the note values of) the motive
tends to disguise it.

In Baroque music motivic play is second only to the thorough-bass
as a style trademark, the motive itself retaining its melodic and especially its rhythmic identity very clearly (Fig. 23).

In Classic music the clear Baroque motive continues to operate.
However, motivic play itself is largely confined to the "development"

of ideas, especially to the development section of the "sonata-allegro" form (p. 228). Within that development section the motive may be gradually extended, shortened, or recast during its repetitions, as if it were an organic process (Fig. 41, p. 229).

In Romantic music the motive is used not only in motivic play but as a kind of character tag that reappears from time to time in different guises to bind the music by way of a "programme" (mood or story). Berlioz' *idée fixe,* Liszt's *thematic transformation,* Brahms' *basic motive,* Wagner's *leitmotif,* Franck's *cyclical treatment,* all refer to the use of a motive that binds the music, yet undergoes profound changes of character through changes of the melody, harmony, rhythm, dynamics, texture, tempo, and manner of performance.

In Modern music the motive often undergoes what has been aptly termed "the organic growth of a germ idea"—frequently several such growths, as though every ramification of the idea were to be explored. The interest in primitivism in Modern music (as in Modern painting) sometimes makes these ramifications sound like the "doodling" in primitive music (as often in Copland and Bartók).

Fig. 24 is invented to suggest how the same series of tones, loosely identifiable by its pitch contour, might be differently applied or altered as a motive, in different eras.

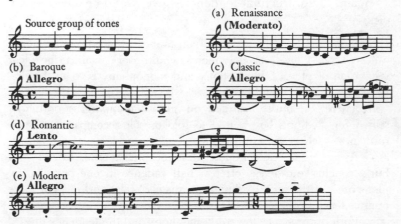

Fig. 24. How the same motive might have been treated in different eras

PROGRESSION BY PHRASE GROUPING

The phrase was defined earlier as "an idea that is more or less complete melodically, rhythmically, and perhaps harmonically, yet one that does not necessarily stand out from its melodic context." Within that meaning, how and why does this basic melodic type *tend* to influence form as the "structural result"? Our best method is to set the generative traits of the phrase in contrast to those of the motive, proceeding point by point (with correspondingly numbered paragraphs):

1. Since the phrase "does not necessarily stand out from its melodic context," it is not necessarily a means of unity.

2. If it is not a means of unity, it is not likely to be repeated often.

3. Furthermore, being "more or less complete" in itself, the phrase is a separable unit that tends to come to some sort of end, with the most probable continuation being another phrase—in fact, probably a new phrase, since a phrase "is not likely to be repeated often."

4. Thus, variety is achieved through the relationship of one phrase to another, whether by opposition, apposition, parallelism, or other complementary grouping.

Again, these structural tendencies give rise to broader tendencies:

5. Since the braidlike texture, constant shifting of position, and different pitch levels of polyphony would work against the clear separation of phrases, homophony and monophony become the preferred settings for the phrase.

6. Therefore, music founded on phrase grouping is ordinarily scored for mediums best suited to solo or solo-accompaniment performance, such as voice and piano.

7. As a more or less complete idea, the phrase tends to end on a fairly conclusive cadence, often a half cadence in one phrase complemented in the familiar "question-answer" relationship by a more final cadence in the next.

8. Both the tendency toward homophony and the tendency toward half and final cadences within phrase groupings favor relatively slow

harmonic rhythm and a stable tonality that moves from plateau (area of but one key) to plateau (like the hummingbird in its steady flight).

9. As a "more or less complete," separable unit not ordinarily interrupted by overlaps, the phrase tends to fall into some regular meter, which makes the "normal" phrase the "square" one of four measures subdivided into two two-measure phrase members. This same regularity also tends to carry over into phrase groupings and into the still higher relationships of the form.

10. In the complementary relationships of phrase grouping and the relative infrequency of phrase repetition, lies a basic urge toward dualism or greater pluralism of ideas, resulting in polythematic rather than monothematic forms.

In summary, this time we reach a general description of progression by phrase grouping and of a kind of form to which *this* style may give rise:

11. A phrase invites continuation by other phrases in a homophonic or monophonic setting, leading to complementary relationships within *phrase groupings* further characterized by regular meters, square construction, and stable tonal plateaus (Appendix II, No. 31,III). This process tends in turn to generate some variety of polythematic and what is here called "hierarchic" design, since the same principle of complementary rhythm and tonality that underlies phrase grouping tends to make the successive phrase groupings fall into still larger sections, and so on, depending on the extent of the form. Necessarily, a hierarchic design is a unified, integrated, and closed form, if only because its largest grouping embraces all the successively lesser groupings.

Two of the foregoing traits of the phrase, its tendency to regularity or squareness (9) and its function in hierarchic design (11), concern us further here. The extent to which phrases depart from a norm of four measures (sometimes two at a slow or eight at a fast tempo) provides a second valuable clue to changing historical styles (comparable to the extent to which the motive changes during its repetitions):

In the proselike chant of the Early Christian Era, regular phrases would have been out of place. When they did eventually make their way into the chant along with metrical rhyming schemes, the chant's decline was at hand.

In the strictest polyphony of Medieval-and-Renaissance sacred music, regular phrases are naturally exceptional. But they occur often in the secular music, especially the instrumental dances, dance songs, and minstrelsy. In fact, regular phrases are commonly listed among the influences of secular music on subsequent sacred music.

In Baroque music the more compelling meter and harmony favored greater regularity in phrase structure. But, as before, this regularity occurs less in polyphony than in music of lighter texture, especially the final dances of the suite and the quicker arias in opera. And even then, after the first four-measure phrase or so, the music usually trails off into light motivic play (Fig. 29, p. 169).

In the pure ethos style of Classic music, the square phrase for the first time became the normal phrase, more so with the law-abiding Mozart than the somewhat nonconformist Haydn. Indeed, it was the square phrase against which Beethoven was already rebelling when he made his well-known complaint about the "tyranny of the bar line" (p. 58).

In Romantic music regular phrases remained the norm. Composers who sought to shake off the curse of regularity usually preferred only to disguise rather than to escape it. Chopin disguises the regularity of one phrase, for example, by not making it exactly parallel in structure to the phrase before it (Appendix II, No. 22)—by varying an internal rhythm, omitting an upbeat, or changing from a *masculine ending* on a strong beat to a *feminine ending* on a weak beat.

In Modern music, regular phrases have generally been avoided except as an archaism by a sophisticate like Satie. Certainly, the return to motivic play, primitive rhythms, or the freedom of prose is hardly conducive to regular phrases.

Fig. 25 is invented to illustrate how a square phrase by Mozart might be (a) drawn out by Bach, (b) deregularized by Haydn, (c) disguised by Chopin, and (d) avoided by Copland. Observe that each phrase in this example is actually a composite of short melodic fragments that may be described as motives. We are reminded at once that in most art music our two styles of progression are likely to cross more or less. Some hint of phrase grouping is almost always present in motivic play, and conversely some motivic play in phrase grouping. Rarely is either style found in such an ideal or pure use, for example, as Bach makes of motivic

Fig. 25. How the same phrase might have been treated in different eras

play in "Prelude in G Minor" from *The Well-Tempered Clavier*, II, or Mendelssohn of phrase grouping in the familiar "Spring Song" from *Songs Without Words* (op. 62, no. 6). As will be noted in the next chapter, the "subject" of a Bach fugue is more likely to approximate a phrase than a motive, as these terms were defined here. Yet the predominant style of progression in a fugue is motivic play (usually based on some element of that subject) rather than phrase grouping. And the resultant form in fugal writing is ordinarily cursive and monothematic rather than hierarchic and polythematic. On the other hand, the basic idea in many Chopin Etudes (p. 239) is a motive (as it also is, for that matter, in the opening of Mozart's *Symphony in G Minor,* K. 550, or the first movement of Beethoven's *Fifth Symphony*). Yet now the predominant style of progression is certainly phrase grouping, with the motive's repetitions falling into clear four-measure phrases. And the resultant form is certainly both hierarchic and polythematic. In each form, the fugue as well as the etude, it is the prevailing texture that seems to determine which style of progression will predominate.

As we have seen, *hierarchic design* is a kind of form made up of complementary groupings within complementary groupings. (Hierarchy means a logical ranking, as from lowest to highest.) The adjoining analysis of *Drink to Me Only with Thine Eyes* shows a very elementary example of a hierarchic design, with the columns progressing from the highest to lowest level reading from left to right. At each level there is a complementary relationship of two units, marked Q. and A. for "question" and "answer" to suggest a psychological relationship often felt in such groupings.

In this same example the phrase groupings, with two four-measure phrases in each, occur at the next-to-the broadest level, or just one level short of the structural result. Larger hierarchic designs have still broader levels (periods, sections, parts, even movements or acts), much as a great country has broader political divisions (counties, states, regions) than a township. Although we have taken the phrase intact as a basic generator, it usually subdivides into half-phrases or other fragments that themselves have a complementary relationship, as is true at the third level in *Drink to Me*. If a still more local level is to be sought, then the analyst is likely to reach what might be called the indestructible atom of music—the *incise,* consisting of at least one strong and one weak beat, or the converse. The danger of breaking down the hierarchic design to that extent, however, is illustrated in this instance by the senseless disruption of the

Structural Result	Phrase Grouping	Half-Phrase Grouping	Incise Grouping
Q.	Q.	Q.	Q. Drink to me on-
			A. ly with thine eyes,
		A.	Q. And I will pledge
			A. with mine;
	A.	Q.	Q. Or leave a kiss
			A. within the cup,
		A.	Q. And I'll not ask
			A. for wine.
A.	Q.	Q.	Q. The thirst that from
			A. the soul doth rise,
		A.	Q. Doth ask a drink
			A. divine;
	A.	Q.	Q. But might I of
			A. Jove's nectar sup,
		A.	Q I would not change
			A. for thine.

song's text. Otherwise the degree of punctuation in the text corresponds interestingly to the hierarchic levels, confirming the sense of the analysis. (To feel the different levels try singing and conducting this song. Its meter is $\frac{6}{8}$, which you will recognize as a compound meter meaning $\frac{2}{\flat}$, as explained on p. 53.)

Such absolute symmetry as you find at the top three levels in this example is, of course, not essential in a hierarchic design— hardly so while art is still art. For one thing, three or even four units may be grouped in a complementary relationship. Three units might be heard, for example, in the sense of question-answer-answer (p. 183) or question-question-answer. For another thing, the question-answer concept itself must not be labored unduly. The second phrase may complement the first, not in one but several ways. Taking the opening pair of phrases in several familiar songs, the second phrase may (1) be identical with the first, as in *Drink to Me;* (2) end on a slight melodic alteration, as in *Home Sweet Home;* (3) end with a more noticeable change of melody, as in *Juanita;* (4) complement a half cadence in the first phrase with a final cadence, as in *Old Folks at Home;* (5) do the same along with a generally opposite movement of the melody, as in *The Star-Spangled Banner;* or (6) both modulate and veer away melodically, as in *America, the Beautiful.* It is the half and final cadences, in particular, that create the sense of rise and fall implied by question and answer.

(A highly illuminating experience for you at this point would be an attempt, purely from information provided thus far, to invent a motive and put it through a bit of motivic play; then an attempt to invent a phrase and complement it with another phrase, followed, perhaps, by further phrase groupings. If it will help you to get started, borrow the motive in Fig. 23 (p. 142) and the phrase in Fig. 12 (p. 74). Results in this sort of experiment, however naïve or crude, rarely fail to give an inside view of the problem that words cannot possibly give.)

STANDARDIZED DESIGNS BASED ON REPETITION AND CONTRAST

Now, turning to musical form in its other sense, what *standardized designs* are found to prevail among the countless individual structural results of progression by motivic play and progression by phrase grouping? As a basis for classifying these designs we return once more to the aesthetic requirement of variety and unity, especially to its corollary, *contrast and repetition.* This corollary contains the germ of a distinction between the form of music and that of the other time arts. Thus, a prime need of literature is to go on, resulting in what are called "open" forms; a prime need of music is to return and repeat, resulting in "closed" forms. To be sure, there are stylized literary works that do return to the beginning, like Keats' poem *Lines on the Mermaid Tavern,* or Theodore Dreiser's *An American Tragedy,* in which the last chapter at least brings us back to a situation like that in the first chapter. And there are some musical compositions that neither return nor repeat. But such examples do constitute exceptions to our rule. Thus, the exceptions in music usually fall into one of three types: pieces so short that they can be digested all in one gulp—not long enough, in other words, to require the bracing of a formal design; fantasias, the very purpose of which is to escape the bonds of "confining" designs; and works that are essentially settings of literary texts or "programmes." Even so, rare indeed is the composition in which at least short melodic or rhythmic figures are not repeated, often more in these three form types than in any others!

Starting with the principle of contrast within repetition, it is now possible to distinguish between three categories of standardized designs, each of which becomes the subject of one of the next three chapters. One grows out of motivic play, another out of phrase grouping, and the third out of both means of progression. The distinction between the three categories lies each time in the answer to the question, What provides the repetition and what provides the contrast?

The first category is that of *forms woven out of motivic play.* Cursive forms in general are not as susceptible of standardized classifications as the hierarchic forms. However, we may include in this category especially the motet, madrigal, fugue, and nearly all idiomatic Baroque instrumental music. Repetition in these forms is provided, first, by a motive or subject that reappears more or less frequently in one or another of the textural voices; and second, by adherence to a certain modal scale, or by eventual return to an original tonal center. Contrast is provided, first, by the shifting about of the motive or subject; and second, by a variety of cadences in modal music, or modulations to other keys in tonal music.

The second category is that of *hierarchic designs based on phrase grouping,* including especially binary, ternary, and rondo forms. In this category, repetition is provided, first, by one or more recurrences of one or more complete sections at the highest level of hierarchic design; and second, by prolonged returns to an original tonal center. Contrast is provided, first, by other sections that alternate with the recurring sections; and second, by modulations away from the original key.

The third and final category is that of the *variation principle,* called a compound process here because it combines both kinds of progression. Within each variation the progression is more often by motivic play than by phrase grouping. At a higher level the hierarchic principle operates in the sense that the variations may group into larger sections. The repetition at regular intervals of some musical idea provides a basis for classifying variation forms. This idea may be a bass line, harmonic pattern, or melody, or any of these taken at will out of a composite theme. Contrast is provided chiefly by varying anything but the recurring element itself, and sometimes even that.

MODERN TRENDS

There have already been occasions, in earlier chapters, to note certain Modern trends—in rhythm, in melody, in harmony, and in polyphony. The approach taken in the present chapter suggests some possible conclusions regarding Modern trends in musical form. First of all, it is as a structural result that Modern form reveals the greatest consequences of the crisis in tonality (p. 98) and the attempts to get around the crisis, of the resistance to regular meter and regular phrases, and of the expansion of melodic concepts.

Standardized designs as such reveal less. Being the fixed molds of form they die hard, anyway, since they have a long tradition in both titles and textbooks. Nor are we likely to find much new in the way of standardized designs. A few experiments in the direction of still greater integration can be pointed to, especially between movements at the highest level in form "cycles" (p. 224). But much as all novels have been reduced to thirty-six and only thirty-six possible dramatic situations by the Frenchman Georges Polti, so musical form might be reduced to a limited number of general designs to which almost any supposedly new type could be referred. If so, that limit may well be at hand, one evidence being the Modern tendency to return to past forms (neoclassicism).

From the standpoint of this chapter the most significant change in Modern music has been a gradual but sure shift from phrase grouping back to motivic play as a means of progression. Whether the trends in tonality and so forth have induced this shift or are themselves the consequence of it may be only a chicken-or-the-egg type of question. But motivic play can account in a rather remarkable way for the fluid tonality, the rhythmic irregularity, the departure from complete melodies stated in complete phrases, and various other of the motive's "symptoms" that prevail in Modern music.

The structural result of this shift has been an equally gradual but sure undermining of the hierarchic designs. Probably the undermining is not a conscious process, since composers continue to use the titles of standardized hierarchic designs—rondo or sonata, for example. However, the effects can be observed clearly enough. Besides the traits just mentioned, there is the prevalence of polyphonic over homophonic texture. There is the tendency toward monothematic music; even when a second idea is present it is usually so bound up with or closely related to the first that it is more of a variant than a contrast or complement. There is in the sonata the more or less continual development of an idea rather than one formal development section or a simple, complete statement followed by a departure to something else. There is strong rhythmic drive, perhaps stronger than ever before in Western music, but chiefly at the pulse rather than the metric level, as in the incessant use of the pattern of a long and two short notes (Appendix II, No. 33,I). There is the frequent interjection of fugal writing, which itself can be a structural result of the motive. There is a tendency to cut short or discard the last complementary unit at the highest level of hierarchic design (for example, the "recapitulation" in Appendix II, No. 33,I). And, above all, there is the effacement of seams and joints, the progression in an unbroken flow, that can be achieved only by motivic play itself, motivic play that has become as malleable and slick as today's plastics.

SELECTED READINGS

Aram Torossian, *A Guide to Aesthetics*. Stanford: Stanford University Press, 1937.

Stephen C. Pepper, *The Work of Art*. Bloomington: Indiana University Press, 1955.

Roger Sessions, *The Musical Experience of Composer, Performer, Listener*. Princeton: Princeton University Press, 1950.

Glen Haydon, *Introduction to Musicology*, Chapters III and IV. Chapel Hill: University of North Carolina Press, 1959 [1941].

George Sherman Dickinson, *The Pattern of Music*. Poughkeepsie: Vassar College, 1939.

Rudolph Reti, *The Thematic Process in Music*. New York: Macmillan, 1951.

Ernest Toch, *The Shaping Forces in Music*. New York: Criterion, 1948.

William S. Newman, "Musical Form as a Generative Process," *The Journal of Aesthetics & Art Criticism*, XII (1954).

Calvin S. Brown, *Music and Literature*. Athens: University of Georgia Press, 1948.

R. O. Morris, *The Structure of Music*. New York: Oxford University Press, 1935.

Hugo Leichtentritt, *Musical Form*. Cambridge: Harvard University Press, 1951.

Norman Demuth, *Musical Forms and Textures*. London: Rockliff, 1953.

Karl Eschman, *Changing Forms in Modern Music*. Boston: E. C. Schirmer, 1945.

Chapter 9

Forms Woven Out of Motivic Play

THE MOTET AND THE MADRIGAL

Having reached the point where we can take up complete musical forms, let us begin with those in which motivic play is the chief means of progression. First to be described are the motet and the madrigal, since these are predecessors of the other motivic forms to be discussed. *Motet* and *madrigal* are titles that have actually been applied to a variety of forms since the Medieval-and-Renaissance Era, including the thirteenth-century "superstructure" motet, with its two or three melodies sung to different texts (!) above a bit of Gregorian chant; and the fourteenth-century eleven-line madrigal in "strophic" (verse) form.

Here we are concerned with the best known and widest use of these titles, that of the late Renaissance on the Continent and in England. In this use motet and madrigal refer to music that is predominantly additive and cursive in form,[1] vocal in four to six parts, *a cappella* (unaccompanied, "in chapel style") polyphonic, and modal in its scale structures and harmonic treatment. The most obvious distinction between the two titles is found in the fact that motet usually implied a sacred text in Latin (or in English in the similar *anthem*), a liturgical use, and an austere style appropriate to church music; whereas madrigal usu-

[1] The terms *additive* and *cursive* are alike here in meaning continuation without return. *Additive* further implies a stringing together of sections, and *cursive* an unbroken flow in the musical texture.

ally implied a secular or at least a nonliturgical text in the vernacular, a cultivated social use, and the freer variety of styles that
secular uses allowed.

Both the text and the music are likely to be additive in these
forms. Only rarely is a form "closed" by the repetition of a section. Nor is it likely to be completely unified, as by a *strophic*
plan, in which each of several different stanzas of text is set to
the same music, or even by the recurrence of the same motive
throughout. In any case, as we have seen (p. 142), the motive
lacks the pronounced rhythmic or melodic character and the
clear identity in Medieval-and-Renaissance music to be quite the
means of unity that it will be in later music. The sense of the text
itself then becomes the most positive unifying agent.

Since the motet and the madrigal are too unpredictable in
their forms to be classified among the standardized designs, the
better solution seems to be a description of them, in the following
paragraphs, according to characteristic methods of procedure. For
the sake of clear illustration the opening of a motet by Lassus for
only three voices is quoted in Fig. 26 (p. 158; Appendix II, No.
14).

1. Ordinarily, a different motive is employed for each line or
shorter division of the text. The imitation that is characteristic of
motivic play results when each of the voices enters in turn, though
in no set order, on this motive. A complete round or so of such
entries on the same bit of text is known as a *point of imitation*. All
together, the successive points of imitation for each division of the
text comprise the several different sections that make up the additive
form. But a clear demarcation of these sections is ordinarily avoided
by means characteristic of polyphony. No sooner do the voices begin
to converge in a cadence as the entries in one point of imitation are
being completed than some voice that has been resting breaks in with
the first entry in a new point of imitation. The lowest voice happens
to have this honor each time (measures 1, 5, and 8) in the two complete points of imitation and the start of a third one that appear in
Fig. 26.

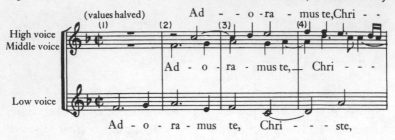

Fig. 26. Procedures in a motet (Lassus, "Adoramus te," for three voices, from *Magnum opus musicum,* No. 44 [53])

2. Occasionally, as at a shift to a momentarily brighter mood in the text, a *homophonic chordal section* replaces a point of imitation. Then the voices move along in block chords (as happens most of the time on the words "et benedicimus tibi" ["and we bless thee"] in Fig. 26), sometimes changing from the usual four-beat to a clear three-beat meter.

3. *Modal harmony* accompanies the use of the old church modes, Dorian, Phrygian, and so on (Lydian in Fig. 26). Although modality

lacks the drive and cohesive influence of the I-IV-V-I orbit in tonality, it offers compensating delights, chiefly in the direction of more subtle, varied melodic and harmonic flavors. Especially at partial and more final endings (as in measure 5 of Fig. 26) can one notice that modality is not limited to the conventional half and final cadences of tonality.

4. Except in homophonic chordal sections, the *separate voices are rhythmically independent*. In Renaissance polyphony a constant unit beat or pulse is ordinarily maintained, but the textual and musical sense of the individual lines implies irregular metric groupings that do not necessarily coincide. In fact, the words are often lost in performance because of the overlappings, so that the pleasure of the music then becomes chiefly that of sheer sound. (Bar lines were actually not used in this music, although modern editors find it convenient to put them in, either allowing them not to coincide or arbitrarily making them coincide, as in Fig. 26, so that performers can stay together. A mystery nearly as puzzling to us today as the construction of the Egyptian pyramids is the almost total absence of full scores of Renaissance music. How could the composer work out his intricate polyphony without seeing the several parts superimposed vertically?) When the voices do converge on the same strong beat, that beat usually marks the moment of dissonance in the preparation-dissonance-resolution formula (p. 117) or the coming to rest on the last chord of a cadence. In Fig. 26 the voices do coincide rhythmically in the more homophonic, second point of imitation; and they do converge on the strong beat of measure 8, which is a suspended dissonance. But otherwise, just as the words do not coincide, so, for example, the high voice begins its own measure later than the middle voice in the first point of imitation (disregarding the editor's bar lines).

5. The most tangible and frequent influence of the text is that called *word painting*. This term means an adapting of the music to illustrate the sense of a word, perhaps by an inflection of the melody, a shift in the rhythm, or a special color in the harmony. The word painting may be literal, as in the melodic descent of a third on the word "cuckoo." It may be psychological, whether obvious or subtle, as in a high tone on the word "high" or "heaven," a dissonant harmony

at an expression of anguish, or a convergence and separation of lines on the words "together and asunder." Or it may be symbolical, as in the familiar device of crossing two voice parts, each singing three stepwise tones, to represent the holy cross ($\begin{smallmatrix} E & & E \\ & \diagdown D \diagup & \\ C & & C \end{smallmatrix}$). (A slightly different crossing of the two lower voices occurs on the words "sanctam crucem" in measure 10 of Fig. 26.)

If we were to go further into the nature of the motet and the madrigal we might begin by exploring the distinctions between these two forms. Thus, in the madrigal, freedom from church restrictions meant a broader choice of texts, harmonic colors, and rhythmic patterns. Moreover, differences in the vernacular tongue, the prevailing literary tastes, and the madrigal's place in society resulted in distinctly national styles.

1. In Italy the madrigal (such as that of Cipriano de Rore) associates with an aristocratic society and its passionately amorous poetry; with warmly lyrical melodies appropriate to the many liquid elisions and clear vowels of Italian speech; and with the daring chromatic harmonies introduced late in sixteenth-century Italian music.

2. In France, the *chanson,* as it was called (such as that by Clément Jannequin), associates with neatly defined melodies and distinct, narrow, rounded, nasal enunciation; with gay fanciful texts well suited to word painting, and even with nonsense syllables; with the quantitative poetry of Ronsard and others; and with the typically French *clarté* of near-homophonic texture.

3. In the German *lied,* as it was called (such as that by Hans Leo von Hasler, or the ever-lovely *Inspruk, ich muss dich lassen [Innsbruck, I Must Leave Thee]* by Heinrich Isaac), the steady, sturdy, robust melodies and deeply expressive harmonies relate to the guttural, heavy speech and the spiritual leaning of the texts.

4. In "merry" Elizabethan England the madrigal (such as that by Thomas Morley) marked one of that country's greatest contributions to music. There the wide, flat vowels and relatively inert consonants seemed to favor simple, cheerful, almost folklike melodies in nearly

square rhythms, including "fa-la" refrains. However, these traits gave way somewhat to a strong Italian influence that was felt late in the century.

FUGAL FORM

The *fugue* originated as a Baroque successor to the motet and the madrigal. But its scoring is more variable, some fugues being for voices with or without instrumental support, and others for one or more instruments alone. As for its typical form, in one overly packed sentence, it is a monothematic, polyphonic, cursive composition in which several expositions of a "subject" alternate in nearly related keys with several modulatory episodes that progress by sequential motivic play on some fragment related to that subject.

As a first step toward breaking that definition down, we may compare the fugue with the motet or madrigal. To begin with, the subject and the exposition in the fugue are successors to the motive and the point of imitation in the motet. But the subject is ordinarily a more distinctive idea (melodically, rhythmically, and harmonically) than the older type motive. Consequently, it can and does serve as a main unifying element in the total form, recurring almost intact instead of being replaced by a new idea in each exposition.

The episodes of motivic play that lead from one exposition to the next are something new in the fugue. They become necessary with the rise of strong major or minor tonality and the need to modulate from key to key. The motivic play itself is of a stricter sort than any in the motet; its imitations are more faithful and exact. In addition, its concentration on elements of the subject helps to reduce the entire rhythmic course of the fugue to one or two main patterns, making for a stronger metrical drive than the motet had.

As a result of these changes there is a more positive musical unity in the fugue than in the motet, a unity that more than compensates for the lack of a binding text in instrumental fugues. Furthermore, the partial sense of return that comes with each new exposition of the same subject somewhat counteracts the additive effect of a string of expositions alternating with episodes. So does the sense of return that is achieved by the key organization in tonality. And so does the cumulative drive to a late climax, to be noted shortly. Yet, with all this, the fugue is still better thought of as *fugal form*. It is still more of a structural result than a standardized design. Like the motet, it lends itself to description better as a series of procedures than a mold to be filled:

1. The *subject* of a fugue is something more than a motive, being closer to a complete idea (Figs. 23, 27, 28, 48a, and 48b, pp. 142, 163, 166, and 270). From it as many as two or three motives may be derived in the different episodes. Often it trails off just short of the symmetry and clear ending of a phrase, thereby not forsaking the braidlike flow of the texture. The subject may be short or long, and in one or two sections. With it may be associated a complementary bit of counterpoint called the *countersubject,* like that sung when the words "For He alone" first appear in Fig. 27 (Appendix II, No. 16). When the countersubject appears often enough and seems important enough to be called a second subject, as it does in this instance (and in Appendix II, No. 23), the fugue may be called a *double fugue.* Other "double," "triple," or even "quadruple" fugues are so called because two or more subjects are taken up one at a time in virtually separate fugues, after which all are heard simultaneously. This was to be the plan in the incomplete "quadruple" fugue in Bach's monumental *Art of the Fugue,* the third subject of which is none other than B-A-C-H (B=B♭, H=B♮).

2. In an *exposition* the two or more "voices" of the fugue enter successively on the subject, somewhat in the manner of characters in a play. They come in at different pitch levels and in any order that alternates either of the high ranges (soprano or tenor) with either of the low ranges (alto or bass). In the initial exposition every voice makes an entry. Farther on in the fugue two entries or only one entry may be all that constitutes an exposition. In the Baroque fugue,

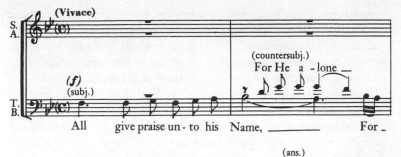

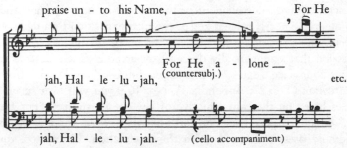

Fig. 27. The subject and countersubject in a choral fugue (Haydn, "Achievèd is the Glorious Work," from *The Creation,* No. 28 [or 27b])

since the tonal scheme usually touches at least once on every or almost every one of the five nearest related keys (p. 95), there is an average of from three to five expositions plus the episodes with which they alternate.

Each alternate entry of the subject in the exposition is called an *answer* because its pitch level is heard as a complement to that of the previous entry (although this relationship is a cumulative one in the growing polyphonic texture, and not a "closed" one as in the question-answer relationship of phrase grouping). If the subject suggests a tonic harmony the answer comes in on a dominant harmony, or vice versa. The answer may even undergo slight melodic adjustments if necessary to confirm this relationship. Each pairing of subject and answer usually ends in a brief *codetta* of free counterpoint before the next subject enters or an episode begins. Here is the order of events in the exposition that opens the four-voice "Fugue" of Bach's *Passacaglia and Fugue in C Minor* for organ (Appendix II, No. 23; see Fig. 32, p. 192):

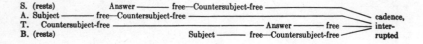

3. An *episode* usually follows an exposition without a break in the polyphonic flow, beginning just as the voices have converged at a cadence, often a deceptive cadence. Most episodes leave out one of the voices, engage some element of the subject in motivic play, and modulate to the nearly related key of the next exposition by a melodic and harmonic *sequence* (which, as was noted on pp. 96–97, is a progression that systematically descends or ascends as it repeats). In Haydn's four-voice fugue "Achievèd is the Glorious Work" from *The Creation* (Fig. 27; Appendix II, No. 16), you will hear several episodes based on the initial motive of the countersubject, "For He alone," which is passed back and forth between two or three voices as it gradually rises or descends with the modulation. Listen, too, for the short, striking episode near the end of the second "Kyrie eleison" in Bach's *Mass in B Minor* (Appendix II, No. 43a), where the sopranos make a high, syncopated entry on a motive from the subject, and each successively lower voice follows at the interval of a fifth.

4. Several factors tend to make a fugue cumulative in its total effect. One is its persistent rhythmic drive, typically culminating in Bach's fugues with a dramatic and climactic pause shortly before the ending (Appendix II, No. 23). Another is the tonal drive of an organized key scheme, which often fits very well the idea of a "grand

cadence" (pp. 93–94). The culmination of this tonal drive may be a dominant "pedal point," as during the moments when the rhythmic drive is grinding to its climactic pause on some half cadence, and/or a tonic "pedal point" during the characteristic prolonging of the final cadence (Appendix II, No. 16). (Named for its frequent use in the pedal keyboard part of organ music, the *pedal point* or *organ point* is a bass tone sustained under successive harmonies that start and end in consonance with it but otherwise may create sharp dissonant relationships.) A third cumulative factor is the foreshortening effect, during the course of the fugue, of expositions with but one or two entries. And a fourth factor, one with decided intellectual appeal, is the increasing use of *contrapuntal devices* toward the end. These devices include entries of the subject upside down or even backward (which the hearer seldom recognizes), augmented or diminished (p. 142), and in stretto. *Stretto* means an exciting overlapping of the subject's entries, each subject interrupting the one before it.

The contrapuntal devices, like the other procedures described, may or may not occur in any particular fugue. To illustrate several of them at once, an unusual exposition is quoted here (Fig. 28) from Bach's *Art of the Fugue*, which great, final collection by him presents a whole series of fugues and canons all based on the same subject. The tenor enters at once on the subject in diminution. It is answered by the soprano in stretto, inversion, and normal note values. The alto enters on the subject, melodically and tonally adjusted, in diminution, inversion, and stretto; and it is answered by the bass in stretto, inversion, and augmentation (continuing beyond the portion quoted here). Dotted brackets encompass each subject or answer. Whole-rests indicate silent "voices." Solid brackets encompass a motive derived from the end of the subject, which occasionally serves as a countersubject. Note the motivic play on the dot-dot-dot-dash figure in measures 4 to 6.

The heyday of the fugue was the Baroque Era, but composers have been fascinated by it ever since, whether as a complete form in itself or as a section (fughetta), especially a means of develop-

(Keyboard?)

Fig. 28. Procedures in a fugue (Bach, "Contrapunctus VII," from *Art of the Fugue*)

ment, in another form. It figures importantly in the music of Haydn, Mozart, Beethoven (chiefly his last works), Mendelssohn, Schumann, Brahms, and many Modern composers. The fugue as an independent form is customarily preceded by a fantasia, prelude, toccata, or other "warm-up" piece that provides an ideal foil for its intellectual severity. This combination is best known in another musician's bible by Bach (see pp. 111, 116, 123, and 165), *The Well-Tempered Clavier*, which contains forty-eight preludes and fugues in two volumes, every major and minor key being represented twice. (These can all be played on the same instrument only if its tuning is equal-tempered, as mentioned on p. 43; hence the title of Bach's collection.) Among later such collections, done in full cognizance of Bach's, are two Modern ones of distinction, Hindemith's *Ludus tonalis* and Shostakovitch's *Twenty-Four Preludes and Fugues,* op. 87.

BINARY DESIGN IN BAROQUE INSTRUMENTAL PIECES

Another type of form in which motivic play is the most characteristic progression may be found in the lighter Baroque instrumental music, whether for stringed keyboard instrument, chamber ensemble, or orchestra. Included in this music are the dances and more intimate pieces that are grouped into suites (p. 204), with maximum contrasts, from one to the next, of tempo, rhythmic pattern, and character. Such familiar dance titles as allemande, courante, saraband, and gigue belong in this category. Also included in the lighter Baroque instrumental music are the approximately 550 clever keyboard "exercises" by the Italian Domenico Scarlatti, which further bear the title of "sonata," though merely in the early sense of "instrumental piece." And also included are the colorful, often "programmatic" (descriptive) keyboard pieces by the Frenchmen Couperin and Rameau.

What usually distinguishes this music from the fugue is not only a thinner, more lax polyphony but an over-all binary design. Both the fugue and the lighter music are essentially cursive, yet the latter, perhaps as the very structural result of its disintegrated polyphony, makes a clean break into two sections. Its division is marked off as much by a binary tonal plan and a somewhat parallel treatment of material as by the external device of double bars and repeat signs (‖: first half :‖: second half :‖), indicating that each half is to be repeated upon completion. This last indication, however, could actually lead to several possible designs, since either or both repeats were regarded as being optional

then, depending on the occasion, just as they are when this
music is played today. The result might be A-A-B-B, A-A-B, or
A-B, though probably not A-B-B.

The somewhat parallel treatment of material in the two halves
amounts chiefly to a restatement of the initial motive at the out-
set of the second half, and the use of a characteristic closing figure to end each half alike. As for the tonality, the relationship between halves is more one of opposition than parallelism. The
first half modulates to the dominant or relative key, where it
ends with the force of a half-cadence, whereas the second half
mirrors this process by starting in the related key and modulating
back to the tonic. The "fall" back to the tonic is almost too easy
to be convincing when done directly. To avoid unbalance and a
sense of insufficiency the composer usually returns by a circui-
tous route on the "dark" or subdominant side of the key, increasing the sense of conquest. He approaches the tonic for the moment as if he were making a "rise" to the dominant. In this way,
he completes the fundamental orbit of tonic, dominant, subdominant. All of which commonly results in an asymmetrical
binary design, with the second half longer, sometimes three or
four times longer, than the first. Here, then, is a typical plan:

||: Initial motive, motivic play modulating to near key, characteristic
   closing figure with half-cadence on near key; :||
||: initial motive inverted, motivic play modulating indirectly around
   "dark" side back to tonic, closing figure with final cadence in tonic
   key. :||

As for the motivic play itself in this lighter Baroque music,
only two or three voices are ordinarily employed. The dance or
other piece often starts with an entry on the main motive in one
voice and a distinct imitation in another, in the subject-answer
manner of the fugue. But thereafter the motivic play is likely to
be of a casual sort, with the rhythmic pattern of the motive being
maintained much more faithfully than the melodic outline (Fig.

29). The dances in Bach's numerous suites are the chief exception to this generalization, for in spite of French and Italian influences he seldom relaxed the texture to this extent. On the other hand, in the harpsichord pieces of Couperin, Rameau, and Scarlatti, after two or three entries on the initial motive, the voices often lapse into passages of parallel sixths or thirds with only an occasional contrapuntal gesture here or there (Appen-

Fig. 29. The "gallant style" in harpsichord music (D. Scarlatti, *Sonata in D Major,* K. 443)

dix II, Nos. 17, 18). This is the pseudo polyphony of the thin but highly ornamented Rococo music and of the less adorned gallant style (opp. Plate 4 and p. 118).

It is especially interesting to observe the effects of this transitional style, this midpoint between strict motivic play and fully homophonic phrase grouping, in the extraordinarily fresh and varied one-movement "sonatas" of Scarlatti. Not infrequently one finds regular, four-measure phrases, complete melodies, sharply contrasted ideas, sectional divisions marked by full stops on half or final cadences, and distinct tonal plateaus. These traits are intimately bound up with the ingenious keyboard techniques, the hammering home of ideas, the daring sonorities and harmonic progressions, and the general buoyancy that give Scarlatti a distinguished niche among innovators of the keyboard.

SELECTED READINGS

R. O. Morris, *Contrapuntal Technique in the Sixteenth Century.* London: Clarendon Press, 1934.

Hans David, *The Art of Polyphonic Song* (a music anthology with valuable prefatory comments). New York: G. Schirmer, 1940.

Edmund Horace Fellowes, *The English Madrigal Composers.* New York: Oxford University Press, 1948.

Charles Kennedy Scott, *Madrigal Singing.* New York: Oxford University Press, 1931.

Alfred Einstein, *The Italian Madrigal,* 3 vols. (the third consisting entirely of complete examples). Princeton: Princeton University Press, 1949.

George Oldroyd, *The Technique and Spirit of Fugue.* New York: Oxford University Press, 1948.

Manfred Bukofzer, *Music in the Baroque Era,* Chapter X. New York: W. W. Norton, 1947.

A. E. F. Dickinson, *Bach's Fugal Works.* New York: Pitman, 1956.

Donald Tovey, *A Companion to "The Art of Fugue."* New York: Oxford University Press, 1931.

Alfred Mann, *The Study of Fugue.* New Brunswick: Rutgers University Press, 1958.

Chapter 10

Hierarchic *Designs* *Based* on *Phrase* *Grouping*

BINARY DESIGN IN HOMOPHONIC MUSIC

Hierarchic design, as you will recall, results when phrases fall into complementary groupings, and these into larger complementary groupings, and so on. Here at once lies the basic distinction between the binary design that results from motivic play and the kind now to be discussed. The former is essentially cursive within each half, not sectional and subsectional. Here, too, lies the reason why hierarchic design can be more but not less than binary. The fugue might conceivably be represented by the single letter A, since it is typically an uninterrupted, cursive, and monothematic form. But a hierarchic design will always fall into A-B, A-B-A, or some other grouping if each of its levels is to express a complementary relationship.

You will also recall that a hierarchic design is necessarily an integrated rather than an additive form since, by derivation, its largest grouping comprehends all its successively lesser groupings. Such additive extremes as the indefinite series A-A-A-A . . . or A-B-C-D . . . cannot qualify as hierarchic designs and, in any case, have generally been ruled out as musical forms except as ways have been found to add variety or unity, respectively. Where the series A-A-A-A . . . does appear, it is likely to undergo changes in a set of variations (Chap. 11) or to be used in a strophic plan—for example, in the American ballad *Frankie and Johnny,* with a new incident in each verse to maintain the interest. The series A-B-C-D . . . can hardly be tolerated unless some recurring element is included or alternated with each unit (as in the Baroque "rondeau" described on pp. 179–181).

From the standpoint of integration, the *binary design* A-B is likely to seem less closed than an A-B-A ternary design. It is less of a complete, independent form in itself because it is clearly strong in contrast yet provides only such incidental repetition as may come from the recurrence in B of fragments from A. In other words its variety is in disproportion to its unity. This does not necessarily mean that the hierarchic A-B design is less satisfying, but simply that it tends to continue, whether by repeating or going on to something else. Conversely, the A-B-A design does not suggest continuation and does not lend itself to repetition *in toto*. When it does repeat, the juxtaposition of two A sections each time—A-B-A̅ A̅-B-A—quickly becomes monotonous (too much unity).

It is not surprising, then, that hierarchic binary designs occur above all in folk and community songs, so many of which continue through several stanzas of text—thus, are meant to be repeated several times. In fact, this use of binary design brings us right back to the additive strophic plan. However, now we are concerned with a broader, more nearly self-sufficient level of hierarchic design than, say, the single phrase grouping into which the melody of *Frankie and Johnny* falls.

Binary designs occur in art music, too, though less often than one might expect of so fundamental a design. They occur, for instance, in the theme of the theme-and-variations form (Appendix II, Nos. 26; 32,II), since each variation must lead on to the next and not stand as a separate design by itself (p. 199). Similarly they often occur in sonata music in each subform of the compound ternary designs minuet-trio-minuet and scherzo-trio-scherzo (Appendix II, No. 31,III). And they occur in the unit design of the strophic plan when it is used in art-songs, as in Schubert's *Ave Maria*, or in opera arias, as in Papageno's opening song from *The Magic Flute* by Mozart. Binary design may also be found in opera arias that are intended not to interrupt the flow of the action as much as the more familiar A-B-A or "da capo" type does. An example is Otello's soliloquy in Act III of Verdi's *Otello* (Appendix II, No. 39f).

Although much more extended examples can be cited, most binary designs of the sort just discussed do not extend to more than one or two levels above that of phrase grouping in the design hierarchy. Most community songs, for instance, are only a pair of phrase groupings. *Flow Gently, Sweet Afton* is less usual in that each half is a pair of phrase groupings.

This much can be generalized about the tonality of binary designs based on traditional harmony: Somewhere after the start in the tonic key there is likely to be a cadence or a fresh start on the dominant or "relative" harmony (p. 92); and somewhere before the end in the tonic key there is likely to be a clear reference to subdominant harmony. There you have, as always, the fundamental orbit of harmonic movement. To illustrate, *Hark! the Herald Angels Sing* cadences on the dominant at the end of its first phrase group (on the word "reconciled"), and makes a strong reference to the subdominant at the beginning of the final, repeated phrase of the second phrase group.

And this much can be generalized about the variety and relationship of the phrases: Infrequently all phrases are quite different from each other. The unity is provided only by the complementary effect of phrase opposition. Almost never are all phrases alike, since there is then no appreciable means of variety. Most often, any two or three of the phrases are identical or at least similar. In the symmetrical nature of phrase grouping the number of phrases in each half of the binary design is likely to be about the same. When either half has more, it will ordinarily be the second. But this design is not nearly so given to asymmetry as the binary design based on motivic play. The chief exception is the Classic minuet or scherzo, which often harks back to motivic styles in the Baroque dance.

Again, let us take some examples from familiar community

songs. All five phrases are different in *O Come, All Ye Faithful,*
which has one grouping of two phrases (ending on the last syllable of "Bethlehem") and one grouping of three phrases. The
first and last phrase are identical in *O, Little Town of Bethlehem,*
the four phrases of which produce the design a-b-c-a. *Abide with
Me* has the phrase design a-b-a'-c, with the prime mark indicating
that the repeated phrase is only similar but not identical to the
first phrase. More explicitly, this first phrase ends on the tonic
chord, whereas the repeated phrase veers to the subdominant
side of the tonality. An a-b-c interpretation is quite possible too.
Drink to Me Only with Thine Eyes (diagrammed on p. 149) has
the frequent phrase design a-a-b-a, with only one different phrase.

Since a phrase or part of a phrase in the first half of a binary
design often recurs at the end of the second half, there is sometimes confusion as to whether this is simply a reference to the
first half or a valid return, making the design actually A-B-A.
This question is not mere hairsplitting but very pertinent to our
understanding of binary and ternary design. As a matter of fact,
many older textbooks used to, and some present ones still do,
maintain that the least reference or return at the end to the
opening converts a binary into an A-B-A design. But this view
must be rejected for more than one reason. In the first place, the
final reference is often only part of a phrase, as it is in Schubert's
Ave Maria. And even when it is an entire phrase, as in *O, Little
Town of Bethlehem,* to make that phrase a separate part in the
design creates a violent distortion of what the Englishman E. J.
Dent called the quatrain principle (in his article listed at the end
of this chapter). This distortion seems all the less justified in that
no one questions the binary classification of all the other songs
that conform to the same quatrain principle but do not happen
to restate fragments from the first half at the end.

To account for this distortion older theorists coined such classifications as "incipient ternary form," calling the first part a
phrase grouping, yet each of the other parts only a phrase. But as
in all analysis of musical form, what really matters is how the de-

sign is *heard*. This is where our discussion of phrase grouping and hierarchic design should shed some further light. The letters A-B and A-B-A represent a complementary grouping of units at the highest level in hierarchic designs. The A and the B are at the same level. By making the A mean one level at first and a more local level at the end, you are asked to hear a complementary relationship between, say, a phrase grouping and a half-phrase grouping (p. 148). This is somewhat like equating a lieutenant and a sergeant in the military hierarchy. It simply does not happen.

Since our ear insists on relating only units at the same level, it will hear a final phrase or half-phrase only in its position as part of a question-answer or other grouping. And there lies what may be the crux of the distinction between a final reference to the first part in a binary design and a valid return in a ternary design. A final phrase will not "feel" like a return to an opening phrase, even when the notes are identical, because it occupies a different position in phrase grouping, *an answer rather than a question position*. When the reference to the opening phrase occupies a similar question position, then and only then can it sound like a return.

TERNARY DESIGN (A-B-A)

Our fussy but necessary distinction between binary and *ternary design* now brings us to the latter with something of a head start. The highly stable and self-sufficient *A-B-A design,* with its equal measure of contrast and repetition, may be found to some extent in nearly all eras and categories of music. For our purposes six broad uses of it may be listed:

1. A-B-A is easily the preferred design of the Romantic *intimate* or *character piece* for piano, violin, or other solo instrument (Appendix II, No. 19). Many of the pieces that are most familiar to today's musical layman fall into this class, including such old favorites as Chopin's "Raindrop Prelude," Rubinstein's *Melody in F,* and Schumann's *Träumerei.*

2. A-B-A is often the plan of the slow movement in Classic and subsequent sonata music—for example, the middle movement of Mozart's *Concerto in A Major,* K. 488, for piano (Appendix II, No. 34,II).

3. As we have seen, A-B-A is also the compound design of certain dance-type movements in the suite or sonata that include a *trio* or alternate dance as the middle section. (The word trio was introduced in the seventeenth-century minuet originally to mean a section in three-voice texture, but has come to mean simply a middle section.) Typical among innumerable examples are the "Gavotte I" and "Gavotte II" (or the "Musette") in Bach's *English Suite in G Minor,* the "Menuetto" and "Trio" in Haydn's "Surprise Symphony," and the "Scherzo" and "Trio" in Beethoven's *Sonata in D Major,* op. 28 (Appendix II, No. 31,III). Ordinarily, the return to the first part was not written out in this form but merely indicated by some such labor- and paper-saving instruction as "menuetto dal capo al fine," meaning that the performer should go back to the beginning and stop at the word "fine" ("ending"), which marks the end of the A section. Later composers—Schumann and Brahms, for example— sometimes used two trios in the scherzo, making a total five-part design A-B-A-C-A.

4. A-B-A is the design par excellence, though by no means the only design, of opera, oratorio, and cantata arias. The special name for this use is *da capo aria,* since the same short cut prevailed that was used in the dance-type movements. However, the Baroque tradition was to alter the return to A by improvising ornaments and other variations. Later, the name was retained but the return to A came to be written out, chiefly because the composer preferred to do his own varying.

5. A-B-A is a design often found in art-songs of the nineteenth century (Appendix II, No. 20). In fact, the terms *lied* (German for "song") or *song-form* are commonly appropriated to mean any A-B-A design. These terms, however, are misleading, since there must be at least as many art-songs that have other designs (pp. 247–248).

6. A-B-A has been the usual design of light dance music since the early nineteenth century (although the choruses of jazz qualify as binary design according to the distinction maintained here). Chopin's

"Minute Waltz," his "Military Polonaise," and many of his *Mazurkas* are examples. On the other hand, Chopin's *Grand Valse brillante* and Johann Strauss's *On the Beautiful Blue Danube* are really cycles of waltzes tied together by recurrences of sections as well as by an introduction and a coda.

Although most of these uses of the A-B-A design are found in Classic and Romantic music, it is not safe to generalize that Baroque forms were binary and later forms were ternary. Bach used the ternary design when it suited him, as in the plan toccata-fugue-toccata that makes up the opening movement of his great *Partita in E Minor* for harpsichord. And Chopin, among others, used the binary design on occasion, especially in smaller forms (Appendix II, No. 1).

The tonal plan of the A-B-A design is more uniform than that of the binary design. Ordinarily the two A sections are in the tonic key and the middle section stays on the dominant or relative side of the tonality, making a tonal plan that is A-B-A in itself. Each section is something of a tonal entity. The first section may end with a final cadence in the tonic key or may shift at the last moment to the key of the new section so as not to make quite such a decisive break in the form. The latter method is used in the expressive *Elégie* for cello and orchestra by the late French Romantic Gabriel Fauré (Appendix II, No. 19). The second section is even more likely to sidestep a final cadence so as to preserve the flow during the return to the first section. In the same work Fauré actually builds the end of the second section into a climax so that the re-entry of the main theme begins on the climactic note itself, this being the actual moment when the tonic key is restored. In this, as in so many other nineteenth-century A-B-A designs, the sense of a complete aesthetic experience is made still more complete by the picture-framing effect of a short prelude and a short postlude or *coda*.

Ternary design usually attains more hierarchic levels than the binary design, which means that it is generally more complex and lasts longer. This fact is made clear by a diagram of one of the compound dance-trio movements, which typically contain three binary designs within their over-all ternary designs:

A (minuet)	B (trio)	A (minuet "da capo
‖:a:‖:b:‖	‖:a:‖:b:‖	al fine," but tradition-
		ally without the re-
		peats)

As explained earlier, binary is likely to be more appropriate than ternary design in the separate sections because it suggests continuation of the form. Complete ternary designs in any of these sections are rather rare, the chief exceptions being certain Classic minuets and scherzos that do have an unequivocal departure and return within the second half of the A section (as in the "Scherzo" of Beethoven's *Sonata in A Major,* op. 2, no. 2, for piano). But all together, and with both an introduction and a coda included, the ternary design is capable of considerable extension (as in Mendelssohn's *Songs Without Words in G Minor,* op. 53, no. 3). In fact, we shall see that the "sonata-allegro" form itself came to be regarded as a grand A-B-A design after about 1800 (p. 230).

The contrast of material between the A and B sections is likely to be more distinct in the ternary than in the binary design. Usually the B of A-B-A takes a deliberately opposite turn. In Schumann's lied called *Dedication* (Appendix II, No. 20) the middle section, corresponding to a sobering turn in the text, changes to a moderately distant key (p. 95), uses even triplets in the accompaniment instead of the more excited dotted rhythmic pattern in the A section, lowers the voice range about a fifth, employs a melody in longer notes that proceed in a more nearly stepwise fashion, and drops the dynamic level from *mf* to *p* . In Chopin's familiar *Etude in E Major,* op. 10, no. 3, the middle section is a display of virtuosity in sharp contrast to the pure melody of the first section. Just the converse holds true of Rachmaninoff's celebrated *Prelude in G Minor,* op. 23, no. 5. And in Mendelssohn's *Songs Without Words in B Minor,* op. 67, no. 5, the melody in the B section not only changes to major but is a very free inversion of that in the A section (Fig. 21, p. 112).

THE RONDO IDEA

The essence of the *rondo* idea is the alternation of a catchy, fetching *refrain* (or rondo) with a series of contrasting *episodes.* You hear that principle at work when a song like *The Old Gray Mare* is sung, each verse (episode) relating a new adventure before leading back to the constant refrain, "Many long years ago." This same principle relates more or less remotely to other form principles described earlier. Thus, the rondo idea would seem to include the A-B-A design, although the latter has but one "episode." Also, rondo as a word stems from round, which form concerns, in its own way, a tune that keeps coming "around" (p. 116). And lastly, the rondo idea recalls the alternation of expositions and episodes in the fugue. But this is only a nominal resemblance. In actuality, there are all those differences that grow out of the distinction between progression by motivic play and progression by phrase grouping. Later we shall see how the "sonata-allegro" form does border on a developed type of the rondo (p. 228).

The rondos that we usually hear today have a predecessor in the Baroque *rondeau,* which is a type often found in the chamber and keyboard works of Couperin and Rameau. As an example, the familiar harpsichord piece *Le Tambourin* by Rameau may be cited, although there are much larger and more expressive examples. The rondeau was more an additive than an integrated form—A-B-A-C-A-D . . . —since episodes were added indefinitely, and usually without repetition. Its effect could easily grow monotonous, especially as each refrain and each episode was likely to be a square-cut section of eight measures, with a

full halt on a final cadence. Although the refrain recurred only
in the tonic key, there was some tonal variety if not organization
in the frequent use of a nearly related key for an episode. On the
other hand, there was less thematic contrast than might be expected between refrain and episode, partly because the motivic
play that still persisted in the Rococo style was not favorable to
polythematic writing (p. 141).

By contrast, the rondo that developed in Classic and Romantic music was a thoroughly integrated and generally more appealing form. There are many independent instrumental solos of this
sort, such as Beethoven's hilarious *Rondo a capriccio* for piano,
op. 129, called "Rage Over a Lost Penny"; or Mendelssohn's
popular *Rondo capriccioso,* op. 14, for piano. Rondo form is also
encountered frequently in sonata music, occasionally in slow or
moderate movements, as in Franck's *Symphony in D Minor;* and
especially in lighthearted, frolicsome finales, including those of
Mozart's *Concerto in A Major,* K. 488, for piano and orchestra
(Appendix II, No. 34,III), and Beethoven's *Sonata in D Major,*
op. 28, for piano (Appendix II, No. 31,IV). Moreover, the
rondo idea has proved to be a convenient skeleton form for programmatic compositions, notably for works whose programs are
episodic anyway, like Richard Strauss's "tone poem" *Till Eulenspiegel's Merry Pranks* (Appendix II, No. 37).

Just why the rondo should be so much more appealing than
the rondeau is well worth our noting, especially as the main differences reflect the integration that comes with hierarchic design.
These differences may be listed one by one:

1. Instead of a new episode after each refrain, at least one of the
episodes may recur later in the form. Thus, B recurs in the favorite
plan A-B-A-C-A-B-A-Coda that Beethoven used in the final movements of his *Sonate pathétique* for piano, his *Violin Concerto in D
Major,* and his *String Quartet in C Minor,* op. 18, no. 4 (where the
square-cut sections recall the rondeau). This recurrence helps to
close the form.

2. Consistent with this change, the tonal plan is also closed. While the refrain keeps recurring in the tonic key, the B episode occurs first in the dominant or other nearly related key and later in the tonic key. In between these tonal landmarks the tour is extended by the C episode, which is usually in some moderately distant key.

3. The final refrain is expanded into a *coda* (conclusion), sometimes a veritable finale. This is usually a free fantasia on elements of the refrain tune. Its effect is to summarize and round off all that went before.

4. The refrain does not usually come to a dead stop, as it does in the rondeau, but leads, or rather dissolves, into the ensuing episode by a *bridge passage*. The episode in turn usually makes some kind of *retransition* back to the refrain.

5. Special means are utilized to enhance and point up the return to the refrain each time, which is made pleasurable in any case by the charm of the tune itself. One means is the use of a dominant pedal (pp. 164–165) to create more expectancy. Another is the culmination of the retransition in some sort of virtuoso run, often a chromatic scale that ends by melting into the refrain. Still another is the *false return*, an amusing device whereby the composer seems to miscalculate and retrieve his tune on a wrong key, leaving him no choice but to ease off, redirect himself, and return, smirking as it were, to the "right" key. All of these means are exhibited brilliantly in the finale of Beethoven's *Piano Concerto No. 3 in C Minor*.

6. Frequently the composer varies the refrain itself, whether by varying its melody or harmony, by cutting it short to avoid the risk of monotony in later returns, or by going so far as to transpose it to various keys. In Mozart's unusual *Rondo in D Major*, K. 485, for piano, all three methods may be heard. In general, however, transposition of the refrain to other keys tends to upset the stability of the rondo.

7. Over the entire A-B-A-C-A-B-A plan a still larger A-B-A design is often imparted by giving special weight to the C episode. This is done by making C a complete ternary form in itself, by making it longer than its neighboring sections, and by making it tonally conspicuous through the use of a more distant key than that of the first B episode.

Here is the "floor plan" of a rondo by one of the greatest masters of that form, Beethoven. The work is his *Rondo in C Major,* op. 51, no. 1, for piano (Appendix II, No. 21). Note that each section of this hierarchic design is itself a binary or ternary design (as shown on the subindented lines), that there happens to be no return this time to the B episode, and that every refrain is melodically varied.

A, tonic key, C major
  a-b-a dissolving into a bridge to
B, dominant key, G major
  a-b ending on dominant-pedal retransition to
A, tonic key, C major
  a (shortened to one phrase grouping) ending on a final
    cadence in C major.
C, tonic minor key, C minor
  a-b-a ending on retransition to
A, "false return" in lowered submediant key, A-flat major
  a (shortened to one phrase grouping) ending on dominant-pedal retransition to
A, tonic key, C major
  a-b dissolving into
Coda, tonic key, C major
  thematic fragments and modulations, concluding in tonic
    key, C major.

"INTUITIVE" ARRANGEMENTS OF SECTIONS

There has been occasion so far to mention several standardized hierarchic designs, including A-B, A-B-A, A-B-A-C-A, and A-B-A-C-A-B-A. Although there is a very definite theoretical limit to the ways in which only three or four different sections can be arranged, it should be obvious that these few designs hardly exhaust the possibilities. For instance, in Medieval-and-Renaissance music the A-A-A-B plan of the fourteenth-century type of madrigal was much in favor (p. 156), as was the A-A-B "barform" of German minstrelsy (p. 110). It is just as obvious that composers who let the content determine the form, who prefer to create "intuitively" rather than fill established molds, may happen upon these or still other equally valid arrangements of sections—A-B-C-A or A-B-A-C-D-A, for example. In terms of the approach that has been taken here, these composers do not start with a standardized design in mind but let the phrase generate its own structural result. Or, to recall a cautious note injected in Chapter 1, they do not necessarily read the textbooks before doing their creating.

Chopin was one of a number of Romantic composers who seem to have conceived in this way. His larger piano works in one movement seldom fall into any of the standardized designs. His shorter works do, and so do most of the movements in his three sonatas, although in the latter the sense of obligation to fill a mold is sometimes only too apparent. Evidently he preferred to let his peerless feeling for form lead him on when he wrote his polonaises, ballades, and similarly extended works. In different ways, Schumann, Berlioz, Liszt, Richard Strauss, and Mahler were also composers who seem to have let the content determine the form in many works.

One of the richest and most mature works of Chopin is his *Ballade in F Minor,* op. 52 (Appendix II, No. 22). The design that results in this work may be summed up as Introduction-A-A-A-B-A-B-Coda. In Fig. 30 the initial thematic material of each section is illustrated. A brief description of the sections will help you to keep track of them as you listen to the work. However, you must be cautioned that the analysis of a work of this sort depends in part on subjective judgments. Another person may hear its form somewhat differently.

The Introduction is a single phrase grouping on the dominant, giving a peculiar satisfaction to the arrival of section A in the tonic key of F minor.

Section A is a grouping of three phrases that can be heard in the relationship of question-question-answer. This section repeats at once with only very slight melodic changes. An interlude too transitory to be heard as an independent section leads through recollec-

Fig. 30. The main themes in an "intuitive" design (Chopin, *Ballade in F Minor*, op. 52, for piano)

tions of A to another repetition of A. This time A is much enriched in its texture by added inner lines and the new dissonances they create. It climaxes in a bridge passage that modulates to section B.

Section B, on the subdominant major key (by change of mode), is a grouping of three phrases that can be heard in the relationship of question-answer-answer. When it is over, an extended 16th-note passage follows (35 measures) that must be regarded as a retransition to A rather than a new section, both because of its modulatory character and because of the fact that it ends on the same material that had served for the Introduction.

This final statement of section A is extremely free and varied. It begins harmonically at a tangent and in short canonic exchanges that represent about as much interest in counterpoint as is to be found in the markedly homophonic writing of Chopin. Soon after A has regained the tonic key it breaks out into a series of ever-more rhapsodic *fioriture* such as only he could write.

The climax of this final statement of A is section B, this time in the submediant key, D-flat major. Section B is now stated so heroically that its relation to the original, "dolce" B section could easily pass unnoticed. This section culminates in some thunderous runs and mighty chords. A dramatic shift from *fff* to five chords played legato and *pp* introduces the Coda.

The Coda, once more in the home key, falls into two main divisions according to the nature of the keyboard figuration—first a rapid, difficult passage in double notes for the right hand, and second a single line in still faster tempo.

SELECTED READINGS

E. J. Dent, "Binary and Ternary Form," *Music & Letters*, XVII (1936).

Percy Goetschius, *The Homophonic Forms of Musical Composition*. New York: G. Schirmer, 1926.

Percy Goetschius, *The Larger Forms of Musical Composition*. New York: G. Schirmer, 1915.

Gerald Abraham, *Chopin's Musical Style*. New York: Oxford University Press, 1940.

Kathleen Dale, *Nineteenth-Century Piano Music*. New York: Oxford University Press, 1954.

Chapter 11

Variation, a Compound Process

SIMULTANEOUS REPETITION AND CONTRAST

Since variety within unity is essential to all art forms, some sort of *variation* must occur in all music. It may occur in the contrast of a new section, timbre, key, or other feature. It may occur in the continuous unfolding of an idea, as in motivic play, improvisation, or sonata-type development. Or it may occur in the changes that accompany the repetition of an idea. Even in this last, more restricted sense, some variation will be found to occur in most music. No true creator lets his ideas repeat without varying them at least some of the time in some manner. We have already seen variation of this sort in changes that a motive may undergo, in deviations from a "normal" square phrase, in alterations of a fugue subject when it is an answer, in ornamentation of an aria's *da capo*, in different versions of a rondo refrain.

What, then, serves to distinguish the variation forms we are about to discuss from all other musical forms? The answer lies in both the extent and manner of the variation. In the variation forms recognized as such, the process of varying goes on throughout, not sporadically. Furthermore, it operates mainly in its most restricted sense, that of *changes accompanying the repetition of an idea*. The effect of this last principle on the structure is twofold. First, any variation form is more accurately a series of separate variations occurring at regular intervals—occurring, that is, with the successive repetitions of the initial idea or theme. And second, a variation form is monothematic, for its prime object is to reveal what and how much can be done with a particular theme.

Variation in this restricted sense provides one example in a time art of contrast and repetition that occur not alternately but simultaneously. Something about the theme must be altered when it repeats, if there is to be variation. At the same time enough about it must be retained to keep it still recognizable. Only when both the contrast and the repetition are perceived simultaneously is variation heard as such. To illustrate, suppose we take "A" as a theme for five variations. During each of its recurrences as least some one of its features will have to be retained and at least some one feature will have to be altered:

Theme: A

Var. I: ∀

Var. II: ↘

Var. III: ⌐\

Var. IV: ◁⫿⫿

Var. V: ⌐⌐

In musical variation, both the *constant* and the *altered factors* will be those same building blocks to which we return time and again—a rhythmic pattern, a melodic line, a harmonic succession. In the interest of over-all unity, the factor that is constant is likely to be the same factor in every or almost every variation of a set. Conversely, in the interest of variety, the factor that is altered is likely to be a different factor in each variation. For this reason, a variation form is best classified according to which factor remains constant. That basis of classification, in fact, is the one used for the remaining section headings in this chapter.

The constant factor generally proves to be one of four main possibilities: (a) a bass line, (b) a harmonic pattern, (c) a binary melody, or (d) a theme that is a composite of all these. Taking the first half-phrase of *Drink to Me Only with Thine Eyes* as our theme, Fig. 31 is invented to show how each of these might serve as the constant factor. Only the bass of the theme is retained in the first variation, only the harmony in the second,

Fig. 31. Four variation techniques as they might be applied to the opening of *Drink to Me Only with Thine Eyes*

only an elaboration of the melodic outline in the third, and merely the structure itself plus the general harmonic direction of the half-phrase in the fourth.

Variation as defined thus far would seem to be an essentially static principle of form. The complete idea or theme to be varied does not function as a generator quite in the manner either of the motive or the phrase. It merely repeats, apparently as many but only as many times as the composer finds new possibilities for varying it. What can come of this procedure but an open, additive structure, somewhat related to the strophic plan in vocal music?

Although no slur against additive form per se is intended, in the dullest sets of variations a peculiarly static effect cannot be denied. However, in the many great sets that honor music literature, any notion of static form fails to take account not only of the wonderfully imaginative treatments of the theme by the masters but of certain shaping forces both within each variation and over the whole set. These forces bear witness that the generative influences of the motive and the phrase will out no matter how each is used. In fact, both influences are at work while the fundamental principle of variation is in operation in the restricted sense meant here. The result is a *compound structural process.*

Briefly stated, within each variation the progression tends to be that of motivic play; over an entire set, complementary groupings of variations are established that favor a broadly sectional organization. More specifically, within each variation the particular factor that is altered, whether it derives from the theme itself or related material, ordinarily takes the form of a motive. Thus, in Fig. 31 the altered factor—rhythmic, melodic, or harmonic—in each new variation on *Drink to Me* is summed up in a characteristic figure that would presumably recur throughout that variation. In this way each variation concentrates on only one of the many facets that a theme may reveal. However, it cannot be said that the motive follows its bent toward motivic play with complete freedom. Sometimes the motivic play is indeed very rich, as in the Bach *Passacaglia* described in the next section (Appendix II, No. 23). Sometimes it is very lax, as in the Paganini *Variations* noted on page 197 (Appendix II, No. 25). But in any case it must submit to or be fitted to the structural mold of the initial idea, which is usually a clear phrase or phrase grouping in a "square" number of measures—four, eight, or sixteen.

The tendency of an entire set of variations toward sectional organization (hierarchic design is too hard and fast a term here) becomes evident in several kinds of broad groupings. Thus, there may be a grouping of slow variations followed by a fast grouping, or meditative variations followed by virtuoso ones, or loud ones followed by soft ones, and so on. Furthermore, although sets of variations do not ordinarily make the organized tour of keys that qualifies here as tonality, they do take advantage of key contrasts, especially the change of mode on the same tonic. Thus, Bach's monumental "Chaconne" from *Partita in D Minor* for unaccompanied violin solo has a first group of variations in D minor, then a middle group in the tonic major, and a concluding group in D minor again, making an over-all A-B-A tonal plan. One other practice helps to give a rounded or closed form to a set of variations. That is the practice of concluding with a fantasia or fugue on the theme, which sometimes has the effect of one grand, final splurge, as it were.

THE RECURRING BASS LINE

First we may take up one of the oldest variation forms, that in which a melodic line keeps repeating in the bass while progression by motivic play, or less often by phrase grouping, is carried on above it. Various terms have been applied to this form or to its *recurring bass line*—basso ostinato (obstinate bass), ground bass, chaconne, and passacaglia, among them. Another term, "cantus firmus variation," has been used to designate a form often employed in English Renaissance music for the virginal (harpsichord). The cantus firmus in this form is a fixed melody, commonly in long notes, that may appear in any one voice or rove from one to another instead of repeating only in the bass.

Sometimes the recurring bass line is only a fragment of a few tones. This type easily grows tiresome when it repeats throughout a composition, as in Arensky's *Basso ostinato,* op. 5, no. 5, for piano, on the six quarter-notes D-C♯-B-F♯-G-A. But it is an effective means of continuity and climax when used in a special passage or section of a work. Listen, for example, to the left-hand 16th-note octaves that repeat on four descending tones for seventeen measures and then seventeen more at the middle of Chopin's celebrated *Polonaise in A-flat Major,* op. 53.

More often, especially in Baroque music, the recurring bass line makes a complete phrase of four or eight measures. Furthermore, the Baroque type is characteristically a descending line in three-four meter and in a minor key. In some instances the expression *melodic* bass line must be understood with reservations. The line is always melodic in the sense that it is a coherent series of tones. But these tones may be primarily the roots of a series of chords that recur with the bass, and not interesting enough in their own right to satisfy as an independent melody.

A renowned, deeply expressive example of variations on a recurring bass line is Dido's "Lament" from the end of Purcell's opera *Dido and Aeneas.* Here the bass line does have pronounced melodic interest. Above it the soprano projects a more extended melody in clear phrases that do not coincide with those of the bass. The effect of this ever-recurring bass is to accent the poignant, irrevocable fate of Dido.

For a further look into this category of variations let us turn to another example, one of the grandest in music literature. This is Bach's *Passacaglia and Fugue in C Minor* for organ (Appendix II, No. 23), often played both in its original form and in recent orchestral transcriptions. An eight-measure bass line, with a Rock-of-Gibraltar sturdiness, appears first alone (Fig. 32); then repeats as the constant factor during twenty variations, all based on motivic play. These terminate on the starting note of the fugue subject, which proves to be none other than the first half of the bass line (the first eight notes, to be exact). The fugue takes about the last five minutes of this fifteen-minute work.

Several of Bach's procedures not only forestall any possible

Organ (pedal)

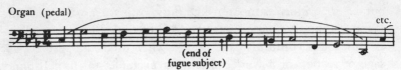

(end of
fugue subject)

Fig. 32. A recurring bass line (Bach, *Passacaglia and Fugue in C Minor,*
for organ)

monotony that might result from twenty-one regularly spaced
occurrences of the same melodic line, but help to bind the variations into one tight-knit structure. First of all, breaks are avoided
between variations by starting the new motive of each new variation just before the recurring bass has ended in the previous one.
Second, certain variations tend to pair off (1 and 2, 6 and 7, 10
and 11, 19 and 20) because the same altered factor or motive
serves in the motivic play of both. When this happens, the latter
of the pair is likely to differ only in a general reversal of direction
or shift of register. Third, by "poetic license" the recurring line is
actually taken out of the bass and shifted to other registers during
variations 11 to 15. It appears in the soprano in variations 11 to
12, in the alto in variation 13, and in the tenor in variation 14;
and it leaps from one extreme to the other on every tone in variation 15! Fourth, this line is itself varied sufficiently to take part
in the motivic play in variations 5, 9, 13 to 15, and 18.

Finally, and most important, a cumulative effect results from
Bach's gradual shortening and filling in of note values. In vari-
ations 1 and 2 the rhythmic pattern of the motive is ♪|♩.♩ 𝄾;
already in variation 3 the overlapping motives complement each
other so that every 8th-note is filled in— ♫♫♫; by a
similar process the resultant rhythm becomes ♫♫♫
in variations 4 and 5, ♫♫♫ in variations 6 to 15,
𝄾♫♫♫ in variation 16, ♫♫♫ ♫♫♫ ♫♫♫
in variation 17, ♫♫♫ in variation 18, and ♫♫♫
♫♫♫ in variations 19 and 20.

The fugue caps this work in a stunning manner. Can you tell

it apart from the variations if you are not told which section is being played? Such exercises focus attention on basic structural distinctions. For example, if it is the fugue that is being played you will be able to distinguish it by knowing that its subject is only the first half of the bass line, that this subject occurs only in its intermittent expositions and not constantly at regular intervals, that it occurs in different ranges and not almost exclusively in the bass, that it occurs in different keys and in the major as well as the minor mode, and that the collective rhythm in all four voices is the same throughout—steady 16th-notes—except at the climactic stop near the end (p. 164).

THE RECURRING HARMONIC PATTERN

In variations on a *recurring harmonic pattern* the constant factor is a succession of chords. This succession has the force of a firm, sometimes elaborate cadence, starting and ending in the tonic key and reconfirming this key with unusual conviction in every variation. Again, the Baroque practice, and the one that still prevails, is to cast the succession in four or eight measures, in a minor key, and in three-four meter. The very fact that the harmonic pattern repeats tends to bring forth a similar or identical supporting bass line in some of the variations. This suggests a certain overlapping of categories, which must be expected in any case, since composers have not felt obliged to stick to one or another category exclusively in any one set of variations.

While the harmonic pattern repeats, all else may change. A new bass line, inner voice, or soprano melody may be found. The rhythmic pattern may change with each variation. And above all, the *figuration* may change. By figuration is meant those arpeggios, scales, and other, more intricate technical devices that are the logical means of varying and elaborating chords. These figurations, in whatever rhythmic pattern they assume, constitute the chief motivic material in this type of variation. Because they tend to range beyond the compass of any one voice, they achieve the motivic play more often by sequence than by exchanges between different voices. Hence the texture is less likely to be polyphonic than in variations on an ever-recurring bass line. In the latter, the usually greater melodic interest of the bass itself invites the use of motives above it that are more melodic than figural.

Bach is also the composer of one of the great sets of variations on a recurring harmonic pattern, the "Chaconne" for unaccompanied violin that was mentioned on page 190. Double-, triple-, and even quadruple-stops (p. 37) are often used in this work to state the harmonic pattern. Another great set is Beethoven's *Thirty-two Variations in C Minor,* for piano. Among still other sets are several based on stock harmonic patterns that have served many composers. One such pattern is named *Folia* (or *Follia*), known best in the variations by Corelli that make up his *Sonata for Violin and Thorough-bass,* op. 5, no. 12. Another is the theme of Paganini's *Caprice in A Minor,* op. 1, no. 24, for violin, used in extended sets of variations by Brahms and Rachmaninoff among others.

As an example to consider here, let us take the finale of Brahms' *Fourth Symphony* (Appendix II, No. 24). The harmonic pattern of this movement, quoted in Fig. 33, repeats thirty times, culminating in a sudden, short, dramatic coda marked "Più Allegro." Again, a larger organization is very much in evidence. In fact, the variation groupings follow the usual order of the separate movements of a symphony. The first eleven variations have the generally vigorous character of an opening movement and are scored mostly for the full orchestra. Variations 12 to 15, in which the meter changes to three-two, make a lovely "slow movement," distinguished by solo and chordal passages in the winds. Variations 16 to 23, once more in three-four meter, have a "scherzando" (playful) character, with crisp, staccato passages throughout the orchestra beginning with variation

Fig. 33. A recurring harmonic pattern (Brahms, *Fourth Symphony*, op. 98, IV)

19. And variations 24 to 30 have the victorious, lyrical sweep characteristic of many finales.

Brahms virtually announces these groupings by making the first variation of each very much like the original statement of the harmonic pattern. Sometimes the top line in the original distribution of the chords becomes the bass line. Occasionally the bass is a pedal point on the keynote E. There are a few complete breaks between variations, but most of the time each variation leads directly into the next so as to keep the flow going. Like Bach, Brahms furthers the larger organization by pairing off certain variations (for example, 8 and 9), making only a change of range, direction, or other detail in the second one. In the coda, parts or complete recurrences of the harmonic pattern can still be discovered.

THE RECURRING BINARY MELODY

When variations are written on a melody that is generally in the soprano range, that melody is likely to differ from a recurring bass line in several ways. First of all, it is usually in binary form, with each half being a repeated phrase grouping. Secondly, it is more in the nature of a pronounced tune, meaning that it has stronger metrical organization and a more distinctive pitch outline. And third, this tune is ordinarily not original with the com-

poser but is one already made familiar in an opera, dance, favorite song, or other public source (which claim, however, can also
be made for certain recurring bass lines and harmonic patterns).

Variations on a *recurring binary melody* seldom go beyond extrinsic changes and ornamentations of the melody itself. The supporting harmony may change from time to time, but not so much
as might be supposed. If the melody is of a fairly disjunct sort, as
it often is in these pronounced tunes, then it pretty well dictates
its own harmony. The style of accompaniment may change from
time to time, too: But this possibility seems to have appealed very
little to composers of the kind of variation we have in mind here.
In fact, in several violin works, the piano accompaniment is written only once, with the instruction simply to repeat it as many
times as there are variations! Exceptional in this regard are
Ravel's *Bolero* (Appendix II, No. 2) and the opening movement
of Shostakovitch's *Symphony No. 7*, obviously modeled after the
former. In both, the melody repeats almost without change and
only the attendant factors are substantially altered—orchestration, dynamics, style of accompaniment, and occasionally the
harmony. However, a certain intentional monotony is sought in
these pieces.

In short, the melody in this type of variation form is at once
the constant and the altered factor. Its outline must remain recognizable through whatever alterations and elaborations it undergoes. The alterations may amount to a pruning of less essential
notes, a change of accidentals and even of mode, or a transformation of the metrical scheme from a duple to a triple scheme or
vice versa. The elaborations will be notes added in one way or another—for example, appoggiaturas, trills or other ornaments,
stepwise passages that fill in melodic leaps, and flourishes such as
runs or repeated notes during long tones and rests. In his bravura
Introduction and Variations on "Nel cor più non mi sento" for
unaccompanied violin solo, Paganini already uses most of these
means merely to present the tune, a favorite aria that he could be

sure was known to every member of his audience. His elaborated version of the theme, including simultaneous bowing and plucking (*arco* and *pizz.*), may be compared with the original in Fig. 34. The variations themselves, which exploit double stops, harmonics, wide leaps, and numerous other resources of the violin virtuoso, are too elaborate to compare at sight here, but you

Fig. 34. The decoration of a recurring melodic outline (Paganini, *Introduction and Variations on "Nel cor più non mi sento"* [aria from Paisiello's opera *Molinara*] for unaccompanied violin)

will have little difficulty recognizing them by ear as variations (Appendix II, No. 25).

The objects of such tinsel and frippery are plainly the good fun of toying with a melody and the opportunity for display of pyrotechnics. Not only Paganini but all of the nineteenth-century virtuosos performed and usually wrote such variations. The musical level of them is often remarkably low. Yet they can have great charm, as Mozart, Chopin, Liszt, Tchaikovsky, and others have shown. Scarcely a familiar tune has escaped exploitation in somebody-or-other's "Variations on the favorite air, . . ." or perhaps a "Pièce de concert" for trumpet, with its inevitable chromatic scales and triple-tonguing. For instance, a surprising number of composers seems to have had a hand at the old folk song and opera tune that you know best as the nursery rhyme "Twinkle, Twinkle, Little Star."

An amusing set for you to hear and see—instructive, too, as regards comparative styles—is Edward Ballantine's *Variations on "Mary Had a Little Lamb,"* for piano, in two volumes, each volume in the styles of ten different composers ranging from Bach to Gershwin and Stravinsky.

OPTIONAL PRINCIPLES IN THE THEME-AND-VARIATIONS

In the *theme-and-variations* any or all of the variation techniques discussed thus far may be applied, depending only on the grasp of form, the imagination, and the resources of the composer. Two general types may be distinguished. One is the more formal, older type represented by such magnificent and lengthy masterpieces as Bach's *Aria* [by Goldberg] *with Thirty Variations,* which is built mainly on a recurring bass-and-harmonic pattern, Beethoven's *Thirty-three Variations on a Waltz by Diabelli,* op. 120, and Brahms' *Variations* [25] *and Fugue on a Theme by Handel,* op. 24 (all three works being for keyboard). The other is a freer, more recent type to be noted shortly. In both types the means of larger organization already observed—the broad groupings, the pairings, the overlappings, the occasional tonal contrasts, and the climactic finales—are all utilized to the fullest.

The more formal type of theme-and-variations is sometimes little other than the type based on a recurring binary melody. But typically it exploits more or all of music's elements. Its theme is usually presented in homophonic texture and in a hierarchic binary design, both halves of which are repeated—||:A:||:B:||. (We have already seen [p. 172] that the A-B-A design would have the disadvantage of being too complete in itself and of juxtaposing two A sections for every B section.) Most themes are borrowed from other composers.

A brief analysis of a capital piano work by Mendelssohn, his *Variations sérieuses,* op. 54 (Appendix II, No. 26), will help to illustrate this important form. There are seventeen variations in all, the last of which leads directly into a brilliant coda that rounds out the entire work and concludes in "presto" tempo. The theme is somewhat exceptional in being original and in not calling for the repetition of either half.

Vigorous rhythms and a gradual advance in tempo from "Andante sostenuto" (Fig. 12, p. 74) to "Allegro vivace" mark the first nine variations. In this grouping the general outline of the theme's melody is always more or less discernible. The first two variations merely enliven the texture with 16th-notes, then 16th-note triplets. The third variation is a motivic dialog between the hands in staccato octaves and chords. The fourth consists of staccato motivic play in two voices. The fifth consists of chords alternated "Agitato" between the hands. The sixth reaches a climax on explosive, widely separated chords. The seventh maintains this climax with an energetic pattern of chords and arpeggios. And the next two variations pair off on driving triplets of 16th-notes.

Variations 10 and 11 depart further from the melodic outline, the first being somewhat fugal, the second songful. As often happens in the theme-and-variations, when the melody is not retained so clearly or at all, the structure of the theme itself becomes the main constant factor—the binary design, the tonal plan with its half and final cadences, and the general organization of the phrases. Variation 12 chiefly retains the harmony. Variation 13 restores the melody, now in the tenor register with a staccato 32d-note figuration above it. Variation 14 is an "Ada-

gio" interlude in the tonic major key, after which the three remaining variations accelerate to the coda.

The freer, more recent type of theme-and-variations hardly
submits to any systematic description. One can only say that each
variation finds its point of departure in some different facet of
the theme, from which it unfolds in the manner of a fantasia.
As noted at the start of this chapter the free unfolding of an
idea is actually a principle of variation quite different from
"changes accompanying the repetition of an idea." Elgar's
"Enigma" *Variations* and Richard Strauss's tone poem *Don
Quixote,* both for orchestra, are well-known examples of this
free type.

Related to the theme-and-variations is the *organ chorale prelude*. This form, based on the Lutheran hymn or *chorale* (p.
274), reached its peak in the incomparable and extensive organ
literature by Bach. It is an elaboration of a chorale, played prin-
cipally before the singing of that chorale by the congregation.
Note that the chorale itself is not stated first as a theme but is
simply understood as the basis for some kind of variation. In
other words the chorale prelude may be no more than one or
perhaps two variations on an understood theme. Only rarely is
it an actual set of variations.

Among a number of procedures used by Bach, the chorale
melody may be played right through to the accompaniment of
an enriched and decorative texture (*Christ Lay in the Bonds of
Death,* S. 625); one or more fragments of the melody may be
treated fugally (*Only to God on High Be Glory,* S. 716); or a
continuous melodic and harmonic background may be established, in the course of which the successive phrases of the chorale are introduced intermittently and in bold relief. In this last
method the background itself may derive from fragments of the
chorale (*A Mighty Fortress Is Our Lord,* S. 720), or it may be
quite independent of the chorale, as in *Sleepers, Wake!* (S. 645),
the opening of which is quoted in Fig. 35. Our example includes

Fig. 35. Variation treatment in a chorale prelude (Bach, *Sleepers, Wake!* for organ, S. 645)

the first two phrases of the robust chorale melody, preceded and separated by rests while the background continues.

SELECTED READINGS

Percy Goetschius, *The Larger Forms of Musical Composition.* New York: G. Schirmer, 1915.

Robert U. Nelson, *The Technique of Variation.* Berkeley: University of California Press, 1948.

Harvey Grace, *The Organ Works of Bach.* London: Novello, 1922.

Edwin Evans, *Handbook to the Chamber & Orchestral Music of Johannes Brahms,* 2 vols. London: William Reeves, 1933 and 1935.

Kathleen Dale, *Nineteenth-Century Piano Music.* New York: Oxford University Press, 1954.

Stainton de B. Taylor, *The Chorale Preludes of J. S. Bach.* New York: Oxford University Press, 1942.

Chapter 12

Instrumental Cycles of the Baroque Era

THE GROUPING OF CONTRASTING MOVEMENTS

Instrumental cycle is the term used here to mean a work for instruments in several movements. There are exceptional instrumental works, even solo piano works, that last more than forty minutes, yet do not divide into movements—for example, Beethoven's "Diabelli Variations" (although these thirty-three variations might be described as diminutive movements in themselves), Busoni's conglomeration of musical styles known as *Fantasia Contrappuntistica,* and Villa-Lobos' Latin-American fantasia *Rudepoêma.* But, generally speaking, it is the instrumental cycles that represent the most extended, developed, and profound works of "absolute" music (music governed by its own laws rather than such outside influences as a text).

A musical form in several movements may be regarded as a complementary grouping at the highest structural level. This grouping originates in two nearly opposite trends of the Medieval-and-Renaissance Era. One trend may be seen in a cell-like expansion of certain basic forms. Thus, the *canzona francese,* an Italian instrumental version of the French chanson (p. 160), ultimately came to divide into "parts" of contrasting meters, tempos, and textures. In some such way single ideas have grown and split into the chapters of a novel, the acts of a play, the episodes of a story in painting, or the rites of a liturgy.

The other trend may be seen in the combining of certain related forms. For instance, one origin of the Baroque dance suite (p. 204) may be found in the sixteenth-century practice of combining a stately, sweeping dance in duple meter, such as the *pavane,* with a rollicking, leaping dance in triple meter, such as the *galliard.* Similar urges to group things of like nature have led to anthologies of poems about the sea, museums of Modern painting, and so on. Although the Baroque suite and sonata have much in common both in the time and circumstances of their origin, it may help to think of these instrumental cycles as originating, on the one hand, in a process of coming together, and on the other, in a process of growing apart.

The problem of how to group movements to good advantage recalls that a time art must be planned according to "the normal increase and decline of the listener's attention" (p. 137). A vigorous movement is usually put first so as to capture that attention. A serious movement may well follow, since by then his concentration will be brought to its peak. Next a lighter movement of contrasting nature will probably be a desirable relief. And finally a rapid, driving movement may be needed to maintain the attention unflagged to the end. This is not to say that one number or order of movements prevails in either the Baroque or Classic Eras. Several standard plans will be noted here. But these are not wholly dissimilar, and it is significant how infrequently composers have dared to depart from the general requirements of the attention span, especially in the later movements.

Stated differently, the ever-present requirements of variety within unity must be satisfied as much at the broad level of movement grouping as at the local level of motivic play or phrase grouping. Contrast between these movements will be achieved as always by any of such familiar means as changes of meter, of tempo, of key, of texture, of motive or theme, and of prevailing mood or character. And unity will be achieved by a general consistency of style, medium, and purpose, as well as by any of the more specific means that happen not to be changed. Unity has often been furthered, for example, by the use of the same or similar motives in some or all of the movements in a cycle.

SUITES OF DANCES

The word *suite* means a set or series of something, as in the expression "suite of rooms." The Baroque suite is a set of contrasted dances and occasional freer movements, scored for solo or ensemble performance. It exists in several related forms, often under another title, such as *lesson* in England, *partita* in Germany, *ordre* in France, *sonata da camera* in Italian chamber music, and *French overture* in German orchestral music.

Dances of different styles were contrasted in the past much as a jazz orchestra may switch from slow to fast to waltz music on the dance floor today. However, many of the dances in the Baroque suites that survive are idealized dances, somewhat as Gershwin's *Rhapsody in Blue* is idealized, concert jazz. They are self-sufficient, and generally too rich in texture for the dancer who wants only the accompaniment of an uncomplicated meter. Most of the dances in Bach's large-scale *Partitas* and *English Suites* for harpsichord, as well as those in his somewhat lighter *French Suites* for harpsichord and *French Overtures* for orchestra, are decidedly of this sort.

As long as the earlier Baroque dances were still intended for actual dancing, their grouping into suites was left to the performer and the requirements of the occasion. Then, the composer merely published a half dozen of one kind of dance all in succession, a half dozen of another kind, and so on, to be combined as desired. By the start of the eighteenth century a grouping of dances that was favored in Germany won international acceptance. Four dances became recognized as the core of the suite, all having undergone refinements in France, where dancing and ballet have always had a preferred place among the arts. These dances are the allemande, courante, saraband, and gigue. Their

form is the motivic binary sort typical of lighter Baroque instrumental music (pp. 167–170).

When other movements were added to this core they were
chiefly some kind of fantasia or prelude to introduce the suite,
and one or more dances of a newer, lighter type between the
saraband and the gigue. Among the lighter types, some of which
came much closer to literal dance music, there were the gavotte
in four-four, the bourrée in two-two, the loure in six-four, and
the minuet in three-four meter, all of which Lully had popularized in his later-seventeenth-century French operas. The rondeau
and chaconne also found their way into the suite from time to
time.

To judge from its title, the *allemande* was regarded by the
French as a German dance. This first in the core of four main
dances was a descendant of the *pavane*. It is usually a firm, dig-
nified dance in four-four meter, beginning with a short upbeat
and characterized by motivic play on a distinctive rhythmic
pattern, often one with dotted notes. Indeed, dotted rhythms occur so often in the initial movement of Baroque instrumental
cycles that that use of them may be regarded as a Baroque man-
nerism.

As its name suggests, the *courante* is characterized by a running patter of notes. Two types are distinguished. The Italian
type (properly spelled *corrente*) usually reveals a steady, rapid patter of 8th-notes in three-four meter and a fairly homophonic texture. The French type cultivates a subtle, intentional ambiguity
by frequent alternations between compound meter, $^6_4$ ♩ ♩ ♩ ♩ ♩ ♩,
and simple meter, $^3_2$ ♩ ♩ ♩ ♩ ♩ ♩ (comparable to the distinction between six-eight and three-four meter noted on p. 53).
This ambiguity is carried into the mercurial interchanges of the
motivic play.

The *saraband* is the slowest and most expressive of the core
dances, a stately, nearly homophonic dance in three-four or three-
two meter. A characteristic rhythmic pattern in this dance is

♩ ♩· ♩ , with its emphasis on the second beat. The slow pace invites the rich use of those ornamental dissonances and other "graces" that are indicated by signs in Baroque music (p. 118).

The *gigue* makes a lively finale indeed! (Pronounce it to rhyme with "league," the first "g" being like the "z" in "azure.") A descendant of the Irish jig, it gallops along in compound, usually six-eight, meter. Its treatment is often more or less fugal. At the beginning of the second half the principal motive is characteristically stated in inversion. As with the courante, a distinction is made between a lighter, more fluent Italian type (*giga*) and a fuller French type that is somewhat slowed by dotted rhythms.

In Fig. 36 is shown the opening of each dance in *Suite in G Minor* for harpsichord by the Belgian Jean-Baptiste Loeillet (Appendix II, No. 28). Besides the standard core of dances the suite includes a "Minuetto." The "Courante" and the "Gigue" are both of the Italian type. Observe that no movement changes key. At most there is not likely to be more than a change to the opposite tonic mode in an inner movement of the suite.

TRIO SONATAS IN CHURCH AND AT COURT

The *trio sonata* was the favorite form of Baroque chamber music, even surpassing in popularity the "solo" violin sonata accompanied by thorough-bass. It is so called because it is written in three main parts, two for two soprano instruments and one, as always, for thorough-bass. Of course, as we have seen (pp. 121–122), this setting usually meant more than three instruments. The thorough-bass traditionally presupposed at least a harpsichord (or organ in church) to realize the chord figures and a cello to reinforce the bass line. The two high instruments were most often violins or flutes, but, thanks to optional Baroque scoring, could be almost any two instruments of high range, reasonable balance, and sufficient flexibility to handle the parts. Although one of the two parts was marked "first" and the other

Fig. 36. Patterns of the dances in a Baroque suite (Loeillet, *Suite in G Minor*, for harpsichord)

"second," these parts interlace, cross, and "compete" much of the time, making for little or no distinction in their respective ranges (Fig. 37).

Two main types of trio sonata were distinguished, the *sonata da camera*, best translated as *court sonata*, and the *sonata da chiesa* or *church sonata*. The court sonata was nothing more than the dance suite described earlier, in trio setting. Countless court sonatas were turned out by countless composers, mostly for the pleasure of the amateur musicians among the aristocracy and employees in the many large or petty courts around Europe (Plate 15). The majority of these works, like the popular Loiellet *Suite* just cited, are effective enough even though run-of the-mill in quality and stereotyped in plan. Some few, such as those by

Fig. 37. A passage from a church sonata in trio setting (Corelli, *Sonata da chiesa No. 5,* op. 3, for two violins and cello or bass lute, with figured bass for organ)

Corelli, Vivaldi, and Handel, reveal an originality, humor, and virility that well justify the present-day revival of interest in them.

The church sonata was actually played in church, though to what extent as part of the liturgy is not now known. Multiple performance of the parts in the manner of an orchestra was probably a frequent practice in larger churches. In keeping with the spirit of the church, the realizing instrument was more likely to be the organ than the harpsichord. Also, the movements were designated by their tempos and not by dance patterns, which nevertheless were more likely than not present in the music itself. In reality, the court and church sonatas of the late Baroque

Era came to overlap more and more in the nature of their respective movements until the chief difference between them became that between light, thin-textured music and weightier music of a more polyphonic texture. It is not surprising, then, that the terms *da camera* and *da chiesa* were eventually dropped from titles.

Around 1700, under the influence of Arcangelo Corelli, one of the noblest of many Italian melodists and violinists, the church sonata became established internationally in what proved to be its almost universal form. This form consisted of four movements in the order of *slow-fast-slow-fast*. The slow *first movement* is ordinarily short, purely cursive in form, intensely expressive, and replete with those dotted rhythms that can be expected in Baroque introductory movements. Essential to its expressiveness are the frequent poignant dissonances resulting when one violin lags behind the other momentarily (suspension) while the two instruments are progressing in the same direction a third or sixth apart. The excerpt in Fig. 37 from an opening movement of a church sonata illustrates this very characteristic procedure. Incidentally, the full score you find here was still rare in Corelli's day and for almost another century. The cost and relative clumsiness of music printing then meant that only the separate parts for each player were ordinarily published.

The *second movement* is likely to be the longest. It is usually in cursive, fugal form, in even meter, and in a serious, energetic style. Corelli's fugues are looser and less developed than Bach's (for other mediums, that is, since only two trio sonatas are credited with certainty to Bach). His subjects are generally less sharply defined, often undergoing changes or being omitted later in the movement. The texture usually slips into chordal or scale figurations. But the energy does not abate and the timing of the entries is always shrewdly managed.

The *third movement* is most often only a brief, serene, homophonic transition to the finale. Its meter is usually triple and may

be marked by the characteristic rhythmic pattern of the saraband.
Its form may subdivide into a binary design or be purely cursive.
If there is any change of key in the sonata movements it will be
in this one. The whole movement may be in a nearly related key
or it may simply start or end on the dominant of a nearly related
key.

The *fourth movement* is sometimes a lively dancelike binary
form in triple meter, often a true gigue in everything but the
title.

The Corelli church sonata, from which Fig. 37 is quoted, fully
illustrates the four types of movements just described (Appendix II, No. 29). Its third movement is cursive and its fourth
movement is an untitled gigue, though not in binary form in this
instance.

THE CONCERTO GROSSO

The *concerto grosso* is the most representative form of
Baroque orchestral music. Among the other main forms were
chiefly the suite and the opera overture. The French overture,
which came to mean suite in Germany, began as an opera overture, made up only of one of those slow, dotted, introductory
movements and a quicker fugal movement (Appendix II,
No. 44a). The "sinfonia," or "Italian overture" as it is called to
distinguish it from the French overture, was a lighter, differently
planned opera overture in three movements, fast-slow-fast.

Like the trio sonata, the concerto grosso owed much to Corelli
and his contemporaries, and especially to Vivaldi, who lived a
generation later in Venice. Today Vivaldi is gaining more and
more attention as one of the most important Italian composers
of the Baroque Era. His more than 450 (!) concerti grossi (including solo concertos) are usually like the sinfonia in having
three movements, fast-slow-fast. Within these movements certain forms can be singled out as occurring more often than others.

However, like the motet and fugue, the movements of the concerto grosso should first be considered from the standpoint of structural procedures rather than set designs.

If ever a form grew out of practical circumstances it is that of the concerto grosso. To appreciate this fact one must understand that most orchestras in the eighteenth century were privately supported institutions in court or church establishments, which then provided almost the only means of employment for musicians. The prince, duke, or other head who maintained the orchestra had to find most of the players among those of his servants who could fiddle or pipe in addition to their other duties. In each section of the orchestra he could ordinarily afford to hire only one professional first-chair man, who would be very much needed to carry the others along. The result was two distinct classes of players. One class, made up of the relatively many fair-to-poor players, constituted the "concerto grosso," which literally meant "full orchestra" and was also called *tutti* or *ripieno.* The other class, made up of the relatively few experts, constituted the *concertino* or "little orchestra," known also as *principale,* and as *soli* because there is one performer to a part.

Now, you would suppose that to combine an average and an expert group in the same music would only work out unsatisfactorily for both. Actually the combination nicely suited certain interrelated musical procedures for which Baroque composers had a penchant. One of these was the use of *antiphony,* meaning the alternate performance of motives, phrases, or larger sections between two groups. Another was the principle of *terrace dynamics,* abrupt shifts from one level of intensity to another. And a third was the *echo* device, evidently employed almost every time a passage was repeated exactly or in sequence.

The result of all this was a musical "rivalry" or opposition inherent in the very word concerto. (The word *concertato* or *concertante* is often used to mean motivic play, which is the prevailing style of progression in the concerto grosso and one manifestation of what is meant by musical "rivalry.") You can hear this "rivalry" especially in the alternation of "tutti" passages that are solid, steady, and loud, with "soli" passages that are light, quick, and decorative if not entirely designed for virtuoso display. The typical scoring of the soli passages is the trio setting we met in the trio sonata (Fig. 38).

As already noted, Vivaldi's concerti grossi established a pattern like that of the sinfonia, three movements in the order fast-

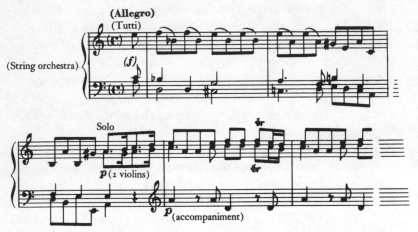

Fig. 38. The opposition of *tutti* and *soli* in a concerto grosso (Vivaldi, *Concerto No. 8*, for string orchestra and two solo violins, from *L'Estro Armonico*, op. 3)

slow-fast. With regard to over-all forms, the structural result of the opposition between the tutti and soli groups often approximates the rondo in the two outer movements. The design A-B-A'-C-A occurs especially often, with the middle A being in the dominant or some other nearly related key. In such forms the tutti group provides the refrains and the soli group the episodes. The middle movement, when it is not merely the transitory type of third movement in the church sonata, is likely to contain expressive solo passages from beginning to end. These may be divided among the soli group or allotted entirely to but one player in this group, and accompanied in the tutti group by some simple melodic and harmonic pattern or *ostinato* (p. 190) freely repeated.

The Vivaldi *Concerto No. 8,* from the opening movement of which Fig. 38 is taken, is representative of the procedures and forms just described (Appendix II, No. 30). Both solo violins share the solos in the lovely middle movement. This is also one of several concerti grossi by Vivaldi that Bach transcribed for organ (S. 593), indicating his great respect for his Italian contemporary (as well as for Corelli, Albinoni, and other Italians whom he copied in his works).

Bach's own six "Brandenburg Concertos" for strings and winds generally have the same three-movement plan as Vivaldi's, while Handel's *Twelve Grand Concertos,* op. 6, have more movements and come closer to suites than to the form that was noted here. The concerto grosso is enjoying a renaissance at the hands of numerous Modern composers. Bloch, Stravinsky, Bartók, Milhaud, and Hindemith are among those who have written works in this vein.

SELECTED READINGS

Manfred Bukofzer, *Music in the Baroque Era,* Chapters VII and X. New York: W. W. Norton, 1946.

William S. Newman, *The Sonata in the Baroque Era.* Chapel Hill: University of North Carolina Press, 1959.

Abraham Veinus, *The Concerto.* Garden City: Doubleday, 1944.

Joseph Culshaw, *The Concerto.* New York: Chanticleer Press, 1949.

See also the books by Marc Pincherle on Corelli and Vivaldi, listed under *Baroque Era* in Appendix I.

Chapter 13

The Classic Sonata: Prototype of Modern Instrumental Cycles

SYMPHONY, CONCERTO, QUARTET, AND OTHER MEDIUMS

The various Baroque instrumental cycles discussed in the previous chapter were succeeded in the masterworks of Haydn, Mozart, and Beethoven by the Classic cycles now to be discussed. The latter all relate to a Classic concept of the *sonata* that still survives in spite of a certain resistance to this concept during much of the Romantic Era. The statement can hardly be disputed that the Classic sonata idea is not only one of music's greatest landmarks in its own right but a prototype for the most serious and extended cycles of absolute music since the Classic Era.

The word sonata is used in three different ways that are treated separately in the three sections of this chapter and need to be kept in mind at all times in order to avoid a confusion of terminology. First, as just suggested, sonata is used as a *generic term* to cover a number of variously titled forms that differ primarily only in their instrumental medium. Second, sonata is used somewhat as it was in the Baroque Era to mean a particular *cycle of contrasted movements*. And third, sonata is used in the term "sonata-allegro" form to designate a *standardized design* associated primarily with the first movement in the Classic and later sonata cycle.

Starting with the first and broadest of the uses, what are the main forms that belong in the family of the sonata? These may be listed according to instrumental medium. Naturally there are the works that bear the title *sonata* itself. They will ordinarily be scored for one solo instrument, chiefly piano, or one other solo instrument with piano as a partner. *Duo* is the title sometimes given to a sonata for two equally important instruments. *String trio, string quartet, string quintet, string sextet, piano trio, piano quartet,* and *piano quintet* are the titles for various chamber music sonatas without or with piano, the instrumentation for which groupings was given on page 122. Furthermore, a *symphony* is a sonata for full orchestra and a *concerto* a sonata for soloist and orchestra. Even the more independent type of opera overture since the early Classic Era may relate to the Classic sonata concept, for it has often been conceived in the "sonata-allegro" form.

These various guises of the sonata do differ in certain secondary respects, chiefly in their average length, in certain details of texture and structural procedure, and in the number of movements each is likely to have. Such differences, as noted presently, grow out of the differences in scoring itself.

Most of the cycles in the sonata family were brought to a first peak by Haydn, Mozart, and Beethoven. The lines of influence within this great triumvirate of Classic composers is suggested by a comparison of their life dates. In parentheses are given the approximate years when each passed from his more formative stages into young maturity. In spite of their age differences, Haydn and the phenomenally precocious but shorter-lived Mozart matured at nearly the same time. Each ultimately came under certain influences of the other, as shown, for example, by the singing-allegro passages (p. 113) in Haydn's later sonata cycles and the more elastic phrases (p. 146) in Mozart's. Yet, basically these two belong among the composer pairs who have defined opposite styles in their eras (p. 22). Haydn's music is likely to be more robust and stocky than Mozart's, more full of dramatic contrasts, introspective fantasy, and piquant irregularities. Expressed in musical terms these differences reflect, for example, Haydn's greater liking for folklike melodies, remote if less subtle modulations, extreme and sharply contrasted dynamics, and surprising turns in any of music's elements for the sake of wit and caprice. By contrast, Mozart's opposite musical inclinations resulted in a

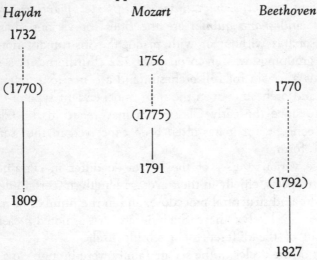

Haydn	*Mozart*	*Beethoven*
1732		
	1756	1770
(1770)	(1775)	
	1791	(1792)
1809		
		1827

more urbane yet deeply sensitive style, and more regular, consistent forms at all of the hierarchic levels. Beethoven marked a meeting ground of much that was outstanding in each of these men. Coming into his own some twenty years later, he began by synthesizing their styles.

Standard in the concert repertoire of Classic sonata cycles are the later symphonies and string quartets, plus a few of the piano sonatas by Haydn and Mozart, the later piano concertos by Mozart, and nearly all the instrumental cycles by Beethoven. These last include nine symphonies (among them the third or "Eroica," fifth or "Fate," and ninth or "Choral"), five piano concertos (the fifth being the "Emperor") and one violin concerto, sixteen string quartets, nine piano trios (among them the "Archduke"), four string trios, ten sonatas for piano and violin (among them the "Kreutzer") and five for piano and cello, and thirty-five solo piano sonatas (among them the "Pathétique," "Moonlight," "Waldstein," "Appassionata," and "Hammerklavier").

In the course of time, as the sonata cycles expanded in length, complexity, and import, each composer found himself putting more and more into fewer and fewer such works. Haydn, like his contemporaries, dedicated a half dozen at a time to the main personages at court. He left more than a hundred symphonies, whereas Mozart left about fifty, Beethoven nine, Schubert eight, Mendelssohn seventeen, Schumann and Brahms each four, Franck one, Bruckner eleven, Tchaikovsky six, Dvořák nine, Mahler ten, and Sibelius seven. Virtually all important Modern composers have written one or more sonata cycles in each main category. Some, like Hindemith, Shostakovitch, Prokofiev, Vaughan Williams, Bartók, and Milhaud, have concentrated most of their instrumental efforts in this direction.

THE CHOICE AND ORDER OF MOVEMENTS

Whereas the average number of movements was three to seven in the suite and three to five in the concerto grosso and church sonata of the Baroque Era, it has remained two to four in the Classic types of sonata cycles. When the Classic cycle is a solo concerto or any of the solo types actually called "sonata," there are usually only three, sometimes only two, movements, partly because there is less variety of timbre to provide further contrast in another type of movement or to hold the interest longer in the total form. Classic cycles of chamber and orchestral music ordinarily have four movements. In the chronology of Beethoven's sonata cycles the number of movements stays about the same in the trios and symphonies, but tends to increase in the string quartets and decrease in the piano sonatas.

The three movements in the solo sonata cycles are usually in the same order of *fast-slow-fast* that we found to be typical in the Baroque concerto grosso and opera sinfonia. This order also nears the slow-fast-slow-fast order of the Baroque church sonata when a Classic three-movement sonata is preceded by a slow introduction, as is Beethoven's *Sonate pathétique* for piano. As for the additional movement in the chamber and orchestral cycles, the minuet or scherzo is used almost invariably. It usually becomes a second inner movement in the total order of *fast-slow-moderate-fast.* Occasionally the inner movements are switched, producing the order fast-moderate-slow-fast (Appendix II, No. 33), which nears that in the four-movement core of the Baroque suite. As an exception to the foregoing generalizations, a small number of piano sonatas in only one movement may be cited, including the six last piano sonatas out of the ten left by the Russian Scriabin.

With regard to the choice of form in each of the several movements, one must start by acknowledging that every recognized design in instrumental music since Bach's day has been used in every movement at one time or another. However, certain forms may be described as typical in each movement of the "typical" sonata, those growing out of phrase grouping now predominating over the Baroque forms growing out of motivic play. The *first movement* is traditionally cast in "sonata-allegro" form, which is described in the remaining section of this chapter. The fact that this movement is usually fast explains the somewhat misleading designation for the form—misleading because the same form may also occur in the slow or moderate movement. The use of some other form in the first movement is surprisingly infrequent. One instance is the "Andante with Variations" that opens Beethoven's *Sonata in A-flat Major,* op. 26. But even the very familiar "Adagio" movement that opens his *Sonata quasi una Fantasia,* op. 27, no. 2 ("Moonlight"), proves to be a "sonata-allegro" form in miniature. The use of a short or extended slow introduction, usually a free cursive passage that leads right into the first movement, is not infrequent.

The *slow movement* is most often an A-B-A design (Appendix II, Nos. 31,II; 34,II) or a variation form (Appendix II, No. 32,II). As suggested earlier, it may also be an adapted "sonata-allegro" form (Appendix II, No. 33,III). In his slow movements (for example, op. 10, no. 3; op. 13; op. 59, no. 1; op. 97; op. 106; op. 125; op. 127; op. 132) Beethoven established a peerless model of songful, profound melody supported by strong harmony in fast harmonic rhythm (p. 87). Composers have sought ever since to emulate him in this side as in other sides of his genius. However, slow music strikes at the very heart of the musical creative process, revealing sooner than any other sort the depth and worth of the composer's ideas. A mediocre composer may be able to keep up a front with noise, pulse, and tone color in fast music, but only the true creator will not sound dull, restless, affected, or sentimental when he is compelled by a slow tempo to commit his ideas openly and completely, in melody and harmony as well as rhythm.

The *moderate movement* used by Haydn and Mozart was the *minuet,* or rather the compound A-B-A design of minuet-trio-da capo (p. 178). Beethoven, too, used this form in his earlier sonata cycles. It had already become considerably faster and more energetic than the stately, genteel type made familiar by the celebrated example in Mozart's opera *Don Giovanni.* Yet Beethoven largely changed over in his later cycles to the still faster, more intense *scherzo* with trio. Both types are in three-four meter, but in place of the minuet's greater variety of rhythmic patterns, the scherzo tends to hammer vigorously and metallically on the steady quarter-note pulse (Appendix II, Nos. 31,III; 32,III).

Since Beethoven the scherzo has been used almost exclusively as the moderate movement. It, too, has changed. Its literal meaning of "joke" can still be related to the rare, elf-like scherzos of Mendelssohn, but hardly tallies with the sinister, suppressed intensity of Brahms' scherzos or the grotesque caprice of many a more recent scherzo. The "Allegretto" of Shostakovitch's *Symphony No. 5* (Appendix II, No. 33,II) returns to the earlier sense of scherzo with its bumpkinish, clodhopping theme for cellos and basses alone, its parody on the usual passage for horns in the trio section, and its ridiculously lilting dance for violin solo complete with glissandos (produced by sliding through all the tones up or down the string).

The *finale* is likely to be in rondo form if the cycle is to end in a light and gay vein (Appendix II, Nos. 31,IV; 32,IV); and in "sonata-allegro" form if the final message is one of triumph (Appendix II, No. 33,IV). The humor and sparkle inherent in the rondo (p. 180) have given this design a preferred place in the finales of solo concertos, where good fun and virtuosity are prime ingredients (Appendix II, No. 34,III). Like the gigue in the Baroque suite and sonata, the finales of the Classic and later sonata cycles, especially the ones that are lightest in character, are often in compound meter. Among Romantic symphonists, Brahms in particular, the ideal of working toward a triumphant finale as the culmination of the entire sonata cycle seems to have been uppermost. There was a conscious striving for maximum integration and that one biggest climax (p. 112). Certain Romantics are known to have sensed a letdown, a slackening of purpose, in some of Beethoven's finales—that of *Sonate pathétique,* for instance. This charge was not leveled, however, at the veritable cantata for chorus, orchestra, and vocal soloists that concludes his "Choral" or *Ninth Symphony* and set a precedent for his Romantic successors, especially Mahler. Mozart, Beethoven, Brahms, and Hindemith are four among many composers who have availed themselves of fugal writing as a means of building up the finale. Like the first movement, the finale is occasionally prepared by a slow introduction.

An extremely interesting question now arises. To what extent are the movements bonded together in the sonata, over and above the accident of their succession in time? We can point at once to some general factors favoring over-all unity. The movements are customarily in the same key except for the slow one, which is usually in a nearly related key. There will naturally be that minimum of stylistic consistency that results merely from a constant instrumental medium and from the fact that a composer cannot range outside of his particular vocabulary of music's elements. And, of course, just hearing the movements played in succession again and again will eventually bind them together through habit of memory. But these factors are not sufficient in themselves to make any one grouping of movements seem like the inevitable and only possible grouping. Thus, one must acknowledge that a sonata movement by Haydn can usually be interchanged with an equivalent one by Mozart without serious detriment to either sonata cycle, and perhaps without detection.

Beethoven does achieve a more positive bonding of the movements. To begin with, he has a well-known tendency to associate a particular mood and certain styles appropriate to it with a particular key. Thus, the "fateful drive" that characterizes his *Fifth Symphony* in C minor can also be heard in most of his other C-minor cycles, among them the piano sonatas op. 10, no. 1; op. 13; and op. 111. Second, Beethoven exhibits an increasing differentiation between styles of texture. For example, his *Seventh Symphony* and *Eighth Symphony* are scored for the same-sized orchestra but the former, in keeping with its more dramatic content, has a generally richer texture, giving the impression of more "weight" of sound. Its texture is richer not simply because there are proportionally more *f* and *ff* passages scored for full orchestra but because there is more contrapuntal activity throughout the *Seventh Symphony* and a relatively faster harmonic rhythm.

Third, Beethoven shows more than an occasional tendency, whether unconscious or deliberate, to interrelate the themes of the several movements. We are not concerned so much here with the phenomenon of three string quartets and a separate quartet movement all related by the same theme (op. 130, 131, 132, 133), nor with the deliberate reference in the finale to passages from earlier movements, as in the "Choral Symphony," but

Fig. 39. Thematic relationships within and between the movements of a sonata (Beethoven, *Sonate pathétique,* op. 13, for piano)

rather with a sonata like "Pathétique," in which the same melodic fragment seems to recur more or less clearly in nearly all of the main themes. Fig. 39 illustrates representative passages where this fragment may or may not have been in the composer's mind (though it is all too tempting to labor such relationships):

(a) the introduction and (b) to (d) the three main themes in the first movement, (e) to (g) two main themes and an incidental accompaniment figure in the slow movement, and (h) to (1) two main themes and three incidental figures in the rondo finale. (To be sure, this particular "how-dry-I-am" motive, as at [c] and [h] in Fig. 39, occurs very often in music. Compare Figs. 35 and 44a [pp. 201 and 245] for instance, or the thematic material in Bach's *Partita in C Minor*, S. 826, for harpsichord.)

Finally, on rare occasions Beethoven related the movements of his sonatas by ascribing to them an extramusical "programme" (pp. 235–236). The five movements of his *Pastoral Symphony*, no. 6, carry these inscriptions along with the usual tempo designations: "Cheerful sensations awakened upon arrival in the country," "At the brook," "Merrymaking of the peasants," "Thunderstorm and gale," and "The shepherd's song—joy and thanks after the storm." There are even some appropriate, literal sound effects. Another example is his *Farewell, Absence, and Return Sonata*, op. 81a, for piano, in which the three moods are represented in the three movements, and the three syllables of "Le-be-wohl" ("Farewell") are even written over the three note idea at the start. There is no doubt that the use of a programme has at least the psychological effect of binding the movements for the listener.

All of Beethoven's means for binding the movements have been used with varying success by later composers. Toward the end of the nineteenth century the interrelationship of themes in sonata cycles became almost an end in itself. We find it to some extent in Brahms' use of a "basic motive," a very short figure that may initiate several of the themes or appear in the supporting texture. It is much more evident in Liszt's "thematic transformation" and in the "cyclical treatment" by Franck and his disciples (p. 143). A few attempts have been made to interrelate the movements in an over-all structural plan. Thus, Hindemith's *Third Piano Sonata* incorporates the fugal section of the third movement in the double fugue that makes up the finale. There may be a question, however, as to whether the conscious introduction of thematic relationships and structural interlocking is not largely an extrinsic means of accomplishing something that will always have to be accomplished internally and organically, anyway. That is to say, perhaps real unity will always have to grow out of something like the inherent behavior of our basic generators, the motive and the phrase.

"SONATA-ALLEGRO" FORM

"Sonata-allegro" form is the usual term for what has so far been the broadest application of hierarchic design within a single piece or movement of absolute music. It is the term adopted by Romantic theorists, who presented it as a highly standardized design in their textbooks. Let us start with their view of it, then return to it more in the sense of a structural result and in somewhat more detail.

As a standardized design, "sonata-allegro" form is a broad ternary, A-B-A plan that may or may not be preceded by a free *introduction* and is likely to be summed up in a free coda. The first A section, called *exposition,* states the main themes and their accessory material in the following order: *principal* or "masculine" theme, *bridge* modulating to the dominant or other nearly related key, *subordinate* or "feminine" theme in the new key, and *closing theme,* ending on a half or final cadence in the new key. Repetition of this exposition is traditionally called for by repeat signs, but more often than not it is disregarded by performers. The B section is that special feature of "sonata-allegro" form known as the *development.* It usually starts in the new key with a statement of the principal theme or one of the other main themes, then dissolves into a succession of modulatory episodes based on motivic play or some other "development" of one or more ideas from any part of the exposition, all very much at the composer's discretion. Culminating a retransition to the tonic key, the A section returns in what is called the *recapitulation*. Here the material of the exposition is repeated, but with the essential difference that the subordinate and closing themes remain in the tonic key, necessitating appropriate adjustments of the modulatory bridge.

Careful theorists have allowed, of course, for many incidental variations and elaborations within this plan. But like all standardized designs, "sonata-allegro" form must be understood only as an abstraction of a considerable variety of structural results. The main shortcoming of the foregoing definition lies in placing so much emphasis on a particular number and order of themes, rather than on the fundamental processes that embody these themes. The essence of a drama is not conveyed, for example,

Fig. 40. Dualism of themes in a Romantic sonata: (a) "masculine," (b) "feminine" (Brahms, *Sonata in C Major for Piano,* op. 1, I)

merely by enumerating the main characters in the order that they appear, however important these characters may be to the plot.

Now, we can gain the clearest insight into "sonata-allegro" design if we consider further how the textbook abstraction of it must necessarily differ from the variety of structural results in actual music. If the typically Romantic dualism of "masculine" theme versus "feminine" theme (Fig. 40) were indeed the essence of "sonata-allegro" form, then one would expect to find that idea in the earliest unmistakable examples of this form if he found nothing else. Similarly, one would expect to find the return to these themes which the textbook definition treats as indispensable. Actually, the earliest examples that really *feel* like "sonata-allegro" form—those by Bach's youngest son, Johann Christian Bach, for instance—seldom exhibit either of these traits and frequently have no really distinctive themes at all. Even when we come to the mature Classics, we find that Haydn often repeats the principal theme where we would expect the subordinate theme to occur; that he frequently omits a theme or inverts the order in the recapitulation; and that Mozart tends to extend the "closing theme" beyond the length of the other two themes put together. Only when we come to the Romantics themselves do we find fairly general correspondence between music and theory, although then the design becomes just another mold to fill for Chopin, Grieg, and many a composer temperamentally indisposed toward such a broadly integrated scheme.

The real reason why the early Classic form already "feels" distinctly different from any main movement of the Baroque instrumental cycles lies in the new treatment of texture and tonality. And in the terms of this book, that new treatment results from the choice of the phrase rather than the motive as the basic generator of progression (p. 144). Furthermore, from a historical standpoint there is little question but that the singing-allegro style (p. 113) as anticipated in early eighteenth-century Italian opera was a potent influence in the switch from the motive to the phrase in early Classic writing for instruments.

As is to be expected, since the phrase is the basic generator, the *texture* is predominantly homophonic in "sonata-allegro" form. It is not surprising, then, that the Alberti bass is a frequent accompaniment device in the Classic sonata (p. 113). There may well be a considerable amount of contrapuntal activity, too, but usually not enough to overcome the authority of the phrase. Only when a theme is being "developed" is motivic play likely to take precedence.

The *tonality* in "sonata-allegro" form moves ordinarily by distinct plateaus. Again, only when the themes are being "developed" does a different principle operate. Then the state of tonal flux characteristic of motivic play can be expected. Together, the tonal plateaus define that organized tour of keys that is implied here by tonality. Significantly, the earliest Classic sonatas make at least a tonal return or recapitulation if not a thematic one. In other words, even these early examples return at least in the sense of coming back to the tonic well before the end. Masters of "sonata-allegro" form seem to have been very alert to the balance of "light" and "dark" keys. Beethoven almost invariably gets to the subdominant or "dark" side in the coda. Brahms' tendency to overweight the "dark" side helps to explain a somber quality in many of his "sonata-allegro" forms. Brahms is also somewhat exceptional in not avoiding the tonic key in the development section.

The "sonata-allegro" form is *polythematic* in consequence of the phrase's structural tendencies. However, the notion of just two main themes and a closing theme is misleading. In the first place, this notion tends to devalue the closing material, which may well be the most important of all (as in the first movement of Haydn's "Military" *Symphony in G Major*). And secondly, the themes often occur in thematic groups rather than singly for the very reason that phrases tend to fall into groupings. A Mozart "closing theme" generally proves to be a whole string of closing themes.

The nature of a "sonata-allegro" *theme* helps to explain the existence of the development section. This theme is something more than a phrase because it does stand out in its melodic context in order to qualify as a theme (see p. 139). It stands out because it is likely to be a complex of distinct motives. In this sense it is like the fugue subject, although one does not usually associate sonata themes with fugue subjects, since the styles and harmonic rhythms of the textures in which each type appears are so different. The important thing about the sonata theme is that it is capable of appearing both intact and piecemeal. It appears intact during the phrase grouping that prevails in the exposition and recapitulation, and piecemeal in the development section, where the separate motives typically generate some kind of motivic play. When the theme is itself no more than a single motive such as the "V-for-Victory" or ". . . —" motive that opens Beethoven's *Fifth Symphony,* then motivic play or sequence is likely to go on through much of the movement. This is a frequent occurrence in Modern sonatas (p. 153).

The *development section* was stated to be a special feature of "sonata-allegro" form. As a matter of fact, if it were not for this feature and the characteristic humor of the rondo, the two designs would come rather close to each other, as they sometimes do, for example, in Beethoven's music:

Rondo Form		*"Sonata-Allegro" Form*
A (tonic key); bridge B (nearly related key) A (tonic key)	Exposition	A or principal theme (tonic key); bridge B or subordinate theme (nearly related key) closing theme (same new key)
C (moderately distant key)	Development in foreign keys	
A (tonic key); bridge (adjusted tonally) B (tonic key) A and coda	Recapitulation	A (tonic key); bridge (adjusted tonally) B (tonic key) closing theme and coda

The development section does not ordinarily introduce new material but explores and exploits any or all of the ideas in the exposition until they unfold like living organisms. Most development sections are episodic, with each episode being defined by one kind of thematic treatment during one modulation or series of modulations. Motivic play in the strict Baroque sense (p. 142) is too narrow a description for what goes on when a master develops his themes. A motive from one of these themes may not only be repeated in sequence or by interchange between two or more melodic lines, but it may be spun out into a new, greater theme, it may be "sewn" on to another of the motives, it may be systematically dissected, or it may be transformed in character. In Fig. 41 the process of dissection is illustrated. The theme, as you see it in full under (a), is first stated twice, the second time in minor; then (b) the last half of it is stated

Fig. 41. Dissection of a theme as a process of development (Beethoven, *Sonata in D Major*, op. 28, for piano, I)

three times; (c) the last half of this is stated four times in motivic interchange; (d) the *first* half of this is stated twelve times in sequence or exact repetition; (e) the same is stated in a new, syncopated pattern between the hands twenty-one times; (f) the same summed up in a single three-beat, syncopated tone is stated eleven times, then three more times in longer values!

Beethoven and Brahms made much of the *coda*, prompting one theorist to call it a "terminal development." What with the digression into the subdominant key and a new view of the thematic material, the coda often caps their movements with something like the force of an O. Henry punch line (Appendix II, No. 31,I). For a particularly choice example of such a punch line, though not in a "sonata-allegro" form, listen to the quasi-jazz figure near the end of the slow movement in Beethoven's *Fifth Symphony*.

As a hierarchic design the "sonata-allegro" form is described by some as *ternary* and others as *binary*. Insofar as it originally related to the binary form of the dances in the Baroque suite (as a brother, however, rather than a son), it was certainly binary in concept. It was still thought of as binary during most of the Classic Era, as evidenced by the frequent absence of a clear thematic return and by the mechanical fact that the exposition was enclosed in one set of repeats and the longer second half in another. (This second half included everything that was or would become development and recapitulation.) Early in the nineteenth century the distinction between the three main sections became a conscious and deliberate one, after which there can be no question about a ternary concept. In any case, the design is a remarkably cumulative one. Among Romantic sonata writers, not only is the notion of a dualistic opposition between masculine and feminine furthered, but the "sonata-allegro" form becomes a field of battle on which one theme eventually emerges triumphant (as in Scriabin's frenzied climaxes). Two climactic spots stand out in this form. One is the instant of return, toward which the tonality has been moving with the excitement of a horse returning to stable. The other is the coda.

The "sonata-allegro" form varies somewhat with the medium. It is capable of more extension in chamber and orchestral than solo music since the greater choice of colors can hold the listener's interest longer. The greater length chiefly results from more development of the material, not only in the development section itself but while or after each theme is presented in the outer sections (as in the long first movements of Beethoven's "Eroica" and "Choral" symphonies). The equal significance of each instrument in the string quartet invites a fairly polyphonic texture, while the duo lends itself to antiphony in the presentation of themes.

The solo *concerto* shows the greatest influence of medium. Traditionally (if not consistently) the exposition is stated first as a tutti by the orchestra, all in the tonic key, then as a combination of soloist and orchestra with the usual modulation to a nearly related key. The coda becomes a *cadenza*, formerly improvised, in which the performer "takes off" by himself, using the occasion to display his utmost virtuosity while developing the thematic material in a loose sort of way. The concerto invites antiphony between soloist and orchestra as well as decorative commentaries by either while the other may be playing one of the themes. Not seldom, as in Liszt's popular first *Concerto for Piano and Orchestra*, in E-flat Major, the orchestra serves primarily as "straight man" in its statements of the main ideas while the soloist does all the elaborating and takes all the liberties. The strong appeal of concertos, especially the idea of the virtuoso soloist, makes them a major source of box office receipts. This fact, in turn, tends to limit the repertoire to a few sure-fire, tried-and-true "war horses," even including two or three that are as full of clichés as this sentence.

As usual, it is the pianist who has the richest assortment from which to choose, including (within that limited repertoire) the last three of Beethoven's five piano concertos, two each by Chopin and Brahms, one each by Schumann and Grieg, the first of two by Liszt and of three by Tchaikovsky, and the middle two of the four by Rachmaninoff. Other keyboard concertos have achieved almost as much popularity, like those by J. S. Bach, Mozart, Ravel, Prokofiev, and Khatchaturian.

String players are much more limited by the repertoire, while wind players have virtually nothing that can insure box office receipts, their solo literature being relatively small at best. Among favorite concertos for the violinist are those by the "three B's" and by Mendelssohn, Tchaikovsky, Dvořák, and Saint-Saëns. The cellist has mainly concertos by Haydn, Schumann, Dvořák, and Saint-Saëns to play. Mention should also be made of the few outstanding concertos for more than one soloist and orchestra, including Bach's for two violins in D minor (S. 1043) and several for from two to four harpsichords, Mozart's *Sinfonia concertante for Violin and Viola* in E-flat major (K. 320d) and *Concerto for Two Pianos* in the same key (K. 316a), as well as Brahms' powerful *Concerto for Violin and Cello* in A minor, op. 102.

SELECTED READINGS

Percy Goetschius, *The Larger Forms of Musical Composition.* New York: G. Schirmer, 1915.

Donald Tovey, *Essays in Musical Analysis,* 7 vols. New York: Oxford University Press, 1936 and later.

William S. Newman, *The Sonata in the Classic Era, . . . Romantic Era, . . . Modern Era,* vols. II-IV in *A History of the Sonata Idea* (see p. 213). In preparation.

William S. Newman, "Climax in Music," *The Music Review,* XIII (1952).

C. M. Girdlestone, *Mozart's Piano Concertos.* London: Cassell, 1948.

Donald Tovey, *A Companion to Beethoven's Pianoforte Sonatas.* London: Associated Board, 1935.

Edwin Fischer, *Beethoven's Pianoforte Sonatas.* London: Faber and Faber, 1959.

D. G. Mason, *The Quartets of Beethoven.* New York: Oxford University Press, 1948.

George Grove, *Beethoven and His Nine Symphonies.* London: Novello, 1948.

Julius Harrison, *Brahms and His Four Symphonies.* London: Chapman and Hall, 1939.

Part IV

Forms Influenced by Extramusical Factors

Chapter 14

Instrumental Fantasy and Description

PROGRAMME VERSUS ABSOLUTE MUSIC

With the discussion of Classic sonata cycles, we have completed our survey of the principal forms of *absolute music,* forms that are dependent entirely on music's own laws for their variety and unity. We come now to various degrees and kinds of *programme music,* which is music that does undergo varying influences from outside factors. As soon as a story, description, mood, occasion, or other association becomes essential to the concept of the composer and to the understanding of the listener, extramusical considerations have entered into the total form. Then music ceases to be a completely pure art but becomes involved in the nature and structural tendencies of other arts. Our motive and phrase continue to function as basic generators of form, but they account for less and less in the final structural result as the programme's influence comes more and more to the fore.

One may oppose programme music as a "muddying" of the arts or defend it as an ideal synthesis in art and a necessary clarification of music's meaning. Ethos eras tend to reject it and pathos eras to cultivate it. Perhaps the *Pastoral Symphony* and the "Farewell Sonata" (p. 223) were evidences that Beethoven, founded in the ethos spirit of Classicism, was keeping abreast of the new pathos spirit of Romanticism. However, Beethoven was himself one of many composers who have resented efforts to impose detailed programmes on their music. In the *Pastoral Sym-*

phony he preferred not to tag each passage with a literal meaning, but remarked in his sketchbook that "a listener must discover the situations for himself." Schumann, in the heart of the Romantic Era, expressed discomfort over the detailed programmatic explanations that Berlioz supplied with his *Fantastic Symphony*. And even Richard Strauss, one of the foremost creators of programme music, supplied little more than titles in his "symphonic poems."

But the layman is not always ready to accept the fact that music is a language in itself; that it is a completely valid art only when it is its own best means of communicating the aesthetic message it is meant to express. He asks, "What is the music describing? What did the composer have in mind?" No wonder publishers often feel obliged to add titles like "Moonlight," "Return to Paris," "Fleecy Clouds"—titles that could be almost anything else with as much reason. Even those pieces that Mendelssohn so deliberately collected under the title *Songs Without Words* have been given programmatic titles! (This whole question is somewhat analogous to that of representation and nonrepresentation in recent painting.)

To be sure, the terms absolute and programme represent interdependent concepts in music. As with variety and unity or space and time, neither extreme is possible. The most absolute of absolute music is bound to have some programmatic connotation, though this may be only a general sense of pleasure or pain, joy or sorrow, calm or turbulence. And the most programmatic of programme music must involve some inner laws of music, at least those governing the basic behavior of rhythm and pitch, or there would be no music at all. But the extent to which a programme may influence musical form does vary widely. Surprisingly, the influence does not seem to be great in a work like *Till Eulenspiegel's Merry Pranks* by Strauss, which proves to be a capital (though very subtle) rondo form quite apart from its story interest. On the other hand, the influence is considerable in most film music, where the story must occupy the observer's central attention, pushing everything else into the background. If film music were generally composed in closed, self-sufficient forms it would compete with the story for the observer's attention. This is said despite occasional concert performances of extracts from such highgrade film music as *The Plow That Broke the Plains, Alexander Nevsky, Hamlet, Our Town,* and *Spellbound.*

Whatever the extent of the programme's influence on the musical form, it must not fight with the inner tendencies of the music. Strauss's rondo form and the Till Eulenspiegel story make an ideal combination because the refrain-and-episode idea makes the natural vehicle for telling about Till and his succession of misadventures. But a rondo form could be very disconcerting in a composition that was meant to depict a single mood, with no justification in the programme for either the refrains or episodes. If music is to have validity and substance of its own, the composer can let the programme direct him only to the most appropriate musical form, from that point on composing whatever music best suits the form, in his artistic judgment.

FREE FORMS BORN OF MUSICAL AND TECHNICAL FANTASY

Somewhere on the road from absolute to programme music lies a variety of generally short instrumental pieces that are born largely out of sheer pleasure in fantasy. These pieces fall somewhat outside of absolute music to the extent that they break away from the usual structural results of motivic play or phrase grouping. Yet they do not qualify as programme music, since the fantasy that governs their course cannot be called an extramusical influence.

Among the most frequent titles for the fantasy pieces are *prelude, toccata, fantasia, impromptu,* and *capriccio.* Each title suggests a slightly different kind of fantasy. Prelude suggests music that prepares the mood, although many preludes, like orchestral overtures, exist alone without other music to follow. Toccata— from *toccare,* to touch, as in playing the keys—suggests music to warm up the fingers. Fantasia brings us back to the fantasy element that underlies all these pieces. Impromptu suggests spontaneous fantasy. And caprice emphasizes the whimsical side of fantasy.

Toccata, fantasia, and capriccio are titles encountered especially in early Baroque music. There it was that the first great strides were made toward a literature of independent instrumental pieces as well as a vocabulary of idiomatic instrumental techniques. Originally, the significance of the titles "fantasia" and "capriccio" was that of freedom from a text; for heretofore the text itself had been a main prop of musical form, as in the motet and the madrigal. But, paradoxically, this new freedom proved to be the impetus for much more binding means of form, since it focused attention on the problem of how to achieve tangible unity in absolute music devoid of a text. Consequently, not a few pieces called "fantasia" or "capriccio" actually fall very clearly into one or another of the types we have discussed previously, whether cursive or hierarchic. The same may be said for the prelude and impromptu, which in Chopin's hands, for example, are most often closed, symmetrical, hierarchic designs.

Hence, a distinction must be made here between those pieces that merely differ from the recognized forms in their titles and those that actually arise out of fantasy, unbridled by any "laws" of form. What is the nature of this fantasy? One can generalize that in its most unbridled state there will be little or no repetition at the higher levels of form—no periodic recurrence of a fugue subject, no complementary return of a large section, and no theme repeated in variations. Without this repetition and without a programme, fantasias cannot last very long. The longer the work, the more is the need for organized architecture in music (p. 148). In any case, if there is to be a coherent flow of musical thought some repetition will always be present, even if that repetition is discoverable only in the most minute fragments of rhythm and melody.

Also characteristic of fantasy is a vacillation, often abrupt, between styles of progression. The massive organ toccatas that were composed throughout the Baroque Era, especially by Frescobaldi and Bach, are distinguished by alternations of sections in some kind of homophonic chordal figuration with sections in motivic play if not actual fugal form. At other times, fantasy may be primarily an exploration into any of music's elements, resulting in experimental modulations, irregular rhythms, endless melody, unusual orchestration, and so on.

Another kind of fantasy is that which delights in the exploitation of idiomatic techniques. Pieces for keyboard are likely to grow out of figures peculiarly suited to it, such as hand crossing, rapid alternation of the hands, staccato chords, repeated notes, and double notes. Pieces for violin are likely to grow out of any of the innumerable styles of violin bowing, or the use of pizzicato, or harmonics, or rapid string crossing (recall Appendix II, No. 25). In Fig. 42 is some idiomatic writing for piano by the Hungarian composer and piano virtuoso Franz Liszt (Appendix II, No. 35). This example comes from a relatively free form in which the melody merely repeats at irregular intervals and in different guises. Four different but equally "pianistic" versions of the same bit of melody are quoted here (with the melodic tones encircled each time). The highly imaginative etudes of Chopin and Liszt are especially fruitful explorations of idiomatic piano techniques.

Of piano preludes there is an especially venerable and rich literature. The custom has arisen of writing sets of twenty-four preludes in all the major and minor keys. Those of Bach that precede the fugues in the two volumes of the *Well-Tempered Clavier* have already been mentioned (p. 166). Chopin's twenty-four preludes, sometimes played at one overly long sitting by re-

Fig. 42. Idiomatic writing in a piano fantasia (Liszt, "Au bord d'une source" ["At the edge of a fountain"], from *Années de pèlerinage,* vol. I)

citalists, include many familiar gems (Appendix II, No. 1). Some are dramatic, some expressive, some virtuosic. Debussy's twenty-four preludes reveal a whole new world of piano writing. However, their expressive titles (including *Girl with the Flaxen Hair, The Dance of Puck,* and *The Engulfed Cathedral*) and their remarkable depiction of moods and impressions put these pieces distinctly in the category of programme music. The twenty-four preludes each of Shostakovitch and Kabalevsky may be mentioned among other effective Modern examples.

Tone poems that reflect moods

Programme music divides into the sort that depicts general moods and the sort that describes literal, specific things and actions. Both sorts may be found in the Romantic orchestral works known as *tone poems* or *symphonic poems.* By these compound designations we are reminded of the close bond between literature and music in the Romantic Era (opp. Plate 5). Also, we are made aware of the compromise that many Romantic composers preferred to make with the Classic sonata idea, notwithstanding the substantial number of full-fledged symphonies produced throughout the nineteenth century. The same generalization can be made of the concerto, which frequently took the form of a fantasy, as in Liszt's *Fantasia on Hungarian Folk Tunes*, d'Indy's *Symphony 'Cévenole' on a French Mountain Song*, or de Falla's *Nights in the Gardens of Spain* (each for piano and orchestra).

Sometimes a printed poem actually appears, like a frontispiece, in the score of a tone poem, as in *Les Preludes* by Liszt and *Les Djinns* by Franck. In the latter work the dynamic plan actually follows the visual diamond shape of the poem as its successive lines "crescendo" from two words to a peak in a full-length line, then gradually contract again. Certain literary subjects recur time and again, as they do in all Romantic art, especially those of the irresistible lover Don Juan (or Don Giovanni) and the man who sells his soul to the devil, Faust. The tone poem usually lasts from a quarter to a half hour and occurs all in one movement, although divisions comparable to the movements of a symphony are frequently to be found. Thematic transformation (p. 143) and interrelationships may be expected wherever there are such divisions.

The two names most linked with the tone poem are Liszt and Richard Strauss, Liszt more for the mood type and Strauss for the literal type. Wagner deserves to be included for the vast symphonic stretches in his music dramas. Among other composers of tone poems often played are Debussy, Delius, Elgar, Sibelius, Dvořák, and Smetana.

Efforts to create general *moods, impressions,* or *atmosphere* are fairly recent in music. Some of the first significant examples occur in Early Romantic opera, as in the eerie forest scenes of *Der Freischütz*. But no music has come closer to this aim than that of the Impressionistic movement around the turn of this century.

Impressionism took its start among French painters of the late nineteenth century. In painting it may be defined as a blurring of outlines and an avoidance of photographic detail, on the theory that the power of suggestion leads to general impressions that are stronger than the thing itself. Recall the effect of a drama done with nothing but backdrops and a few cubistic boxes on the stage. From these the imagination can sometimes create far more vivid and impressive scenery than the most lavish but literal walls and props. Or recall an Irish bull attributed to Shaw, "A man runs after a woman until she overtakes him," which makes a very meaningful impression, yet is pure nonsense when analyzed in detail.

The effect of this blurring is to exaggerate the few most essential traits at the expense of the many less essential ones. In a sense this is what the cartoonist does. Thus, three curved lines suffice to give the essential impression of a cottonpicker in the field. In Plate 17, Monet, one of the chief Impressionistic painters, makes the outline of the bridge, smokestacks, and boats clear enough, but all else is blurred in the haze.

How is Impressionism achieved in a time art like music? Again, by the power of suggestion. Think of a person who starts a sentence only to let it trail off unfinished, leaving the hearer to imagine the rest *or even more*. So Debussy, in whose works musical Impressionism begins and culminates, may start a theme and let it trail off, allowing the listener to imagine, perhaps, something more beautiful than could ever have been expressed in notation. Fig. 43 illustrates such a theme exactly as it occurs in Debussy's *Nuages* (*Clouds*) for orchestra (Appendix II, No. 36). It is a mournful fragment, played by the English horn. In that same work we find other means of the musical Impressionist—the blurred key center when the whole-tone scale is used (p. 66), the blurred sonority of muted strings, the blurred harmony resulting from frequent parallelisms such as those of the luscious

Fig. 43. Impressionism as exemplified in a fragmentary theme (Debussy, *Nuages* [*Clouds*], first *Nocturne* for orchestra, reprinted by permission of Jean Jobert, Paris, France, copyright owner; Elkan-Vogel Co., Inc., Philadelphia)

ninth chords in measure 14, and the blurred rhythm resulting from the absence of pronounced patterns and from irregular phrases and changing meters. Besides *Nuages* and the other two *Nocturnes,* you will enjoy knowing *La Mer* (*Sea Pieces*) and *Afternoon of a Faun* among other tone poems in which Debussy depicts moods and impressions.

With this mention of Impressionism must come that of another movement that originated similarly in painting, but as a reaction to Impressionism. *Expressionism* in music began in the early twentieth century, its chief locale being the Vienna of Sigmund Freud and its chief exponent Schoenberg. In both painting and music it may be defined not so much as a depiction of a mood or subject itself but as a subjective, psychological reaction to that mood. Hence the extraordinary distortions of subject matter and ideas. In his painting *Caricature, the Red Egg* (Plate 18), Kokoschka, a key painter in the Vienna group, symbolizes his reaction to a blood-tainted Mussolini, whose purple mask gapes at the right. Expressionism in music has been marked by efforts to break away from the binding forces of metrical regularity and the I-IV-V-I tonal orbit (p. 99). The resulting style is atonal, motivic, compressed, intense, irregular in meter, strongly dissonant by traditional standards, and highly sensitive in its colors and dynamics. Expressionism presents, among other difficulties, the probability that no listener is likely to share the exact subjective reactions that the composer has experienced.

TONE POEMS THAT DESCRIBE LITERALITIES

The idea of describing concrete things or actions in sound is perhaps as old as music itself. Word painting such as we found in the motet (p. 159) can also be found in Gregorian chant and much vocal music since then. Programmatic effects of a literal nature can be found in instrumental music as far back as idiomatic techniques can be found. Among well-known examples, the Elizabethan virginalist John Munday attempted to describe "Faire Wether," "Lightening," "Thunder," and "Calme Wether." The Italian Carlo Farina imitated barnyard and other sounds on the violin. Johann Kuhnau, a predecessor of Bach, wrote *Bible Sonatas* for keyboard that depict in detail the familiar stories of David and Goliath and other Biblical characters. Bach's own *Capriccio on the Departure of His Beloved Brother* is one of many music examples in which the programme concerns farewell and absence. His organ chorale preludes are full of symbolic representations of their subjects, such as a downward leap of a seventh in the bass to depict Adam's fall, a dotted rhythm to express the walk of the cripple, and a winding figure to describe the angels ascending the stairs. Rameau even imitates the hen's clucking in *La Poule*. And countless other examples might be cited from the orchestral accompaniments in opera, ballet, and oratorio.

However, so far, these examples that take us through the Baroque Era do not go much beyond the naïve imitation of sounds and the symbolic representation of action. Once an appropriate musical symbol is decided upon, it is generally treated as a motive and the music goes about its own way. When we come to the Romantics we find increasing efforts to reproduce the actual feel or psychological sensation of the thing described. This applies not only in the depiction of moods or impressions such as Debussy created but in literal descriptions. The *idée fixe* that runs through Berlioz' *Fantastic Symphony* is first stated serenely to represent his beloved, then later in grotesque distortion when he dreams of her as a witch. The motive of the magic broomstick that fetches water in Dukas' *Sorcerer's Apprentice* grows and grows as the water swells to a torrent, until the listener almost feels that he himself is being drowned in the uncontrollable onrush of sound. Arthur Honegger's remarkable *Pacific 231* reproduces so realistically the sound of a huge locomotive getting under way that one critic asked why a simple recording of the

Fig. 44. Literal description in music (R. Strauss, *Till Eulenspiegel's Merry Pranks*, op. 28, for orchestra, reproduced from the piano reduction made by Otto Singer, with the permission of C. F. Peters Corporation, New York)

actual thing would not do just as well. But the tone poem becomes more and more symphonic (extended by purely musical means) as it develops the sensations of gradual acceleration, full speed, then gradual deceleration, and finally the grind to a full halt.

In Fig. 44 the principal descriptive themes are quoted from Richard Strauss's ever-popular tone poem *Till Eulenspiegel's Merry Pranks* (Appendix II, No. 37), mentioned earlier on several occasions. The story appears to be that of a chase that gets hotter and hotter, incident by incident, until success is on the side of the law. Strauss reportedly gave at least tacit approval to a fairly detailed programme offered by a critic, including the idea that (a) in Fig. 44 represents the introduction of the legendary Till; (b) reveals him as his true, shifty, roguish self; (c) presents him posing unctuously as a priest; and (d) shows Till, in fear and angry despair, being condemned by the long bony finger of the law and forthwith hanged on the spot! To be sure, much is lost, in such illustrations, without the orchestral colors. Hear, sometime, how Strauss describes his carping, mincing critics, with shrill flutes and piccolos; and his beloved wife, with the rich, tender sounds of the solo violin—both in his autobiographical symphonic poem, *A Hero's Life*.

SELECTED READINGS

F. Niecks, *Programme Music in the Last Four Centuries*. New York: H. W. Gray, 1906.

Alfred Einstein, *Music in the Romantic Era*, Chapters III and VII (on programme music). New York: W. W. Norton, 1947.

Adolfo Salazar, *Music in Our Time*, Chapters XIII, XVI-XVIII, and XX-XXII (on Impressionism and Expressionism). New York: W. W. Norton, 1946.

"Film Music," article in *Grove's Dictionary of Music and Musicians*, 5th ed. New York: St. Martin's Press, 1954.

Robert Elkin, *The Stories Behind Music*. New York: Rider, 1949.

Chapter 15

Allegiance to Text in Song and Opera

Cursive art-song

The term programme music is not as generally applied to vocal as to instrumental music, but the fact remains that music with a text is certainly more likely to be descriptive than absolute. In this chapter and the next we consider various types of secular and sacred vocal music whose forms are primarily determined by the sense and course of the text. You will recall that certain other vocal types have already been included under forms based on the inner laws of music. Among these are the madrigal and the motet, which are governed at least as much by the nature of motivic play as by the text; the A-B-A type of art-song, including the *da capo* aria, and the A-B type of folk and community songs, which fall into hierarchic designs; and secular minstrelsy, which is but little governed by the text except in the sense that it follows the Medieval verse forms. In the present section is discussed the *cursive art-song* (or *through-composed* art-song, as the Germans say), a type that comes about as near to free form as the fantasy types of instrumental pieces discussed in the previous chapter.

The history of the art-song may be said to include especially the monophonic minstrelsy of the Medieval-and-Renaissance Era, the tender Burgundian chansons of the early fifteenth century (chiefly those by Dufay), the wonderfully free "ayres" for lute and voice of Elizabethan England (such as those by Dowland), the rich and varied nineteenth-century German lied (now a universal term for German art-song), and the late, almost precious nineteenth-century art-song in France (such as was written by Fauré and Debussy) with its influences in America (as in the songs of Loeffler and Griffes).

Of these flowerings by far the best known is that of the *lied*, which received its first great development in some 600 lieder (plural of lied) by Schubert, followed especially by the somewhat more delicate and subtle lieder of Schumann, the folklike lieder of Brahms, and the remarkably intense and varied lieder of Hugo Wolf. Among the most important collections of lieder are a number of extended *song cycles*. A song cycle, in analogy with instrumental cycle, is a series of songs based on a series of related poems. Thus, Schubert's *Winterreise* (*Winter's Journey*) contains twenty-four songs that deal variously with the bleak spirit and death contemplations of a love-forsaken man—with the hot tears he has wept, frozen on his cheek by the bitter cold; the old elm where once he carved the initials of his beloved's name; the raven that will devour him when he has fallen.

Beethoven had prepared for Schubert's song cycles with his own wistful, intimate collection *An die ferne Geliebte* (*To the Distant Beloved*). The six little songs, almost folklike in their simplicity, are actually interconnected musically. After Schubert, Schumann's *Dichterliebe* (*Love Poems*), Brahms' *Magelone*, Debussy's *Chansons de Bilitis*, and Vaughan Williams' *On Wenlock Edge* (for tenor and string quartet) have been favorites among song cycles.

The level of poetry is generally very high in the lied, represented as it is by Goethe, Schiller, and Heine, among others. The success of the lieder singer depends not only on voice and musicianship but quite as much on an ability to project the intimate, personal character of the poetry across the footlights. Without this ability singers like Lotte Lehmann, Elisabeth Schwarzkopf, and Alexander Kipnis (or Maggie Teyte and Gérard Souzay in

French art-song) could not leave their audiences spellbound as they have done, nor maintain such pre-eminence among exponents of the art-song. Incidentally, most songs are published in transposed keys as well as the original key so that they can be sung in any of the standard voice ranges, men's or women's (even when the sense of the text is contradicted).

In all of the lieder the piano accompaniement plays an extremely important role, qualifying the vocal melody by the various means used in homophony (pp. 111–114), setting the mood, and often providing preludes, interludes, and postludes that round out the form. In Schubert's lieder more musical activity generally goes on in the piano than in the voice part. Besides A-B-A and cursive forms, many lieder employ the *strophic plan* —an additive plan in which each of several verses is set to the same music, as in Schubert's *Ave Maria*.

Consider two of Schubert's cursive lieder, both involving dialog concerning death, although the first is a narrative and the second more of a philosophy. *Erlking*, a setting of a ballad by Goethe (and objected to by Goethe!), is a dramatic narrative of a father who raced on horseback to save his child from the erlking, but in the end found that "in his arms the child—was dead!" While the accompaniment maintains the effect of breathless galloping, the singer alternately sings the words of the narrator, the anxious father, the terror-stricken child, and the wily, menacing erlking, each in a different style. As a sample of the varied poetry of the lied, the entire text of *Erlking* follows (from Henry S. Drinker, *Texts of the Solo Songs of Franz Schubert in English Translation* [New York: Association of American Colleges Program, 1951]). This translation does retain the same prosody (syllables and accents) in order to fit the musical setting. But the art-songs in German and Romance languages are seldom actually sung in translation; as in the Renaissance madrigal (p. 160) the music relates too intimately to the original word sounds.

ERLKING (*Erlkönig*), by Goethe

NARRATOR: Who rides in the night so late and wild?
It is the fa-ther with his young child;
the boy lies snug and tight in his arm,
he holds him safe-ly, he keeps him warm.

FATHER: "My son, why hide you your face so in fright?"

CHILD: "The erl-king, fa-ther, there in the night!
the fear-ful erl-king, with crown and tail!"

FATHER: "My son, 'tis but a va-por-trail."

ERLKING: "You dar-ling child, come go with me,
the flow'rs are fair-est there by the sea;
so ma-ny games you and I will play,
and your clothes will all be gol-den and gay."

CHILD: "My fa-ther, my fa-ther, and did you not hear,
what erl-king whis-pered so soft in my ear?"

FATHER: "Now fear not, lie there qui-et, and still,
the night wind stirs the trees on the hill."

ERLKING: "O come, dear boy, come you home with me,
where my daugh-ter waits you, a fair maid she,
with her sis-ters dan-cing the whole night long,
they'll rock you to sleep with their dan-cing and song."

CHILD: "My fa-ther, my fa-ther, O now see you not
the erl-king's daugh-ters in that dark spot?"

FATHER: "My son, my son, it is as I say;
'tis on-ly the wil-lows, old-en and gray."

ERLKING: "I love you so, and want you to go there with me,
and go you not wil-ling, by force let it be."

CHILD: "My fa-ther, my fa-ther, he gave me a blow;
Erl-king has hurt me and bids me go!"

NARRATOR: The fa-ther shud-ders, he rides fast and wild,
he holds yet tight-er his weak moan-ing child;
he reach-es home in fear and dread;
and in his arms there the child is dead!

Death and the Maiden, on a poem by M. Claudius, falls into two parts: the disturbed plaint of the maiden too young to die, sung in short rhythmic groups to agitated, somewhat chromatic, harmony; and the calm reassurance of death, sung almost in a monotone to more peaceful rhythm and harmony. Schubert

Fig. 45. Styles of lieder accompaniments: (a) *The Erlking;* (b) *Death and the Maiden* (Schubert)

used this same music as the theme of the theme-and-variations in the second movement of his *String Quartet in D Minor,* "Death and the Maiden" (Appendix II, No. 32,II). In Fig. 45 are quoted (a) the "galloping" figure in the piano accompaniment of *The Erlking,* and (b) the peaceful harmonies when death

speaks in *Death and the Maiden,* which harmonies also comprise
a brief prelude and postlude by the piano accompaniment.

THE VICISSITUDES OF OPERA

Opera (from *opera in musica,* a work in music) may be defined as drama intensified by music. However, during the so-
called "decadent" phases of opera history the emphasis has
shifted, at which times just the opposite, music intensified by
drama, might be a more accurate definition. The story of an opera
is called a *libretto.* Besides the actor-singers, an opera usually
calls for a conductor and full orchestra to accompany and play
independent instrumental music, including both the *overture*
and descriptive *interludes.* There may also be a mixed *chorus* and
a *ballet* corps.

Among the many types of opera three stand out in particular.
There is *grand opera,* a serious type that often ends tragically.
There is *comic opera,* distinguished not necessarily by comedy
but somewhat arbitrarily by the admission of occasional spoken
lines. Comic opera includes the farcical and satirical *ballad opera*
in England and *opéra-comique* in France, the *singspiel* (song
play) in Germany, and the more recent *operetta,* such as that
made popular by Gilbert and Sullivan. And there is *music drama,*
especially that of Wagner, in which all arts are meant to conspire
toward a "total art form" (*Gesamtkunstwerk*).

In this day of motion pictures, radio, and television the great
impact of opera over the last three-and-one-half centuries as a
main source of entertainment may not be readily appreciated.
The association of music and drama is very old, but opera proper
did not begin until around 1600, when some Italian humanists
created a new musical style out of what they meant to be an imitation of ancient Greek drama. That style was monody (p. 114;
Fig. 46c, p. 258), whose clear projection of the solo voice over a

realized thorough-bass was obviously better suited to dramatic recitation than Renaissance polyphony with its equalization and interweaving of several voices. After the middle of the seventeenth century, opera spread to France, Germany, and England, where Italian and indigenous styles eventually combined.

The tendency to emphasize the singing itself in Italian opera (Plate 16), causing the libretto and the organization of the musical "numbers" to become stereotyped, brought periodic reforms both deliberate, as by Gluck and Wagner, and inadvertent, as in *The Beggar's Opera* by Pepusch and Gay, and Pergolesi's *Servant as Mistress*. (For highly amusing accounts of the state of early eighteenth-century Italian opera be sure to read Joseph Addison's articles in *The Spectator* for March 6, 15, and 21, 1711, available in numerous reprints.) Mozart marks the culmination of eighteenth-century opera. Two other giants, Wagner and Verdi, both born in 1813, dominate Romantic opera, which eventually took a turn toward nationalism, especially in Russia, and realism, especially in France and Italy.

Hope that opera is not becoming an extinct art, as claimed by some, is seen in important new works of recent decades, such as those by Stravinsky, Hindemith, Berg, and Britten; in the astonishing success of a few composers like the Italian-born American Gian Carlo Menotti, several of whose operas, including *The Medium* and *The Consul* have "made Broadway," and one of which, *Amahl and the Night Visitors*, is known to all television viewers as an annual Christmas event; and in the rapid growth in this and other countries of excellent little "grass-roots" opera companies able to serve their communities as the innumerable European companies, at least one in every sizable city, have served in past centuries.

Here are some of the main names of opera history in chart form, listed by country of chief residence, along with one of the best-known operas by each:

Century	Italy	Germany	France	Other Country
17th	Monteverdi *Orfeo*		Lully *Atys*	
	A. Scarlatti *La Rosaura*			Purcell (England) *Dido and Aeneas*
18th				Handel (England) *Rodelinda*
	Jomelli *Fetonte*		Rameau *Castor et* *Pollux*	
		Mozart *Don Giovanni*	Gluck *Orfeo*	
19th	Rossini *Barber of* *Seville*	Weber *Der Freischütz*	Berlioz *The Trojans*	
	Verdi *Aïda*	Wagner *Tristan and* *Isolde*	Bizet *Carmen*	
	Puccini *La Bohème*	R. Strauss *Der Rosen-* *kavalier*		Mussorgsky (Russia) *Boris Godunov*
20th			Debussy	
		Hindemith *Cardillac*	*Pelléas et* *Mélisande*	Britten (England) *Peter Grimes*
		Berg *Wozzeck*	Milhaud *Christophe* *Colomb*	Menotti (America) *The Medium* Stravinsky (America) *The Rake's* *Progress*

CONFLICTS AND COMPROMISES INHERENT IN OPERA

Opera is a hybrid art. It actually embraces several arts, including vocal and instrumental music, literature, acting, dancing, costuming, and scene designing. This fact explains serious conflicts that must be solved or at least reconciled anew in each work.

In any case, one must accept the resulting unrealities or he cannot accept opera at all. Obviously, it is not real for a person to sing everything he says, or to stop in a tense moment and philosophize in an aria about what he is doing. Furthermore, the situations themselves are often implausible, the choruses and dances are sometimes introduced on the flimsiest of excuses, and the singers may look like anything but the parts they are playing. The story itself cannot have the continuity of real life or of a novel, but must be telescoped, even more summarily than in a drama, into a few main scenes. We can only say to all this that art has no obligation to be a photograph of real life.

The simple fact of cost is another problem posed by the complexity of opera. Try to calculate just what the performance of one opera costs the foremost United States company, The Metropolitan Opera Company of New York (and incidentally realize what a public service this company's long-time Saturday-afternoon radio broadcasts have been to the millions of devoted listeners on this continent!). Figure in some one hundred men in the orchestra, the conductor, the large chorus, the ballet corps, the prima donnas and other soloists, the lavish costumes and elaborate stage sets, and the many persons involved in getting all this together and ready. You will understand then why full-scale opera productions have had to be controlled by those who hold the purse strings, which may mean political censorship of tastes; a limited, shopworn repertoire because only the "successful" tried and true operas will satisfy the box office; productions only in large centers and the largest halls; and the necessity for hiring only "name" artists who are sure to sell well (even prompting some American singers to change to the greater glamour of an Italian name). One must regret that even those outstanding opera productions adapted to television, complete with fresh translations into English, have been so few and far between because of high costs.

Another factor delimiting opera repertoire is the story, which is likely to become dated and untimely much sooner than the music. Except on college campuses, operas that come from before Mozart's time are rarely performed now. The first century-and-a-half of opera was devoted mainly to the subjects of ancient Greek drama, whereas Menotti today writes a timely opera, *The Consul,* about the tragedy of a family trying to escape from behind the Iron Curtain. Although the subject matter of Greek drama is often timeless and universal, the same cannot be said for its dubious rehashing in many librettos. To be sure, the much-done story of how Orpheus won back his Eurydice through song, and in some versions lost her again, is a "natural" for opera. But the stories that wear the best seem to be the simple earthy plots of the comic operas. Always fresh is the story of the pert young servant girl who announces that she is quitting just when her master needs her most; after threats, cajolery, and all other inducements fail he finally asks her to marry him, which is what she had sought in the first place (Pergolesi's *Servant as Mistress,* 1733). And always fresh is the story of how some grasping nephews, cousins, and in-laws connive to get the will changed of their newly deceased relative, a rich old man who had left everything to charity—only to discover that the unscrupulous attorney whom they hire proceeds to will everything of importance to himself (Puccini's *Gianni Schicchi,* 1918). Or to single out another among several choice comedies of the twentieth century, in *L'Heure espagnole* by Ravel (1911) the zany intrigue in a clock-maker's shop never fails to bring its audiences to uproarious laughter.

A further problem of opera for us is the matter of translation into English. This is not so easy as you might suppose. Unless the translator is very skillful and imaginative he writes stilted English, or distorts the sense beyond recognition, or reaches climaxes on weak words like "the" and "and" ("to the eternal Honour of our English Particles," as Addison wryly observed), or changes the vowels on tones in extreme ranges to other vowels that cannot be sung well in that range. Furthermore, we have seen that language traits are intimately bound up with melodic traits (p. 160). A lyrical melody designed for the liquescence of Italian speech may bump along when clipped English words are fitted to it. Yet a growing number of protesters declare that "opera in English" must come if opera in English-speaking countries is to survive. Of course, the metaphysical ruminations such as Wagner often writes, especially those sung during rich orchestral passages, are not likely to be caught by the listener regardless of the language.

Actual *conflicts* in opera arise from the mixture of such different arts as drama and music. Or rather, these arts do not mix any more than oil and water do. The history of opera has been the history of how the conflicts between them have been reconciled though never solved. It is interesting to note in this connection how few are the composers who have been their own librettists, as have Wagner and Menotti, and how often there has been inequality or friction between librettist and composer. Two main conflicts are inherent in the mixture of drama and music.

1. Action tends to be continuous; music needs to repeat (p. 151). The traditional way of meeting this problem halfway has been to alternate sections of action, in which the music is reduced to *recitative*, with sections of musical *arias*, in which the action is reduced to commentaries and contemplation. Recitative is speech sung in a declamatory manner, constantly modulatory, narrow in melodic range, free in rhythm rather than bound to regular meter or phrases, and *syllabic* (one note to a syllable) rather than *melismatic* (more than one note to a syllable). It is accompanied by only occasional chords in *dry* or *secco* fashion or by a more consistent texture in *accompagnato* fashion that brings it closer to the tangible phrase grouping of the aria, or what is often called an *arioso*. The *arias* have all the rhythmic and tonal stability of hierarchic designs, whether A-B-A, A-B, or some "intuitive" form (p. 182). In Fig. 46 are the beginnings of a recitative melody and an aria melody, both from

Fig. 46. Vocal styles in Classic and Baroque opera: (a) recitative and (b) aria (Mozart, *Don Giovanni*), (c) air (Lully, *Armide*, I)

Mozart's great tragicomedy, *Don Giovanni,* and an "air" with thorough-bass from Lully's *Armide.*

There have been other ways of meeting this same conflict. Thus, an even greater division is made between action and music in the singspiel and operetta, which use spoken dialog for the action and only *numbers* (arias and other complete forms) for the music. A certain compromise is found in the strophic plan which permits new words in each verse while the music repeats, as happens in Mozart's popular singspiel, *The Magic Flute.* In later opera, especially that of the "reformers," the continuity of action often takes precedence over numbers. The desire for unbroken continuity led to Wagner's *endless melody,* which is melody that flows on and on rather than coming to final cadences at the ends of phrase or even broader groupings. Debussy virtually eliminates numbers in the vocal portions of *Pelléas et Mélisande.* Even the orchestral interludes in this opera, which do have an independent musical interest, serve primarily to maintain continuity by bridging the gaps from one scene to the next. On the other hand, Verdi still bows to the distinction between aria and recitative, although he goes a long way toward concealing that distinction in his later operas. In these he keeps the music going between numbers, and he does so by substituting meaningful, thematically related "joints" for those full cadences and obvious *vamps* that characteristically announce the arias in earlier Verdi masterpieces such as *La Traviata.* (A vamp is a measure or so of um-pah-um-pah or similar introduction played by the orchestra as the singer clears his throat and steps forward to sing his aria.)

This conflict of form is most nearly resolved when the structural means of the music is primarily motivic, as it often is in Wagner's and Puccini's operas. Then the need for repetition in the music is satisfied by the recurring motive, while the cursive style that naturally results is compatible with the continuousness of the action.

2. With regard to the other main conflict, much less time is ordinarily required to stage or relate the action than to work up appropriate emotional support for it in the music. A well-known illustration is provided by comparing the ways that the chief characters declare their love at climactic moments in the great love operas of Debussy (*Pelléas et Mélisande*) and Wagner (*Tristan and Isolde*).

Debussy, giving precedence to the action, drops out all accompaniment and accomplishes his aim with three short words on three soft repeated tones. Wagner, giving precedence to the music, works the orchestra into a frenzy lasting nearly ten long minutes while the characters can do little more than stand facing each other. Thus, Wagner's compromise (probably unwitting, in view of his avowed emphasis on the drama) was to slow down the action. In any case, his operas have been called symphonic dramas because the musical continuity is maintained more by the orchestra and by its web of *leitmotifs* (recurring motives, linked with characters, things, or ideas) than by the voices, which may occur only intermittently and be treated as integral instruments in the orchestra. Among other favorite ways in opera of "stretching out" the words to the slower pace of music are the illogical but vocally acceptable device of repeating the same phrase of text several times, and the use of melismatic writing with many notes to a syllable.

Opera's delights

With so many problems and conflicts in its way, one marvels at the great success of this hybrid art. The answer lies in the unquestioned delights that opera affords. The masterworks manage to hold together remarkably well in spite of these problems and conflicts. Over and above whatever unity may result from the subject matter of the libretto, the music itself may hold together in several ways. First, the use of recurring motives, at least their use to identify characters, has been frequent in opera, although rarely integrated so completely as in Wagner's leitmotif technique. Wagner's all-embracing climaxes characteristically save the fullest, most satisfying statement of important motives until the peak of interest in the story, somewhere near the end (p. 112). Second, the overture (or overtures to more than one of the acts) often gives a kind of précis of much of the musical material that is to figure in the opera. Third, the balance and order of solos, duets, larger soli and choral ensembles, dancing, orchestral interludes, and scene changes is ordinarily planned with great care from the standpoint of variety within unity. Especially note-worthy are the finales of the acts in the best Italian operas, which may build up to an almost symphonic climax through a quick, close-knit succession of increasingly lively numbers. Fourth, tonal unity is sometimes achieved throughout entire operas by the use of one main key as a point of departure and return. Handel and Mozart are among composers who have occasionally employed an over-all tonal plan. And fifth, completely integrated hierarchic designs may be found in Wagner's lengthy, mature operas, from the concept of the whole down to the minutest detail. At least that is the theory of the German scholar Alfred Lorenz, who has written four weighty volumes to establish his point. For example, the over-all plan of the three acts in *The Mastersingers of Nuremberg* proves to be A-A-B, thus a gigantic elaboration of the barform that had been used in the German minstrelsy of the six-teenth-century *Meistersingers* themselves.

At most a book can only itemize the delights of opera. Opera, clearly, must be seen and heard to be appreciated. No doubt there are many readers who have not yet had this opportunity. They will understand opera's lure better when they see and hear the uncommonly accurate characterizations in Mozart's *Marriage of Figaro*, the color and melody of Bizet's *Carmen*, Mimi's pathetic death and Rodolfo's grief in the last moments of Puccini's *La Bohème*, the mixture of broad humor and mellow philosophy in Wagner's *Mastersingers of Nuremberg* and Strauss's *Rosen-kavalier*, the good theater and elemental melodic strength in Verdi's *Rigoletto* and *Aïda*, the amazing adaptation of Shake-speare in the same composer's *Otello* (Appendix II, No. 39) and *Falstaff*, the clever buffoonery and sheer vocal pleasure in Ros-sini's *Barber of Seville*, the shattering psychological deteriora-tion of a good but simple man (amidst a veritable compendium of absolute musical forms) in Berg's Modern masterpiece *Woz-zeck*, and the vast scope and emotional sweep of Wagner's over-whelming tetralogy *The Ring of the Nibelung*.

SELECTED READINGS

Elisabeth Schumann, *German Song*. New York: Chanticleer, 1948.

James Husst Hall, *The Art Song*. Norman: University of Oklahoma Press, 1953.

"Song," article in *Grove's Dictionary of Music and Musicians,* 5th ed. New York: St. Martin's Press, 1954.

Donald Grout, *A Short History of Opera*. New York: Columbia University Press, 1947.

E. J. Dent, *Opera*. Baltimore: Penguin Books, 1940.

Ernest Newman, *Great Operas*, 2 vols. (of the stories and their backgrounds). New York: Vintage Press, 1958.

Ernest Newman, *The Wagner Operas*. New York: Alfred Knopf, 1949.

Irving Kolodin, *The Story of the Metropolitan Opera, 1883-1950*. New York: Alfred Knopf, 1953.

Joseph Kerman, *Opera as Drama*. Alfred Knopf, 1956.

Chapter 16

Sacred Choral Cycles Governed by Text

OFFICE AND MASS IN GREGORIAN CHANT

In this last chapter on musical forms we take up three great categories of sacred choral music, all products of Western Christianity. Each is represented in its broadest aspects by choral cycles made up of movements, acts, or other divisions that are largely governed in their forms by the nature and course of their sacred texts. One cycle is the Mass in the monophonic Gregorian chant of the Early Christian Era. Another is the polyphonic Mass, which flowered as a complete cycle rather late in the Medieval-and-Renaissance Era. And the third is the sacred oratorio and its variants, linked somewhat with the rise of opera at the onset of the Baroque Era.

Gregorian chant represents one of those basic literatures of music that have furnished Western civilization with inestimable funds of melody. In fact, it not only antedated but served as one source for the other literatures, including the treasures of minstrelsy, folk song, and the Lutheran chorale. Gregorian chant itself apparently traces back to Hebrew, Byzantine, and Greek sources. It is the chief variety of Western plainchant, another being Ambrosian chant, instituted by Saint Ambrose of Milan. Pope Gregory I, for whom it is named, may himself have had a share in selecting and classifying many chants from among the ones then in use.

The chants are divided between those of the Office and those of the Mass. The *Office* includes the prayers of the eight daily or canonical hours. Of the chants for the Office many are too elementary from a melodic standpoint to be of special musical interest. The chief exceptions are those for the matins and vespers, especially *Salve regina* (Hail, Queen) and three other so-called antiphons *B. V. M.* (Blessed Virgin Mary). The *Mass,* being the celebration of the Eucharist or Holy Communion, is the principal rite of the Roman Catholic Church and the occasion for most of the musically important chants.

A few words about the Roman Catholic Mass itself should help to clarify a form that has given rise to some of music's most inspired and beloved masterpieces. The Mass is celebrated daily by the priest, but the congregation does not regularly attend more than once a week. Certain portions of the Mass are repeated at every celebration of it. These fixed portions are known collectively as the *Ordinary.* The other portions vary from day to day according to whether that day is dedicated to some special feast, above all Christmas (from Christ Mass) and Easter; to some particular Saint, such as the Blessed Virgin Mary; or to some group of Saints, such as the Apostles or Confessors. These variable portions are known collectively as the *Proper.*

At least in a figurative sense, the parts or "steps" of the ceremony represent the altar steps leading up on the left or Gospel side to the paten and chalice, containing the bread and wine that are said to be changed into the Body and Blood of Christ, and down again on the right or Epistle side for the taking of Communion. The Low Mass is usually spoken throughout, both in the Ordinary and the Proper portions, while the High or Solemn Mass includes singing as well as speaking. Here is the usual sequence of the High Mass, including some parts that have varied in different eras. The parts of the Ordinary are italicized and all the sung parts are asterisked:

Prayers at foot of the altar
*Introit (beginning)
*Kyrie eleison (Lord, have mercy) ·
*Gloria in excelsis Deo (Glory be to God on high)
 Collect (prayers before the Epistle)
 Epistle (lesson from the Scriptures)
*Gradual (chant originally sung from altar steps) and
*Alleluia (praise ye the Lord) or
     *Tract (Scriptural verses sung on graver days)
 Gospel (one of the four Gospels, selected for the day)
*Credo in unum Deum (the Nicene Creed)
*Offertory (offering of bread and wine to God)
 Lavabo (recited as the priest washes his hands)
 Secret (low-spoken prayer before the Preface)
*Sanctus, Sanctus, Sanctus (Holy, Holy, Holy—the end
     of the Preface)
 Canon (doctrine of the "sacrifice")
 Pater Noster (the Lord's Prayer)
 Fraction (breaking of the bread before Communion)
*Agnus Dei (Lamb of God, prayer of sacrifice)
 Pax (kiss of peace)
*Communion (partaking of the Eucharist)
 Postcommunion (prayers after Communion)
*Ite missa est (congregation dismissed, from which the
     Mass gets its name) or
     *Benedicamus Domino (Let us praise the Lord)
 Last Gospel (final part, usually from John i. 1-14)

In summary, the sung parts include five or six in the Ordinary:
Kyrie, Gloria, Credo, Sanctus, Agnus Dei, and sometimes Ite
missa est or Benedicamus Domino; and five in the Proper: Introit, Gradual, Alleluia, Offertory, and Communion.

The chief musical interest in the monophonic Mass of the
Early Christian Era lies in the many varied chants of the Proper,
which are generally richer and far more numerous than those of

the Ordinary. They are richer especially in the sense that they tend to be melismatic, sometimes extremely florid, whereas those of the Ordinary tend more toward the syllabic style (p. 257; Appendix II, No. 40). Most of the chants are settings of Biblical prose texts from the Scriptural Psalms and the great canticles such as the Magnificat, a fact that is consistent with their wonderfully subtle and plastic rhythm (insofar as scholars understand and agree on this rhythm). The forms of the chant are chiefly additive, or strophic, or hierarchic to the extent of being loose but fairly extended rondo designs. With regard to scale structures, the Medieval-and-Renaissance church modes (p. 67) are already present if not fully assimilated in Gregorian chant.

It is significant that the Latin metrical hymn, with its several verses, was only a peripheral development throughout the great flowering of Gregorian chant. This flowering declined rapidly when regular meters were imposed. Among the latest chants to be retained by the Church were five rhymed *sequences* dating from the eleventh to the thirteenth centuries. The sequence originated as a new text set in metrical, syllabic style to the long florid "melisma" or "jubilus" that was vocalized on the final "-a" in an Alleluia (Appendix II, No. 41). The oldest of these, the Easter sequence *Victimae paschali laudes* (*Praise to the Easter Victim*), is well known (p. 75). Even better known is *Dies irae* (*Day of Judgment;* Fig. 47c; Appendix II, No. 42), which has been used repeatedly in music about death (as in works by Berlioz, Liszt, Saint-Saëns, and Rachmaninoff). The last sequence to be adopted officially in the Roman Catholic liturgy (1727) was the *Stabat Mater* (*There Stood the Mother*), well known in the settings of Rossini, Dvořák, and several others. Credit for important restorations of Gregorian chant, after several centuries of serious misconceptions, goes primarily to the Benedictine monks of Solesmes in France, whose official *Editio Vaticana* was prepared early in the present century.

Fig. 47 illustrates three types of Gregorian chant, both in the square notation on a four-line staff that is now generally used for this music, and in the rhythm usually employed when this chant is transcribed to our conventional staff notation. Note that the C

Fig. 47. Types of plainchant: (a) syllabic ("Gloria" from the Ordinary of the Easter Mass *Lux et origo*), (b) melismatic (Alleluia, "Ascendit Deus" for the Ascension), (c) sequence ("Dies Irae" for the Requiem Mass) (p. 5,* 265, and 97,* respectively, in *Graduale Romanum*, Paris, 1924, reproduced by permission of Desclée & Cie., Tournai, Belgium)

clef locates middle C on each four-line staff (p. 69). The note that is actually square-shaped is called a *punctum*. When a dot follows a note here the value of the note is doubled. The lower punctum is sung first when it is directly under another one. In

(b) the heavy diagonal line is part of a three-note group (*liga-ture*), as the conventional notation indicates. The saw-toothed and the littlest notes are thought to call for certain expressive and ornamental styles in singing. Rhythmic incises of two or three notes (p. 148) are indicated in the Solesmes manner by a short vertical line or a horizontal dash over or under the first note of such a group.

THE POLYPHONIC MASS AND REQUIEM

Polyphonic settings of the Mass are chiefly devoted not to the Proper, as were the monophonic Masses in Gregorian chant, but to the five or six parts of the Ordinary. Composers appear to have found more satisfaction in composing works that would be per-formed regularly, not merely on infrequent special occasions. In the Renaissance Masses, which comprise much the largest litera-ture of the polyphonic Mass, the separate parts or movements generally follow the procedure of the motet. Occasionally each of these movements is based on a plainchant of the same name (Kyrie, and so on). More often all the movements of the Mass are bound together by a recurring melody in long notes that runs through the tenor voice line or weaves in and out of the several voices like a colored thread. Here was a certain precedent for both the recurring melodic line in variations (p. 188) and the nine-teenth-century cyclical treatment in sonata cycles (p. 223). The melody or "cantus firmus" (p. 190) used in the Mass was usually borrowed from sacred or secular sources, but was sometimes in-vented by the composer. Many Renaissance Masses are named according to this melody—for example, Josquin Des Prés' *Missa "L'Homme armé"* on a very popular French folk song, or Pales-trina's *Missa Ut re mi fa sol la* on six tones of the scale.

Although the Mass has been cultivated much less since 1600, there have been several masterworks of the first order, including Bach's *Mass in B Minor*, Mozart's incomplete *Mass in C Minor*, K. 427, Haydn's "Nelson" *Mass in D Minor*, Beethoven's *Missa solemnis in D Major*, Schubert's *Mass in A-flat Major*, Liszt's "Graner" *Missa solemnis in D Major*, Bruckner's *Mass in F Minor*, and the powerful Modern *Mass* by the Frenchman Poulenc. These are all large-scale works carefully planned for overall balance and integration. Among their movements are frequent choral fugues, which are the mainstay of the later Mass, although Bach's successors seem somewhat formal and stiff in their polyphonic writing by comparison with his incomparably fluent yet sinewy style. There are occasional reversions to the motet type of movement, too. And, on the other hand, there are newer forms of a symphonic nature, including variation forms, hierarchic designs such as A-B-A and rondo, and even approximations of the "sonata-allegro" form.

Bach's own great *Mass in B Minor*, a work that alone would justify his pre-eminent place in the whole history of music, may serve as our chief example here (Appendix II, No. 43). This *Mass* generally adheres to the Roman Catholic form with Latin text, although as a Protestant writing for Protestant worship Bach could not help introducing certain minor adjustments of the text and form, and certain melodies and symbolisms that linked with his own Lutheran tenets. Typically for Bach, several of the sections were actually reworkings of parts from cantatas that he had written earlier. Since the *Mass in B Minor* lasts some three hours, it cannot be given in its entirety in any liturgy. Bach himself led only separate movements in performance. By expanding each movement of the Ordinary so that it divides into several sections, he provides twenty-four sections in all. For example, the *Credo* movement divides into eight separate sections, which begin (translated):

> "I believe in one God"
> "The Father Almighty"
> "And in one Lord, Jesus Christ"
> "And was incarnate"

"And was crucified"
"And the third day he rose again"
"And I believe in the Holy Ghost"
"I acknowledge baptism . . . Amen."

Among the sections, six are solo arias with violin, "corno di caccia," or "oboe d'amore" obbligato; three are solo duets; and the remaining fifteen are choruses in four to six parts. All the movements have orchestral accompaniments. Choruses, solos, and duets alternate in skillful contrasts. They are variously resounding, tender, tragic, joyous, anguished, confident, and calm, revealing seemingly endless resources of style, depths of expression, and strength. Compare the subject of the highly chromatic fugue in the second "Kyrie" (Fig. 48a; Appendix II, No. 43a)

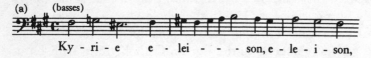

Fig. 48. Contrasting styles in Bach's *Mass in B Minor*: (a) chromatic fugue subject ("Kyrie eleison," No. 3), (b) diatonic fugue subject ("Gratias agimus," No. 6)

with that of the thoroughly diatonic fugue "Gratiamus agimus" from the *Gloria* movement (Fig. 48b; Appendix II, No. 43b). (The latter subject has an especially telling entry when the high "Bach trumpet" states it as a separate, fifth "voice" at two climactic moments in the fugue.) Listen to the heartfelt supplication at the words "miserere nobis" ("have mercy upon us") in "Qui tollis" from the *Gloria* movement (Appendix II, No. 43c). Hear the unshakable faith conveyed by "Credo in unum Deum" (Appendix II, No. 43d), with its use of a strongly modal Gregorian chant; and the symbolical use of the canon for soprano and alto in "Et in unum Deum" (Appendix II, No. 43e) to represent both the oneness and separateness of the Father and the Son. What could be more sorrowful than "Crucifixus" (Fig. 43f, p. 243) from the *Credo* movement, a passacaglia on a descending chromatic bass that recurs thirteen times and gives way to a completely transfigured final cadence? Follow the punctuating octave skips in the bass line and the reverberating, rocking triplets that answer in the women's voices at the opening of "Sanctus" (Appendix II, No. 43g). And hear the tender interchanges of the solo violin obbligato and solo alto voice in "Agnus Dei" (Appendix II, No. 43h).

As a complete cycle, Bach's *Mass in B Minor* is unified mainly by a balance of alternating styles in the individual sections; by adherence to the tonal centers of B minor and D major, with all sections in these or nearly related keys, only; by the repetition of one fugue (nos. 6 and 24), tending to "close" off the Mass; and, of course, by the meaning and the organizing influence of the Ordinary itself. Bach conceived this Ordinary in a larger plan of two parts, with the Kyrie and Gloria in Part I, and the Credo, Sanctus, and Agnus Dei in Part II.

The *Requiem* is a special Mass for the Dead, represented by a small but important literature paralleling that of the regular Mass. It differs from the usual sequence of the Mass in discarding those movements that rejoice (especially the Gloria, Credo, and Alleluia), and adding the somber Tract and Dies irae (Fig. 47c, p. 267). Polyphonic settings of the Requiem ordinarily include the appropriate movements of the Proper as well as the Ordinary, although variations in the text and musical content are greater than in the usual Mass.

The Requiem figures in concert performance more than the usual Mass, chiefly owing to the generally shorter length and to the greater accessibility of its contents to choruses as well as audiences. The Dies irae has had an especially strong appeal, both because of the Medieval sequence that is still chanted in some Requiems and because of further affecting elaborations of this text, including "Tuba mirum" ("O wondrous Trumpet"), "Rex tremendae" ("Lord of Majesty"), and "Lacrymosa" ("Day of Weeping"). Among Requiems most performed are those by Mozart, Berlioz, Verdi, Fauré, and Brahms. Mozart's *Requiem in D Minor* was left not quite complete, and is performed in the version finished by his student Süssmayr. Verdi's *Requiem,* written after the Italian novelist Manzoni died, is remarkably operatic in character. Brahms' *German Requiem,* composed at the time of his mother's death, departs completely from the movements of the Mass, using other passages freely chosen from the Scriptures in the vernacular.

ORATORIO, PASSION, AND CANTATA

Oratorio stems from Medieval-and-Renaissance sources, among which were the liturgical dramas, the mysteries, and the Roman "orations" conducted in the manner of Salvation Army gatherings. But oratorio proper did not originate until after 1600, when it grew up alongside and sometimes inseparably from opera. It may be loosely defined as sacred opera, provided important typical distinctions are borne in mind. The oratorio is generally performed as a concert work in church or elsewhere, not acted out with costumes and stage sets. Since whatever action the libretto may contain cannot be seen, this action is often related by a *narrator,* who sings chiefly in the recitative style that is used to accompany or relate action in opera. Thus, oratorio must achieve its dramatic representation by direct appeal to the imagination of the listener. The *chorus,* which is often slighted if not omitted outright in opera, becomes one of the main vehicles of expression in oratorio, functioning as "the ideal observer" while the subject matter progresses.

Otherwise, oratorio has generally employed all of the musical apparatus of opera—the soloists, orchestra, recitatives, arias, and ensembles. By comparison with opera's greater preponderance of soloists and soli ensembles, and the Mass's greater preponderance of choral groupings, oratorio usually strikes a rather even balance between all vocal mediums. As in opera, oratorio begins with an orchestral overture. Stylistically its development has paralleled that of opera insofar as the same forms are used. However, the religious nature of most oratorios has tended to keep them on a steadier course in music history. They have been less involved in the endless controversies that have beset opera throughout its history and they have not tended to date quite so quickly. Also, the fact that the action in an oratorio libretto is usually of a much quieter sort than in opera means that the total form of an oratorio is determined more by purely musical considerations.

The chief subjects of oratorio are the familiar stories of the Bible, including apocryphal stories; and the lives and works of saints (hagiology), prophets, and other sacred persons. *Jephtha* by the seventeenth-century Italian Carissimi is an example of the first type, and *The Legend of Saint Elizabeth* by Liszt an example of the second type. A special class of oratorio is the *Passion*, dealing chiefly with any of the Gospel narratives of the final events in Christ's life. Two outstanding works in this class are *The Seven Last Words of Christ* by the seventeenth-century German Heinrich Schütz and Bach's *Saint Matthew Passion*. The latter contrasts diametrically with Bach's *Mass in B Minor*, for it is an extremely subjective, searching work, with expressive solos, both arias and recitatives; abrupt dramatic effects, including sudden ejaculations of the chorus; intimate characterizations of both soloists and chorus; and the use of recurring chorales.

The *cantata* bears a relationship to oratorio about like that of the short story to the novel. It is generally on a smaller scale in length, in the size of its forces, and in the scope of its subject. However, though there have been relatively few secular oratorios, there have been many secular cantatas (including both the "Wedding Cantata" and the burlesque "Coffee Cantata" of

Bach). In fact, the cantata began in early seventeenth-century Italy as a secular chamber work in monodic style, characteristically a short set of variations for but one voice over a recurring thorough-bass (although Carissimi's cantatas are freer in form). The French cantata was still primarily a secular, solo, chamber work in the early eighteenth century (as by Rameau). But the German cantata, especially under Bach and his immediate predecessor Buxtehude, became mainly a church work. Bach's nearly two hundred extant cantatas, out of some three hundred that he wrote for more than five years of Sundays and other special days, form the single greatest contribution to the cantata literature. Among the best known of these are *Sleepers, Wake!* (Appendix II, No. 27), *A Mighty Fortress Is Our Lord,* and *Christ Lay in the Bonds of Death.*

All three of the cantatas just named have as their central theme the Lutheran chorale of the same name. The *chorale* was one of Luther's own contributions to the Protestant Church. His object was to provide an easily singable melody set to a text in the vernacular, so that the congregation could join in the devotional singing. A few of these melodies were newly composed, but many more were derived from folk songs or plainchants. They are characterized by strong simple rhythms; clear phrases ending on firm cadences, yet generally free of squareness; syllabic settings of the text; and diatonic melodies. The same melodies had been harmonized as chorales for almost two centuries before Bach wrote his harmonizations (p. 111) and chorale preludes (pp. 200–201). Many Bach cantatas center around a particular chorale, beginning with fugues, variations, and fantasias based on the chorale melody, and concluding with a simple, complete, harmonized statement of the chorale itself. In fact this principle may be observed not only in many other German cantatas of the Baroque Era but to a lesser extent in the contemporaneous German oratorio and Passion, too (as in Bach's *Christmas Oratorio* and *St. Matthew Passion*).

Except for the Lutheran chorale, the Protestant hymn has not commonly served as the central theme in sacred choral cycles. But it has held a key position in Protestant services since the publication of Calvinism's first complete Genevan Psalter (1562; the hundredth tune being none other than *Old Hundred*) and this country's own Bay Psalm Book (1640). Of course, the poetic depth and musical potentials of the Psalms have caused them to be set not only as simple hymns but in much more elaborate arrangements, especially Psalms 23 ("The Lord is my shepherd . . ."), 33 ("Rejoice in the Lord . . ."), 42 ("As the hart panteth . . ."), and 150 ("I will extol Thee . . ."). Actually the majority of hymns used so extensively in English and American Protestant services stem rather from the eighteenth-century English poets Isaac Watts, Charles Wesley, and William Cowper. Many of the hymns now sung in this country were either adapted or originally composed by that chief American music educator of the nineteenth century, Lowell Mason.

To return to the oratorio and cantata: perhaps because of their dramatic qualities and greater suitability to the concert hall, these forms, unlike the Mass, have continued to interest composers right up to the present day, including d'Indy, Walton, Pierné, Honegger, Hindemith, Bartók, Prokofiev, and Stravinsky. Very popular and effective have been Honneger's exotic *King David*, divided into the five stations of the Biblical hero's life; the equally exotic *Belshazzar's Feast* by Walton, with its large orchestra supplemented by two brass bands during the climactic approach to the handwriting on the wall and the fall of Babylon; Prokofiev's *Alexander Nevsky*, treating of a thirteenth-century Russian victory over German invaders; and Orff's "scenic cantata" *Carmina burana*, in which are set some of the hedonistic Medieval poems collected under that title. Three oratorios in particular are known and done the world over, year in and year out—Handel's *Messiah*, *The Creation* by Haydn, and Mendelssohn's *Elijah*. To take one of these, Handel's *Messiah* (Appendix II, No. 44) is the setting of selections freely compiled from both the Old and New Testaments by Handel's wealthy dilettante friend Charles Jennens. Jennens' libretto divides into the customary three parts, the meanings of which are subtle in this work. According to a recent interpretation by the Danish authority Jens Peter Larsen, *Part I* concerns the prophecy and recognition of God's plan to redeem mankind through the coming of Messiah, and divides into the "promise" (Nos. 2-12) and the "Christmas message" (Nos. 13-21). *Part II* concerns the accomplishment of redemption by the sacrifice of Jesus, mankind's rejection of God's offer, and mankind's utter failure to oppose the power of the Almighty, this part dividing into the "suffering and the deed itself" (Nos. 23-35), followed by the "announcement of victory and spreading of the Gospel" (Nos. 36-44). And *Part III* (Nos. 45-53) is not a "description of victory" (as often supposed) but a "hymn of thanksgiving for the final overthrow of Death." There is a narrator in *Messiah,* but the soloists are not identified as they are in *The Creation* and *Elijah.* Some idea of the contrasts, balance, close tonal organization, and general succession of events can be had from a list of the first nine "numbers" (p. 253) in *Part I.* Even in this partial listing can be seen the manner by which the oratorio is built up from cumulative groupings of the separate numbers, variously progressing from solo recitative to arioso, to aria, to small ensemble, to full chorus:

1. "Sinfonia," Grave and allegro moderato; E minor, **c** (four-four meter); French overture for orchestra alone (p. 210; Appendix II, No. 44a)
2. "Comfort Ye, My People," Larghetto; E major, **c**; arioso (cursive aria) for tenor solo (Appendix II, No. 44b)
3. "Every Valley Shall Be Exalted," Andante; E major, **c**; A-B-A aria for tenor solo (Appendix II, No. 44b)
4. "And the Glory of the Lord," Allegro; A major, $\frac{3}{4}$; in motet style, for chorus (Appendix II, No. 44c)

5. "Thus Saith the Lord of Hosts," Andante; D minor, **c**; recitative for bass
6. "But Who May Abide the Day of His Coming?" Larghetto and Prestissimo; D minor, $\frac{3}{8}$ and **c**; free rondo for bass solo
7. "And He Shall Purify the Sons of Levi," Allegro; G minor, **c**; fugue for chorus
8. "Behold! a Virgin Shall Conceive"; D major, **c**; recitative for contralto
9. "O Thou that Tellest Good Tidings to Zion," Andante; D major, $\frac{6}{8}$; free strophic aria for contralto followed by further strophes for chorus

All of the choruses in *Messiah* are in S. A. T. B. scoring except for one ("Lift up Your Heads") that calls for a second soprano part, too. There is only one ensemble, the duet "O Death, Where Is Thy Sting?" Singers relish this music and learn it with relative ease. (Every Welsh chorister has it memorized from beginning to end, says one commentator.) By comparison with Bach's choral writing this seems much less complex. Indeed, Handel and Bach are another of those composer pairs who seem to embrace the extremes of their era in their frequently opposite styles. They differ in almost everything except the fact that they were both born in Germany in 1685 and both went blind in later life. Handel, who trained under fine teachers, traveled widely, and never married, excelled in opera and oratorio, and reflected chiefly Italian influence. Bach, who virtually trained himself, traveled little, and fathered among many children five sons who became important musicians in their own right, excelled in almost all other Baroque forms, and reflected very cosmopolitan influences. Handel's style is generally simpler. The melodic lines are more often diatonic, with few jagged leaps. The harmony stays closer to the primary triads (p. 86); the polyphony is less dense, and the harmonic rhythm in it much slower, making for a generally more homophonic effect. Handel achieved grandeur in his own way, but never conceived on so large yet concentrated a canvas as that of Bach's *B Minor Mass.* He wrote complete fugues less often, and when he did write them they were looser and less developed in form, with less insistence on a single idea.

But none of these remarks is meant to the disadvantage of Handel's music. They concern those differences in style by which any composer achieves individuality of expression. There is strength in simplicity as well as complexity. This truth can be heard in the wonderfully serene and noble melody of "He Shall Feed His Flock" (Appendix II, No. 44e), a pastoral aria written in the easy-flowing twelve-eight meter of the *siciliano* dance; and in the wider-spaced, choral melody of "I Know That My Redeemer Liveth" (Appendix II, No. 44i). Strength in simplicity can be heard, too, in the spontaneous, telling entries and exclamatory words of the chorus "For unto Us a Child Is Born" (Appen-

(Andante)
bass solo (recitative)

and I will   shake,

Fig. 49. Word painting in Handel's *Messiah* (Part I, No. 5, "Thus Saith the Lord")

dix II, No. 44d), in the rhythmic verve of "And the Glory of the Lord" (Appendix II, No. 44c), and in the ceaseless drive of the short motive of two 16th- and two 8th-notes in the ever-popular "Hallelujah" chorus (Appendix II, No. 44h).

There is a particular charm in Handel's "coloratura" or florid melismatic passages on a sustained syllable. These coloraturas (or *roulades*) usually progress up or down the scale on a circular or zigzag melodic figure. Often they are employed as a means of word painting. A brilliant instance among many is the rise on the word "ex-alt- - - -ed" in "Every Valley Shall Be Exalted" (Appendix II, No. 44b). Another occurs with the word "shake- - - -"

in "Thus Saith the Lord" (Fig. 49), and many more occur in that amazing virtuoso aria for bass, "Why Do the Nations So Furiously Rage Together?" (Appendix II, No. 44g)

SELECTED READINGS

Marie Pierik, *The Spirit of Gregorian Chant*. New York: B. Humphries, 1939.

Willi Apel, *Gregorian Chant*. Bloomington: Indiana University Press, 1958.

Liber Usualis (the main present-day compilation of Gregorian chant), edited by the Benedictines of Solesmes. Tournai: Desclée, 1947.

Edward Dickinson, *Music in the History of the Western Church*. New York: Scribner's, 1950.

C. S. Terry, *Bach: the Mass in B Minor*. New York: Oxford University Press, 1949.

Edwin Liemohn, *The Chorale*, through 400 years of musical development as a congregational hymn. Philadelphia: Muhlenberg Press, 1953.

Robert M. Stevenson, *Patterns of Protestant Church Music* (with appendices on Catholic and Jewish liturgies). Durham: Duke University Press, 1953.

Jans Peter Larsen, *Handel's Messiah;* origins, composition, sources. New York: W. W. Norton, 1957.

Percy M. Young, *The Oratorios of Handel*. New York: D. Dobson, 1950.

R. M. Myers, *Handel's Messiah*. New York: Macmillan, 1948.

Winton Dean, *Handel's Dramatic Oratorios and Masques*. New York: Oxford University Press, 1959.

F. G. Edwards, *The History of Mendelssohn's "Elijah."* London: Novello, 1896.

Part V

Postlude

Chapter 17

The Pursuit of Music

AN IMPORTANT AMERICAN INDUSTRY!

We have concluded our survey of music itself. Let us take this final chapter to consider the pursuit of music on the American scene as an industry, a career, an artistic satisfaction, a means of recreation, and a challenge to education.

If all *employment* that directly affects music is considered, music qualifies as one of this country's major industries. Included are manufacturing, servicing, and handling of music instruments and accessory equipment; writing and publishing; entertaining by way of recordings, radio, television, movies, stage, dance hall, and restaurant; and both private and public teaching. The statistics are impressive. In the fifth edition of *Who Is Who in Music* (Chicago, 1951) nearly 5,000 leading composers, performers, teachers, and writers are singled out in this country. Also listed for this country are 106 societies and associations devoted to music, professional, educational, and amateur; 191 music periodicals; 184 (out of many more) educational institutions offering "majors" in music at college and/or graduate level; 1,196 music editors and/or critics on 926 United States and Canadian newspapers; 868 representatives and bookers of concert artists; 565 symphony orchestras, including 100 of major importance; 540 concert and/or marching bands exclusive of school and military units; 80 opera companies; some 130 piano manufacturers and 60 organ builders; 255 manufacturers of band

and orchestra instruments and accessories; 699 recording companies; and 1,522 music publishers.

The young man or woman who looks forward to a *career* centering around the actual performance of music has a number of possibilities to consider. As a musician, he (or she) may teach and coach individuals or classes, either independently or in some educational institution. He may perform as a solo recitalist or in an ensemble, whether in public or through such mediums as motion pictures, radio, or television. He may compose, arrange, or edit music for any of those mediums. He may write articles or books on music of a popular or scholarly nature, or he may serve as a music critic for a newspaper or magazine. And, finally, he may combine any of these, as do most musicians now in the field, whether by preference or out of necessity.

Teaching, both public and private, and performing in ensembles provide the largest number of jobs for musicians. According to a recent estimate there are some 55,000 teachers of piano alone in the country! On the other hand, arranging, directing, and composing for the most patronized mediums of music—recordings, motion pictures, radio, and television—offer the greatest potential pay. But the latter types of musical employment are relatively exclusive, since comparatively few, and only those "at the top," are needed to meet the aims of these consolidated, nationwide services. Performers in ensembles are paid pretty much according to supply and demand, with special premiums for the most skilled. Rarely does a solo recitalist make his living from public performances alone. Composers of serious art music have no illusions about being able to support themselves by royalties from the sale of published compositions. Even in the fields of jazz and light musical shows the percentage of real "hits" is very low indeed.

We are still a relatively young nation in the arts, but have reached the point in music where our best composers, performers, and writers command high international respect. In caliber of performance, manufacture, publication, and library facilities we rank with any other nation. Few orchestras abroad can match those of Boston, New York, and Philadelphia. Few opera companies can match the Metropolitan. Few libraries can match the Music Division of the Library of Congress in comprehensiveness and published materials. One explanation, of course, is that this country has been able to pay the prices of the best men and equipment.

Naturally, we must acknowledge that the riches of our musical life are concentrated in the large urban centers. Only New York and a few other large cities can afford the luxury of radio stations like WQXR, devoted almost entirely to art music. Music has always been first of all a product of urban societies. But radio and television, on the other hand, are helping to spread these advantages, at least in small amounts, to outlying areas. So is the lively recording industry, which enjoyed one big spurt in the late forties with the advent of the long-playing, microgroove recording, and another in the late fifties with the development of "stereophonic" and other new "hi-fi" equipment. And at the same time there has been a healthy growth of amateur community music groups throughout the country, fostered often by secondary schools and colleges. Among these groups are opera workshops, orchestras, discussion groups, composers' clubs, concert series, and so on. As both our urban and rural societies take to art music more and more, we come closer and closer to the point where we can say that this country has "arrived" musically.

"De gustibus non est disputandum"

Granted that we are producing this much music and attendant activity, how worth while is it in an artistic sense? We can agree at once that the standards vary between wide extremes, but we may not be able to agree at all on what *standards* should apply. The venerable Latin expression quoted at the head of this section, "There is no disputing tastes," means in effect that each man has a right to like what he pleases. Are there, then, no bases in music aesthetics for deciding between good and bad? This question arose earlier in connection with melody (p. 72). Possible clues to an answer lie in a still more venerable expression, a question posed by the ancient Greeks: Is beauty in the eye of the beholder or in the thing itself?

If beauty is in the thing itself, if the proverbial rose on the desert isle is beautiful even when it grows unseen, then there must be objective standards for beauty. So writers like Edmund Burke have assumed in their efforts to establish laws of "beautiful" proportion in form (*The Sublime and the Beautiful*), and more methodical aestheticians, such as Schillinger, who have tried to find mathematical laws (pp. 102–103).

But Mr. Average Man may still insist that he likes what, and only what, he pleases. Thus arises an alternative clue. If beauty is in the eye of the beholder, if the rose is only beautiful when it is seen by an approving eye, then there must be subjective standards. Only with the twentieth-century advances in psychology has it become possible to investigate these standards in even a partly scientific manner. Men like Freud have shown how greatly our likes and dislikes can be influenced unconsciously by past associations. A melody may appeal strongly because it happens to resemble another played some time ago at a dance that left pleasant memories. In an opposite way a rhythm or harmony may strike the listener as strangely distasteful.

Undoubtedly both the objective and the subjective considerations influence taste. But what happens when two persons find themselves in complete disagreement as to which is the "better," say, between Bach's "Little" *Fugue in G Minor* and Irving Berlin's "White Christmas"? One argues that Bach's music has lived much longer and the other answers that Berlin's has sold many more copies than Bach's will ever sell. One points to the rich complexity of Bach's music and the other to the simple songfulness of Berlin's, and so on. If there is no absolute standard for an evaluative comparison of like works of art, there can certainly be none for these, since the real difficulty here lies in trying to compare unlike things. One might just as well try to compare pencils and trays.

Bach's and Berlin's pieces differ basically in function. A Bach fugue is *art music*, designed primarily to convey an aesthetic message from composer to listener. It is ideal in the concert hall, but of questionable value on the dance floor. A Berlin song is *social music*, designed primarily for social dancing and light entertainment. It may serve well on the dance floor and in a tune show, but not in the concert hall. In spite of its fetching melody it necessarily complies so exactly with the standardized design of all commercial dance music that it cannot offer that prime interest of any art, a form flexible enough to exploit the structural tendencies of its contents. Of course, the same man can very well like the music of Bach and the music of Berlin, each according to its function and place. But do you see, for example, why the familiar antonyms "classical" versus "popular" are misleading for more than one reason, and why such antonyms as "art" and "social" may be preferable?

Besides the question of absolute standards in taste there is the matter of *cultivating taste*. Taste is developed and refined by experience and knowledge. The novice complains that all music sounds about the same to him in quality; he cannot tell the differences. Actually, his ears take in everything that reaches the trained listener, but he has not yet learned to sort out the various elements of music. In fact, he may respond just as much emotionally, provided the idiom itself is not foreign to him, but he has yet to experience the intellectual pleasure of knowing what he is hearing. To experience that pleasure is the principal reason why one reads a book of this sort.

THE EVALUATION OF MUSIC AND PERFORMANCE

Let us take for granted that our novice wants to partake consciously of music and that he is not satisfied simply to bask in its sound or keep it going merely to still the silence, as it were. Once he does begin to develop an awareness of the make-up of music he should encourage himself to form evaluations of his own, which are the right and privilege of every art appreciator. In so doing, he must steer between two opposite but equally disturbing courses, one being an unnecessary timidity about expressing himself and the other being the sort of hasty, rash judgment that would rock a knowing listener on his heels.

Evaluation implies not only knowledge and experience but some of those intangibles of art that cannot be put down in a book. However, let us see if some sample guides can be formulated at least for intelligent, independent observation of art music, starting first with the nature of the music itself and later turning to the character of the performance. Our method will be the systematic one mentioned in Chapter 1, that of dividing and conquering. Several sets of questions follow. These are representative but, naturally, not all-inclusive. The first four sets concern the ways that the separate elements of music are treated, while the remaining two are intended to get at the broader aspects of form. Try subjecting an unfamiliar work to these questions, preferably a short, simple one at first. You will find this sort of artistic sleuth work to be challenging, provocative, and rewarding. By referring to the historical charts in Chapter 2, which should have considerably more meaning for you by now, you can help to keep the styles, forms, and eras oriented. You may celebrate your admission into the fraternity of educated laymen when, upon hearing an unfamiliar piece, you can respond, "I do not recognize the actual piece, but such-and-such styles and structural methods suggest not that but this era and, in fact, not that but this composer."

1. Starting with *rhythm* (Chap. 4), can you detect a regular pulse? If so, do the pulses group in meters that are more or less regular in the manner of verse, or so irregular as to go on much as prose does? If the meter is regular, is it monotonously so, or is it varied and enlivened by syncopations, accents on weak beats, dissonant suspensions, and sufficient freedom from squareness in the phrase structures? Do the note values fall into perceivable patterns, made distinguishable by dotted notes, triplets, ties, rests, short and long notes, or other rhythmic identification? Is the rhythmic excitement maintained at the same level or does it build up through livelier patterns, shorter note values, and faster tempo?

2. With regard to *melody* (Chap. 5), do the one or more lines fall into perceivable pitch patterns? Are these patterns fragmentary in the manner of motives or more complete in the manner of phrases? (This question, like many other aspects of melody, involves rhythm, too.) Are the patterns generally stepwise or disjunct? Are they generally diatonic or chromatic? If there is an extended melody, does it divide into clear phrases or is it spun out "endlessly"? Is its contour broad and smooth, or is this contour characterized by many shifts of direction? How does the melody tally with the four generalizations that were made about melodic tendencies (p. 73)?

3. With regard to *harmony* (Chap. 6), do the simultaneous tones group into intelligible chords? If so, can a polarity between consonance and dissonance be sensed in these chords? Is the harmonic movement of the simple, fundamental, diatonic sort that suggests the use mainly of primary triads, or can chromatic, substitute, and other chords of unusual color or force be detected? Is the harmonic rhythm slow or fast? Does the music seem to modulate constantly, or to remain on one broad tonal plateau at a time?

4. If the music is not monophonic, is the *texture* predominantly homophonic, monodic, or polyphonic (Chap. 7)? If it is homophonic, can the accompaniment be distinguished as block chords, arpeggios, Alberti bass, or other style? If it is polyphonic, are the lines separately discernible? Can the separate lines be heard to converge at moments of dissonant suspensions? If the music is scored for an ensemble, do the instruments and/or voices combine in balanced sonorities? Do they perform as one complete unit or are they opposed singly and in

choirs? Are the separate instruments exploited for their individual timbres? Does sonority for its own sake become a main consideration in the listening experience?

Now, before going on to the questions about form it may be well to recall the different structural tendencies that follow upon the use of a clear motive or a clear phrase as the basic generator of form (pp. 138–150). These tendencies may be summarized in a simple chart:

Generator	*Texture*	*Progression*	*Meter*	*Harmonic rhythm*	*Tonality*	*Theme structure*	*Form*
motive	polyph-ony	motivic play	irregular	fast	constant flux	mono-thematic	cursive
phrase	homoph-ony	phrase grouping	regular	slow	broad plateaus	poly-thematic	hier-archic

5. With regard to the style of *progression* (p. 140) can you hear a characteristic motive repeated often by means of the sequences or interchanges that constitute motivic play? Or do you hear complete phrases in question-answer or other complementary relationships that qualify as phrase groupings?

6. If the progression is by *motivic play* (Chap. 9), can certain typical procedures be observed that associate with a particular type of form—for example, the successive points of imitation of a motet, the alternations of expositions and episodes in a fugue, or the over-all ||:A:||:B:|| design of a Baroque dance? If the progression is by *phrase grouping* (Chap. 10), can you hear complementary groupings within larger complementary groupings up to the broadest hierarchic level of an A-B, A-B-A, rondo, or other design? If the form appears to be a series of variations (Chap. 11), can you discover a constant factor—a recurring bass line, harmonic pattern, or melody? If you are hearing a cycle of movements (Chaps. 12 and 13), can you determine what factors provide contrast between them, such as change of key, tempo, or character; and what factors may bind them together, such as thematic interrelations or programmatic continuity?

While the foregoing questions should help to sharpen your observation of musical processes and forms, please remember that they are only guides. As has been stressed on several previous occasions, music is not and must not be bound to rules. All forms do not fall into distinct categories so clearly, say, as Haydn's choral fugue "Achievèd is the Glorious Work" (Appendix II, No. 16) or Fauré's *Elégie* in A-B-A design (Appendix II, No. 19). You will find many borderline examples and overlapping of types for the very reason that each form is a particular structural result that may or may not be typical enough to qualify as a standardized design. Furthermore, some forms range beyond the usual tendencies of music's basic generators, subject perhaps to the fantasy of the composer or some programme he is following (Chap. 14). In any case, beware the urge to *force* forms into a particular mold merely for the satisfaction that comes with finding a classification. An author cannot escape that pitfall entirely, because he must organize his book into parts, chapters, and sections. But the human mind need not be restricted to such hard-and-fast compartmentizing.

With these cautions in mind we can purposely choose a borderline example to which to apply our questions briefly. Let us assume that one of the most convincing works by the Modern American composer Roy Harris, his *Third Symphony*, is unfamiliar to you, and sample the opening section of about four-and-a-half minutes (up to rehearsal no. 14 in the G. Schirmer "Study Score"). The answers are numbered not in order but to correspond with the foregoing paragraphs of questions.

1. The rhythmic pulse is regular but the meter is free in the manner of prose, without a strong sense of bar lines, patterns, or special rhythmic devices, yet with gradual increases in the tempo. 2. A single melodic line predominates, spun out almost without a break and kept very clear by its careful balance of conjunct and disjunct motion; it subdivides into fairly broad arches that are often similar but too freely varied to be grouped under the word "motive" or "pattern." 4. After a virtually monophonic beginning, this section starts unobtrusively to take on harmonic and polyphonic interest, develop-

ing bit by bit in this respect (toward a maximum in the later, dramatic, fugal section). 3. The harmonic combinations that result from the increasing polyphonic activity are not classifiable in traditional terms but do maintain, in relatively slow harmonic rhythm, a clear distinction between the tensions of dissonance and the relaxation of consonance. 4. With the increasing polyphonic activity the color of the lower strings, which open the *Third Symphony,* is gradually enhanced by the entries of woodwinds, brasses, and higher strings. 5. While the texture continues to be dominated by a single line, the section progresses by broad, free phrase groupings. 6. Taken by itself, this section is cursive in form (although its return near the end later gives the total work an integrated form).

Of course, partaking consciously of music does not preclude attention to something besides its construction. Remembering that music as a time art must be re-created with each *performance* (pp. 137–138), one can understand why the manner and quality of that performance should also be a matter of great interest to the listener. Furthermore, we all share a very human interest in seeing how successfully the performer manages to cope with the expressive and technical problems that a particular work may pose. There follow further sets of questions intended as sample guides to an independent evaluation of performance. Most of these questions concern matters that are vital to a convincing projection of the music, yet matters that so far refuse to be codified in any concrete fashion.

1. Is the *pitch* accurate, whether sung, bowed, or blown?
2. Is the quality of *tone* appropriate? Is it true to the nature of the instrument? Does it make excessive or faulty use of vibrato? Is it "placed" correctly in singing? Does it exceed or understate the capacity of the instrument? Is it steady at various ranges, at different levels of intensity, and during long-sustained tones?
3. Is the performer's physical agility adequate for the task at hand? Instrumental *technique* is much more a matter of skilled coordination than brute strength. Does the performer seem to be working too

hard for his results? Is he awkward in performance? Can he play clearly and up to speed? Is there a sense of headlong, uncontrolled rushing? Are crucial tones played "in the cracks" often (beyond what must be permitted any performer by way of human errors)?

4. Is the *memorizing* secure? This is the most terrifying aspect for performers who suffer from stage fright (which means virtually all performers).

5. With regard to *rhythm*, when the music contains distinctive patterns, such as those in dance music, are the values distinguished precisely? Is the meter projected with the necessary accents and grouping so that it conveys the sense of physical movement essential to all rhythm? Recalling the different physical movement associated with different tempos (p. 60), does the tempo *feel* right for the particular piece, place, and occasion? Do liberties in the prevailing tempo, such as rubato and accelerando, seem to reflect good artistic and stylistic judgment or distasteful distortions?

6. Is the outline of the *melody* contoured so that the melody can be perceived in its entirety? Such contouring depends primarily on working toward and away from one or more climactic points through gradations of intensity and tempo.

7. Is the *texture* appropriately clear or appropriately clouded (as in some Impressionistic music)? If it is homophonic, does the melody stand out sufficiently? If it is polyphonic, are the lines distinguishable? Is there a sensitivity to harmonic values—to dissonance and consonance, to unusual chords, to cadences and other strong harmonic movements? Such sensitivity is achieved, again, primarily through gradations of intensity and tempo. Is there a sensitivity to color values in the total sonority?

8. Is there an appreciation of *performance styles*? (This question may depend on a knowledge of *performance practices* in history that the layman does not have.) For example, are the niceties of execution observed, including staccato and legato, attack and release, and intonation? If present, are the ornament signs properly solved, such as that for a trill? Is the figured bass appropriately realized, or the cadenza appropriately improvised (or composed)? Is there a proper balance of instruments and/or voices in ensemble music? Is the choice of instruments correct, within reason, for the era concerned?

Thus, Bach's harpsichord music is now chiefly played on the piano for practical reasons, but there are many who prefer to hear it on the harpsichord when that is possible.

9. Does the performer show an awareness of the musical form? Are the entries of motives, subjects, or themes adequately pointed up by dramatic contrasts, metrical accents, projection in the texture, adjustments of tempo, and so on? Similarly, are larger divisions made clear? Is there a concept of the entire form, such as might be apparent in broad contrasts and long-range climaxes, or is the attention to interpretation limited to very local levels of the form?

10. Finally, does the performer inject too much of his own personality or does he fail to communicate his message sufficiently? Both extremes are very disturbing. We may have no interest in hearing So-and-So push Beethoven into the background in order to make known his own extraordinary ideas. On the other hand, the completely passive performer may do everything impeccably yet leave the audience cold for want of an independent personality.

IN SEARCH OF MUSICAL TALENT

The nature of *musical talent* is always a fascinating subject, touching as it does on the age-old question of environment versus heredity. Why could Yehudi Menuhin become a world-famous violinist well before he was ten years old while there are others who will never manage to carry a tune, much less play or sing musically? (Observe that keyboard prodigies are much rarer, for the reason that no half- and three-quarter-size pianos are made to fit a child's hand as violins are.) Or to take more average examples, why does John next door make better headway in music than Bill down the street?

On the side of heredity, psychologists have sought to define and measure what they argue to be inborn capacities, capacities that indicate not achievement but maximum potential. If their research is correct, their tests should apply with quite the same validity for musical novices and initiates. Perhaps you have had an opportunity to take one of the earlier and best-known series of tests, the *Seashore Tests of Musical Talent* (superseded in some respects and according to some authorities by the tests of Jacob Kwalwasser). These include six tests made up on recordings by means of laboratory instruments, each measuring only one variable—pitch, timbre, time, rhythm, loudness, and tonal memory. The author of these tests, the late Carl Seashore of the State University of Iowa, argued that each measures a specific physiological capacity. On the pitch test, for example, the listener attempts to say whether the second of two tones is higher or lower than the first, until the tones gradually get closer than his individual ear struture permits him to distinguish. The six tests mean six different things in music and cannot be averaged together. A person weak in pitch discrimination might be well advised to study a keyboard instrument if he wants to take up music, since the pitches are then predetermined for him. A person weak in timbre is likely to be less sensitive to varieties of tone color, say, in singing; and so on. Seashore has also developed a motor (or neural) test of technical (physical) speed capacities, in which is measured the number of times per second that the hand can tap, working from the wrist.

Of course, environment must figure in musical talent, too, as a sum of all those less tangible factors that make up drive, interest, persistence, and enthusiasm. The public schools know, for example, that the Seashore tests are no indication of how a child will apply his talent. Something further is needed where so much time, money, and equipment are involved if an undue turnover in the membership of school orchestras, bands, and choruses is to be avoided. A simple but effective method with students who volunteer for instruments, for example, is to put them on inexpensive flageolets for the first three months while they are learning the rudiments. In that much time it is rather easy to tell not only who learns to read and finger correctly, but such very practical matters as who remembers to bring his instrument and who keeps from fighting with the boy at the next stand.

Actually, you can estimate your own musicalness fairly well right now. Does music hold positive attractions for you? What classes of music appeal to you the most and what elements in the music? Are you one who likes to sing "around the house"? Do you retain tunes readily? Since repetition figures so importantly in music, the ability to remember a tune is obviously vital to intelligent listening. Are you one who can harmonize in a group that is singing community songs (as is always done in *Down by the Old Mill Stream,* for instance)? This talent indicates, of course, an alertness to harmony and texture. Do you keep step easily on the dance floor or in a marching group? That ability corresponds with fair reliability to a good sense of rhythm. In any event, remember that musical talent is the norm, not the exception. Otherwise, music would never have the universal appeal that it has (Chap. 1).

Modern education is doing more to discover and foster musical talent than ever before. Singing, playing, and music reading are all firmly established in the lower grades. Larger high schools have not only developed unprecedented bands, orchestras, and choruses in the last two decades, but many offer "majors" in music, including one or two years each of theory, history, appreciation, and applied music (private or class instruction in voice or an instrument). A vital stimulus has come from several large-scale, democratic, nonprofit organizations of, by, and for the teachers, students, and performers. Most of these organizations trace back to the Music Teachers National Association (founded 1876), followed by the National Association of Schools of Music, the Music Educators National Conference, the National Federation of Music Clubs, and certain more specialized groups like the National Association of Teachers of Singing and the National String Teachers Association.

As the statistics earlier in this chapter indicated, the number of colleges that offer "major" courses in music is also considerable. In place of the sugar-coated superficial course or two that used to be offered all too often as the sole musical fare, these courses now aim toward a solid foundation in the cultural and technical aspects of music. In place of the social glee clubs that seldom got beyond the musical requirements of *Bull Frog on the Bank,* current choral groups, orchestras, and bands come to grips with some of the world's most important and exciting music—operas, symphonies, oratorios, Masses, chamber music—of all eras.

A notable development of colleges and graduate schools in recent years has been the growth of interest in *musicology,* systematic research into all branches of musical learning (furthered by the American Musicological Society since 1934). Masters' and doctors' dissertations of high caliber have begun to appear that contribute valuably to a further understanding of music. Accompanying this trend has been the development of strong music libraries in universities, libraries made up of the great sets that have been devoted to single composers and national music cultures, books about music, recordings and listening equipment, plus microfilm, periodicals, reference books, and all the other treasures of present-day libraries.

Some of those who enjoy these important educational offerings will themselves participate in music as professionals. Many more will become the amateur practitioners and the enthusiastic listeners who support this most patronized of the arts, for they are now on the road to understanding music.

SELECTED READINGS

Gilbert Chase, *American Music,* from the pilgrims to the present. New York: McGraw-Hill, 1955.
P. S. Carpenter, *Music, an Art and a Business.* Norman: University of Oklahoma Press, 1950.
Gilbert Chase, *Music in Radio Broadcasting.* New York: McGraw-Hill, 1946.

Jacques Barzun, *Music in American Life*. Garden City: Doubleday, 1956.

Paul R. Farnsworth, *The Social Psychology of Music*. New York: Dryden Press, 1958.

M. D. Calvocoressi, *Musical Taste*. London: Oxford University Press, 1925.

Max Graf, *Composer and Critic*. New York: W. W. Norton, 1946.

Oscar Thompson, *Practical Musical Criticism*. New York: Witmark, 1934.

Roger Sessions, *The Musical Experience of Composer, Performer, Listener*. Princeton: Princeton University Press, 1950.

Marshall W. Stearns, *The Story of Jazz*. New York: Oxford University Press, 1956.

James Mursell, *The Psychology of Music*. New York: W. W. Norton, 1937.

Carl Seashore, *The Psychology of Music*. New York: McGraw-Hill, 1938.

Jacob Kwalwasser, *Exploring the Musical Mind*. New York: Coleman-Ross, 1955.

Hazel Nohavec Morgan (ed.), *Music in American Education*. Chicago: Music Educators National Conference, 1955.

Edmund Jeffers, *Music for the General College Student*. New York: King's Crown Press, 1944.

Vincent Jones, *Music Education in the College*. Boston: Birchard, 1949.

George S. Dickinson, *The Study of Music as a Liberal Art*. Poughkeepsie: Vassar College, 1953.

Glen Haydon, *Introduction to Musicology*. Chapel Hill: University of North Carolina Press, 1959 [1941].

Manfred Bukofzer, *The Place of Musicology in American Institutions of Higher Learning*. New York: Liberal Arts Press, 1957.

Appendixes

Some Biographies of Great Musicians

Note: This list, recommended in Chapter 1 for interesting supplementary readings, is arranged by eras and alphabetically by biographee within each era. The choice of books is determined by the importance of the biographee; by the extent to which his musical productions, associates, and environment are included; by the authority of the material; and by its readability and general interest. Two extremes are avoided: on the one hand, the more exhaustive studies such as those by Spitta and Terry on Bach, and, on the other hand, fictionalized biography. Occasionally a collection of letters or a compilation of documents is included because of its broad interest and biographical continuity. The reader is advised to skip from era to era in his choice of books so as to enter into as many different musical circles as possible. For readers especially interested in American music the biographies of American composers are preceded by an asterisk.

RENAISSANCE ERA

Leigh Henry, *Dr. John BULL*. London: Herbert Joseph, 1937.

E. H. Fellowes, *William BYRD*. New York: Oxford University Press, 1946.

Cecil Gray and Philip Heseltine, *Carlo GESUALDO*. London: J. Curwen, 1926.

E. H. Fellowes, *Orlando GIBBONS*. New York: Oxford University Press, 1951.

Henry Coates, *PALESTRINA*. New York: Farrar, Straus and Cudahy, 1956.

Denis Stevens, *Thomas TOMKINS, 1572-1656.* New York: St. Martin's Press, 1957.

BAROQUE ERA

Hubert Langley, *Doctor ARNE.* Cambridge: Cambridge University Press, 1938.

Eva Mary and Sydney Grew, *BACH.* London: J. M. Dent, 1947.

H. T. David and Arthur Mendel, *The BACH Reader.* New York: W. W. Norton, 1945.

C. Hubert H. Parry, *Johann Sebastian BACH.* New York: Putnam's, 1934.

Marc Pincherle, *CORELLI: His Life, His Work.* New York: W. W. Norton, 1956.

Edward J. Dent, *HANDEL.* London: Duckworth, 1934.

Newman Flower, *George Frideric HANDEL.* London: C. Scribner's, 1948.

Percy M. Young, *HANDEL.* New York: Farrar, Straus and Cudahy, 1949.

H. F. Redlich, *Claudio MONTEVERDI.* London: Adler, 1952.

Leo Schrade, *MONTEVERDI.* New York. W. W. Norton, 1950.

J. A. Westrup, *PURCELL.* New York: Farrar, Straus and Cudahy, 1953.

E. J. Dent, *Alessandro SCARLATTI.* New York: St. Martin's Press, 1960.

Ralph Kirkpatrick, *Domenico SCARLATTI.* Princeton: Princeton University Press, 1953.

Marc Pincherle, *VIVALDI: Genius of the Baroque.* New York: W. W. Norton, 1957.

CLASSIC ERA

C. S. Terry, *JOHN CHRISTIAN BACH.* New York: Oxford University Press, 1929.

Paul Bekker, *BEETHOVEN.* New York: Dutton, 1922.

John N. Burk, *BEETHOVEN.* New York: Random House, 1943.

A. E. F. Dickinson, *BEETHOVEN.* London: Nelson, 1941.

Marion M. Scott, *BEETHOVEN.* New York: Farrar, Straus and Cudahy, 1943.

W. J. Turner, *BEETHOVEN*. London: George H. Durand, 1945.

Ditters von Dittersdorf, *DITTERSDORF* (autobiography). London: Richard Bentley, 1896.

Alfred Einstein, *GLUCK*. New York: Farrar, Straus and Cudahy, 1954.

Karl Geiringer, *HAYDN*. New York: W. W. Norton, 1946.

Rosemary Hughes, *HAYDN*. New York: Farrar, Straus and Cudahy, 1951.

Eric Blom, *MOZART*. New York: Farrar, Straus and Cudahy, 1935.

John N. Burk, *MOZART and His Music*. New York: Random House, 1959.

Alfred Einstein, *MOZART*. New York: Oxford University Press, 1945.

W. J. Turner, *MOZART*. London: Victor Gollancz, 1938.

ROMANTIC ERA

Hector BERLIOZ, *Memoirs*. New York: Alfred Knopf, 1937.

J. H. Elliot, *BERLIOZ*. New York: Farrar, Straus and Cudahy, 1938.

Mina Curtiss, *BIZET and His World*. New York: Alfred Knopf, 1958.

Winton Dean, *BIZET*. New York: Farrar, Straus and Cudahy, 1948.

Karl Geiringer, *BRAHMS*. New York: Oxford University Press, 1947.

Ralph Hill, *BRAHMS*. New York: Duckworth, 1948.

Florence May, *The Life of Johannes BRAHMS*, 2 vols. London: W. Reeves, 1948.

Hans F. Redlich, *BRUCKNER and MAHLER*. New York: Farrar, Straus and Cudahy, 1955.

Werner Wolff, *Anton BRUCKNER*. New York: Dutton, 1942.

E. J. Dent, *Ferruccio BUSONI*. New York: Oxford University Press, 1933.

Arthur Hedley, *CHOPIN*. New York: Farrar, Straus and Cudahy, 1947.

Herbert Weinstock, *CHOPIN*. New York: Alfred Knopf, 1949.

Casimir Wierzynski, *CHOPIN*. New York: Simon and Schuster, 1949.

Thomas Beecham, *Frederick DELIUS*. London: Hutchinson, 1959.

Arthur Hutchings, *DELIUS*. London: Macmillan, 1949.

Alec Robertson, *DVOŘÁK*. New York: Farrar, Straus and Cudahy, 1955.

W. H. Reed, *ELGAR*. New York: Farrar, Straus and Cudahy, 1939.

Norman Suckling, *FAURÉ*. New York: Farrar, Straus and Cudahy, 1951.

Norman Demuth, *César FRANCK*. New York: Dennis Dobson, 1949.

*Vernon Loggins, *Where the World Ends; the Life of Louis Moreau GOTTSCHALK*. Baton Rouge: Louisiana State University Press, 1958.

D. M. Johansen, *Edvard GRIEG*. Princeton: Princeton University Press, 1945.

*Edward N. Waters, *Victor HERBERT*. New York: Macmillan, 1955.

L. P. Lochner, *Fritz KREISLER*. New York: Macmillan, 1950.

Walter Beckett, *LISZT*. New York: Farrar, Straus and Cudahy, 1956.

Ralph Hill, *LISZT*. New York: A. A. Wyn, 1950.

James Huneker, *Franz LISZT*. New York: Scribner's, 1911.

*Lawrence Gilman, *Edward MACDOWELL*. New York: Dodd, Mead, 1931.

John Erskine, *Song Without Words* (MENDELSSOHN). New York: Julian Messner, 1941.

Philip Radcliffe, *MENDELSSOHN*. New York: Farrar, Straus and Cudahy, 1954.

M. D. Calvocoressi, *Modest MUSSORGSKY*. Fair Lawn: Essential Books, 1956.

Rom Landau, *Ignace PADEREWSKI*. New York: Ivor Nicholson and Watson, 1934.

Ignace Jan Paderewski and Mary Lawton, *The PADEREWSKI Memoirs*. New York: Scribner's, 1939.

Mosco Carner, *PUCCINI; A Critical Biography*. New York: Alfred Knopf, 1959.

George R. Marek, *PUCCINI*. New York: Simon and Schuster, 1951.

Vincent Seligman, *PUCCINI Among Friends*. New York: Macmillan, 1938.

S. Bertensson and Jay Leyda, *Sergei RACHMANINOFF*. New York: New York University Press, 1956.

Victor I. Seroff, *RACHMANINOFF*. New York: Simon and Schuster, 1950.

RIMSKY-KORSAKOV, *My Musical Life*. New York: Alfred Knopf, 1942.

Francis Toye, *ROSSINI*. New York: Alfred Knopf, 1947.

Maurice J. E. Brown, *SCHUBERT; A Critical Biography*. New York: St. Martin's Press, 1958.

Alfred Einstein, *SCHUBERT*. New York: Oxford University Press, 1951.

Newman Flower, *Franz SCHUBERT*. New York: Tudor, 1928.

Arthur Hutchings, *SCHUBERT*. New York: Farrar, Straus and Cudahy, 1956.

John N. Burk, *CLARA SCHUMANN*. New York: Random House, 1940.

Herbert Bedford, Robert *SCHUMANN*. London: K. Paul, Trench, Trubner, 1933.

Joan Chissell, *SCHUMANN*. New York: Farrar, Straus and Cudahy, 1956.

Cecil Gray, *SIBELIUS*. New York: H. Milford, 1947.

Harold E. Johnson, *Jean SIBELIUS*. New York: Alfred Knopf, 1954.

Henry T. Finck, *Richard STRAUSS*. Boston: Little, Brown, 1917.

Wladimir Lakond (ed.), *The Diaries of TCHAIKOVSKY*. New York: W. W. Norton, 1945.

Herbert Weinstock, *TCHAIKOVSKY*. New York: Alfred Knopf, 1946.

F. Bonavia, *VERDI*. New York: Oxford University Press, 1930.

Dyneley Hussey, *VERDI*. New York: Farrar, Straus and Cudahy, 1940.

Francis Toye, *Giuseppe VERDI*. New York: Alfred Knopf, 1949.

Robert L. Jacobs, *WAGNER*. New York: Farrar, Straus and Cudahy, 1947.

Richard WAGNER, *My Life*. New York: Dodd, Mead, 1931.

William Wallace, *Richard WAGNER*. New York: Harper, 1925.

William Saunders, *WEBER*. New York: Dutton, 1940.

MODERN ERA

*Nathan Broder, *Samuel BARBER*. New York: G. Schirmer, 1954.

Emil Haraszti, *Béla BARTÓK*. Paris: Lyrebird Press, 1938.

Halsey Stevens, *BARTÓK*. New York: Oxford University Press, 1953.

*Julia Smith, *Aaron COPLAND; His Work and Contribution to American Music*. New York: Dutton, 1955.

Edward Lockspeiser, *DEBUSSY*. New York: Farrar, Straus and Cudahy, 1951.

Rollo H. Myers, *DEBUSSY*. London: Pellegrini and Cudahy, 1948.

Victor Seroff, *DEBUSSY: Musician of France*. New York: Putnam's, 1955.

Oscar Thompson, *DEBUSSY*. New York: Tudor, 1940.

*David Ewen, *A Journey to Greatness, The Life and Music of George GERSHWIN*. New York: Henry Holt, 1956.

*Henry and Sidney Cowell, *Charles IVES*. New York: Oxford University Press, 1955.

Darius MILHAUD, *Notes Without Music* (autobiography). New York: Alfred Knopf, 1953.

Israel V. Nestyev, *Sergei PROKOFIEV*. New York: Alfred Knopf, 1946.

Norman Demuth, *RAVEL*. New York: Farrar, Straus and Cudahy, 1956.

Roland Manuel, *Maurice RAVEL*. London: D. Dobson, 1947.

Victor Seroff, *Maurice RAVEL*. New York: Henry Holt, 1953.

*R. Schreiber and V. Persichetti, *William SCHUMAN*. New York: G. Schirmer, 1954.

A. E. Hull, *SCRIABIN*. London: K. Paul, Trench, Trubner, 1927.

Igor STRAVINSKY, *Chronicle of My Life*. London: Victor Gollancz, 1936.

Alexandre Tansman, *Igor STRAVINSKY*. New York: Putnam's, 1949.

Eric Walter White, *STRAVINSKY*. New York: S. Lehmann, 1948.

*Kathleen Hoover and John Cage, *Virgil THOMSON; His Life and Music*. New York: Thomas Yoseloff, 1959.

H. J. Foss, *Ralph VAUGHAN WILLIAMS*. New York: Harrap, 1950.

Appendix II

A Coordinated List of Music to Hear

Note: As indicated in Chapter 1, the object of this list is to illustrate the present book with one balanced representation of great masters and their masterworks, of main eras and styles, and of principal forms and mediums. The list is numbered in one sequence and arranged according to chapters, each work being entered where it most applies. However, you will note that in about a third of the entries you are simply invited to "prehear" or "rehear" works listed under another chapter and section. This system has the double advantage of giving you repeated opportunities to know most of the works and of avoiding a larger list than could actually be heard by listeners with limited time and facilities.

Chapter	*No.*	
2		Early Christian plainchant: prehear nos. 40, 41,
Historical		and 42
styles		Renaissance motet: prehear no. 14
by		Baroque concerto grosso: prehear no. 30
eras		Classic piano concerto: prehear no. 34
		Romantic character piece: prehear no. 19
		Modern symphony: prehear no. 33

Chapter	No.
	1. Ethos and pathos styles in the same composer: Chopin, *Preludes in A Major* and *F Minor*, op. 28, nos. 7 and 18, for piano
3	2. Varieties of timbre: Ravel, *Bolero*, for orchestra
Sound	3. Instrumental choirs and solos: Britten, *Variations and Fugue on a Theme of Purcell*, op. 34 ("The Young Person's Guide to the Orchestra")
and its	
instru-	
ments	

Piano: prehear no. 35

Organ: prehear no. 27

Harpsichord: prehear no. 17

Soprano, mezzo-soprano, tenor, and baritone: prehear no. 39d

4   Baroque dance patterns: prehear no. 28

Rhythmic   4. Romantic and Modern dance patterns:

patterns   a. Chopin, *Mazurka in C-sharp Minor*, op. 41, no. 1, for piano

and   b. Chopin, *Polonaise in E-flat Minor*, op. 26, no. 2, for piano

styles   c. J. Strauss, *Waltz, Southern Roses*, op. 388, for orchestra

            d. Falla, "Danse finale, Jota," from *The Three-Cornered Hat*, ballet music for orchestra

            e. Dvořák, *Polka*, op. 53, for piano

            f. Schubert, *Divertissement à la Hongroise* (czardas), op. 54, for one-piano duet

            g. Albeniz, *Tango in D Major*, for piano

            h. Gershwin, *Three Preludes for Piano* (jazz)

     5. Irregular rhythms in Modern music: Copland, "Dance," from *Music for the Theatre*, for small orchestra

5   Diatonic melody: prehear no. 44e

Melodic   Chromatic melody: prehear no. 43h

styles   Disjunct melody: prehear second theme (as in Fig. 19) of no. 33,I ("I" means the first movement)

Chapter	No.
6 **Harmony** **and** **tonality**	6. Harmonic and tonal movement: Wagner, "Prelude" to *Parsifal*, for orchestra 7. Atonality: Schoenberg, *Quintet for Wind Instruments* (flute, oboe, clarinet, French horn, and bassoon), I ("Spirited") 8. Polytonality: Milhaud, *Sonate* (*1916*), for piano, II ("Moderately") 9. Extended tonality: Hindemith, *Sonata for Violin and Piano* (*1940*), I ("Lively")
7 **Texture** **and** **sonority**	10. Oriental heterophony: Japanese melody, *Matsumae-Oiwake* (no. 4 in the Decca album *Music of the Orient*) 11. Unaccompanied folk song (from Virginia): *The Two Sisters* (in vol. VII of the Library of Congress albums *Folk Music of the United States*) Homophony: prehear first main theme ("A" in Fig. 30) of no. 22 Polyphony: prehear no. 16 Vocal duet: prehear no. 43e Unaccompanied "soli" quartet, S.A.T.B.: prehear no. 15 Six-part chorus with orchestral accompaniment: prehear no. 43g Violin and piano duo: rehear no. 9 String quartet: prehear no. 32 12. Symphony orchestra: Tchaikovsky, *Capriccio italien*, op. 45 13. Atmosphere evoked by sonority alone: Stravinsky, "Introduction" to *The Rite of Spring*, for orchestra
8 **Musical** **form**	Motivic play: prehear "Passacaglia" of no. 23 Phrase grouping in a hierarchic design: prehear no. 31,III A form woven out of motivic play: prehear "Fugue" of no. 23

Chapter   *No.*

A hierarchic design (rondo): prehear no. 21

The variation principle: prehear no. 26

9
Cursive
motivic
forms

14. Motet: Lassus, *Adoramus te* (from *Magnum opus musicum* no. 44 [53] for high, middle, and low voices)

15. Madrigal: Morley, *April Is in My Mistress' Face,* for S.A.T.B.

16. Choral fugue: Haydn, "Achievèd is the Glorious Work," from *The Creation,* no. 28 (or 27b)

17. Binary design in a separate harpsichord piece: D. Scarlatti, *Sonata in D Major,* K.443

18. Binary design in a dance from a harpsichord suite: Couperin, "L'Audacieuse" from *Ordre No. 23*

10
Hierarchic
phrase
designs

Binary themes used for variations: prehear themes of no. 26 and no. 32,II

19. Ternary design (A-B-A) in an accompanied cello solo: Fauré, *Elégie,* op. 24, for cello and orchestra

20. An A-B-A art-song: Schumann, "Dedication," no. 1, from the song cycle *Myrtle,* op. 25, for voice and piano

21. A rondo with the form A-B-A-C-A-Coda: Beethoven, *Rondo in C Major,* op. 51, no. 1, for piano

22. An "intuitive" arrangement of sections in the order of Intro.-A-A-A-B-A-B-Coda: Chopin, *Ballade in F Minor,* op. 52, for piano

11
Variation
forms

23. The recurring bass line: Bach, *Passacaglia and Fugue in C Minor,* for organ

24. The recurring harmonic pattern: Brahms, *Fourth Symphony,* op. 98, IV

25. The recurring binary melody: Paganini, *Introduction and Variations on "Nel cor più non mi sento,"* for unaccompanied violin

Chapter   *No.*

             26. The theme-and-variations: Mendelssohn, *Variations sérieuses*, op. 54

             27. A Baroque chorale prelude for organ: Bach, *Sleepers, Wake!*, S. 645

12   28. A harpsichord suite: Loeillet, *Suite in G Minor*
Baroque   (I "Allemande," II "Courante," III "Sarabande," IV "Minuetto," V "Gigue")
instru-
mental   29. A church sonata: Corelli, *Sonata da chiesa*
cycles   No. 5, op. 3, for two violins and cello or bass lute, with figured bass realized by the organ (I "Grave," II "Allegro," III "Largo," IV "Allegro")

             30. A concerto grosso: Vivaldi, *Concerto No. 8*, for string orchestra and two solo violins, from *L'Estro Armonico*, op. 3 (I "Allegro," II "Larghetto e spiritoso," III "Allegro")

13   31. A Classic sonata for piano: Beethoven, *Sonata in D Major*, op. 28 (I "Allegro," II "Andante,"
Sonata   III "Scherzo. Allegro vivace [and Trio]," IV "Rondo. Allegro, ma non troppo")
in
various   32. A Romantic chamber music work: Schubert, *String Quartet in D Minor*, "Death and the Maiden" (I "Allegro," II "Andante con moto,"
guises   III "Scherzo. Allegro molto [and Trio]," IV "Presto")

             33. A Modern work for orchestra: Shostakovitch, *Symphony No. 5* (I "Moderato," II "Allegretto," III "Largo," IV "Allegro non troppo")

             34. A Classic piano concerto: Mozart, *Concerto in A Major*, K. 488 (I "Allegro," II "Andante," III "Presto")

14   35. Idiomatic writing in a fantasia for piano: Liszt,
Instru-   "Au bord d'une source," from *Années de*
mental   *pèlerinage*, vol. 1
fantasy
and de-   36. An Impressionistic tone poem: Debussy, *Nuages*, first *Nocturne*, for orchestra
scription
             37. A tone poem that describes literalities: R.

Strauss, *Till Eulenspiegel's Merry Pranks,* op. 28

**15
Song
and
opera**

38. Two cursive lieder for voice and piano:
    a. Schubert, *The Erlking,* op. 1
    b. Schubert, *Death and the Maiden,* op. 7, no. 3

39. Selections from an Italian opera: Verdi, *Otello, A Lyrical Drama in Four Acts* (libretto by Boito)
    a. Iago's drinking song, "And let the cannikin clink!" Act I
    b. love duet of Otello and Desdemona, "Now in the thick of the night," Act I
    c. Iago's creed, "Cruel is the God I know," Act II
    d. quartet of Desdemona, Otello, Iago, and Emilia, "On his behalf who has provoked your displeasure," Act II
    e. duet in which Cassio's dream is related by Iago to Otello, "The other night, while Cassio slumbered," Act II
    f. Otello's soliloquy, "God! were all the ills of despair heaped upon me," Act III
    g. Desdemona's willow song, "She wept as she sang her song," Act IV
    h. Desdemona's "Ave Maria," Act IV
    i. duet in which Otello suffocates Desdemona, "Who's there?" Act IV

**16
Sacred
choral
cycles**

40. Syllabic Gregorian chant from the Ordinary of the Mass: "Gloria," from the Easter Mass *Lux et origo*

41. Melismatic chant from the Proper: "Ascendit Deus," Alleluia for the Ascension

42. A rhymed sequence: *Dies irae* from the Requiem Mass

43. Selections from a polyphonic Mass: Bach, *Mass in B Minor* for soloists, chorus, and orchestra

No.

(numbered according to Frank Damrosch's edition, published by G. Schirmer, Inc., New York, 1927)

a. "Kyrie eleison," for S.A.T.B. chorus (item 3)

b. "Gratias agimus" (from the Gloria movement), for S.A.T.B. chorus (item 6)

c. "Qui tollis" (from the Gloria movement), for S.A.T.B. chorus (item 8)

d. "Credo in unum Deum," for S1.S2.A.T.B. chorus (item 12)

e. "Et in unum Deum (from the Credo movement), duet for soprano solo and alto solo (item 14)

f. "Crucifixus" (from the Credo movement), for S.A.T.B. chorus (item 16)

g. "Sanctus, sanctus, sanctus," for S1.S2.A1. A2.T.B. chorus (item 20)

h. "Agnus Dei," for alto solo with violin obbligato (item 23)

44. Selections from an oratorio: Handel, *Messiah*, for soloists, S.A.T.B. chorus, and orchestra (numbered according to J. M. Coopersmith's edition, published by Carl Fischer, Inc., New York, 1941)

a. "Sinfonia," for orchestra (item 1)

b. arioso, "Comfort Ye," and air, "Every Valley," for tenor solo (Part I, items 2 and 3)

c. "And the Glory of the Lord," for chorus (Part I, item 4)

d. "For unto Us a Child is Born," for chorus (Part I, item 12)

e. aria, "He Shall Feed His Flock," contralto solo followed by soprano solo (Part I, item 21)

f. "Behold the Lamb of God," for chorus (Part II, item 23)

g. aria, " Why Do the Nations," for bass solo (Part II, item 38)

h. "Hallelujah," for chorus (Part II, item 42)

i. aria, "I know that my Redeemer Liveth," for soprano solo (Part III, item 43)

j. "Worthy is the Lamb," for chorus (Part III, item 50)

Index

(with glossary and biography aids)

Note: The numbers of pages on which pertinent examples or illustrations occur are italicized. Concert works are indexed by composer, but only those that receive more than passing mention. Community songs and anonymous pieces are indexed by title. In place of a separate glossary, a definition for each term essential to this text can be found in context by means of this Index, usually by turning to the earliest page reference. In place of a separate "Personalia," the full name, nationality of birth, and life dates (where known) of each composer cited in this text are given under his Index entry.

a cappella, 119, 121, 156, *158*; App. II, nos. 14, 15

A-B-A design, 135, 139, 171, 172, 173, 174, *175–179*, 181, 219, 224, 249; App. II, nos. 19, 20

absolute music, 202, 214, 224, 235–237, 247, 261

absolute pitch, 42

accidentals, 71, 72, 85, *89–92*

accompaniment, 107, 109; App. II, nos. 38a, 38b; in art-song, 249, *251–252*; in homophony, *111–114–115*; opp. Plate 5

acoustics, *29–32*, 79

Addison, Joseph, 256

additive form, 23, 108; App. II, no. 14; homophonic, *171–172*, 179, 189; polyphonic, *156–157*, 162

aesthetics, 133–138, 285–287

Agnus Dei, 265, 271

Albeniz, Isaac (Spanish, 1860–1909), 17; App. II, no. 4g

Alberti bass, 14, 113, *114*, 115; App. II, no. 21

Albinoni, Tommaso (Italian, 1674–1745), 213

Alleluia, 265, 266, 267, 271, 278; App. II, no. 44h

allemande, 205, 207

Ambrose, Saint (Italian, 333–397), 17, 263; opp. Plate 1

American music, 17, 55, 109, 128, 248; App. II, nos. 4h, 5; church, 275; education, 296–297; opera, 253–254, 255; Plates 9–14; profession, 283–285

Annie Laurie, 88

anthem, 156

anthologies of music, 9

antiphony, 211, 230

appoggiatura, 88, 118

architecture and music, 15, 18, 23, 49, 133, 134, 136; Plates 1–6

Arensky, Anton Stepanovitch (Russian, 1861–1906), 191

aria, 146, 172; App. II, nos. 39f, 44e; form, 176; in opera, 257–258, 259, 270, 272

arpeggio, 113, 193

arrangement, *see* transcriptions

art music, 285, 287

art-song, 172, 176, 247–249, *251*

atonality, 98; App. II, no. 7

attention span, 137, 202–203

Bach, Carl Philipp Emanuel (German, 1714–1788), 17

Bach, Johann Christian (German, 1732–1782), 17, 226

Bach, Johann Sebastian (German, 1685–1750), 12, 14, 17, 117, 138,

146–147, 176, 177, 209, 218, 223, 231, 232, 239, 294; "Adagio" from *Violin Concerto in E*, 75; "Air" from *Suite in D*, 72; App. II, nos. 23, 27, 43; *Art of the Fugue*, 162, 165–166; cantata, 273–274; "Chaconne" from *Partita in D Minor*, 190, 194; chorale preludes (*Sleepers, Wake!*), 200–201; chorale treatment, 111–112, 274; concerto grosso, 213; dances, 169, 204; dissonance, 117–118; "Goldberg Variations," 198; *Mass in B Minor*, 120, 268, 269–270–271, 273; opp. Plate 3; organ, 44; *Passacaglia and Fugue in C Minor*, 164, 189, 191–192–193; *St. Matthew Passion*, 121, 273; trumpet, 41, 124; versus Handel, 22, 277; versus Irving Berlin, 286–287; *Well-Tempered Clavier* 142, 147, 166–167

Bach, Wilhelm Friedemann (German, 1710–1784), 17

ballad opera, 252, 253

Ballantine, Edward (American, 1886–   ), 198

ballet, 244, 255

band, 125, 126, 127, 128; Plate 14

bar line, 51, 52, 56–57, 159–160

barform, 110, 182, 261

Baroque Era, 14, 16–19, 24, 35, 37, 45, 57, 58, 60, 66, 81, 96, 105; App. II, nos. 17, 18, 23, 27, 28, 29, 30, 43, 44; instrumental cycles, 202–214, 217–218, 226, 238, 239, 244, 263, 274; monody, 114–115; motive, 142–143; phrase, 146–147, 152, 167, 177, 191, 193; Plates 3, 15, 16; scoring, 121–125, 127

Bartók, Béla (Hungarian, 1881–1945), 17, 100, 110, 128, 143, 213, 217, 275

basic motive, 143, 223

bass, 114–115, 120, 122

bass clef, 69–70

bass drum, 42

bass viol, 35–38, 123

basso ostinato, 190–191

bassoon, 40, 69; Plate 10

Beethoven, Ludwig van (German, 1770–1827), 5, 7, 11, 12, 13, 14,

15, 17, 24, 122, 125, 146, 166, 176, 223, 248, 268, 294; App. II, nos. 21, 31; *Ninth Symphony*, 123–125; opp. Plate 4; piano concertos, 181, 231; programme, 223, 235–236; rhythm, 58, 61; rondo, 180–182; sonata, 214–223, 227, 228–230; *Sonata* (op. 28), 176, 180, 229; *Sonata pathétique*, 222–223; *String Quartet* (op. 130), 75; variations, 194, 198, 202; violin concerto, 231

bells, 42

Benedicamus Domino, 265

Berg, Alban (Austrian, 1885–1935), 100, 253–254

Berlin, Irving (American, 1888–   ), 286–287

Berlioz, Hector (French, 1803–1869), 17, 125, 128, 143, 183, 236, 244, 254, 266, 272; opp. Plate 5

binary design, 152; App. II, nos. 17, 18; motivic play, 167–168; phrase grouping, 171–175; "sonata-allegro" form, 230; in variations, 195–196, 199–200

biographies of musicians, 8, 301–307

Bizet, Georges (French, 1838–1875), 17, 120, 128, 254, 261

Bloch, Ernest (Swiss, 1880–1959), 17, 128, 213

Boccherini, Luigi (Italian, 1743–1805), 17

borrowed tones, 92

bourrée, 205

bowing, 36–37, 239; Plates 8, 9, 15

Brahms, Johannes (German, 1833–1897), 12, 17, 22, 176, 231, 232, 248; App. II, no. 24; basic motive, 143, 223; *German Requiem*, 121, 272; sonata, 217, 220, 225, 227, 229; tempo, 61; two-against-three, 114; variations (finale of *Fourth Symphony*), 194–195, 198

brasses, 32–34, 126–127

bridge, 181–182, 224–225

Britten, Edward Benjamin (English, 1913–   ), 35, 253–254; App. II, no. 3

Bruckner, Anton (Austrian, 1824–1896), 17, 217, 269; opp. Plate 5

Bülow, Hans Guido von (German, 1830–1894), 15
Burke, Edmund, 286
Busoni, Ferruccio (Italian, 1866–1924), 202
Buxtehude, Dietrich (German, 1637–1707), 17, 274
Byrd, William (English, 1543–1623), 17

C clef, 69–70, 267
cadence, in modality, 157–159, 173, 177–178, 193, 259; in traditional harmony, 86–87, 94, 117, 141, 144, 150
cadenza, 231; App. II, no. 34
Cage, John (American, 1912-   ), 103
canon, 116, 165, 185; App. II, no. 43e
cantata, 273–274
"cantus firmus," 190, 268
canzon, 202
capriccio, 238
career in music, 283–285
Carissimi, Giacomo (Italian, 1605–1674), 273, 274
cello, 35–37, 69, 121–122, 123, 177, 206; App. II, no. 19; Plates 9, 15
Cézanne, Paul, 20; Plates 7a, 7b
chaconne, 190, 194, 205
chamber music, 75–76; App. II, nos. 7, 9, 29, 32; Baroque, 206–210; Classic and later, 215, 217, 231–232; Plates 8, 9, 10, 15; types, 121–123, 126
chamber orchestra, 123
chanson, 160, 202; opp. Plate 2
character piece, 175; App. II, no. 19
Child, Francis, 109
chimes, 42
choirs, 126
Chopin, Frédéric (Polish, 1810–1849), 17, 21, 75, 113, 121, 143, 175, 176, 198, 226, 231; App. II, nos. 1, 4a, 4b, 22; *Ballade in F Minor*, 75, 183–184–185; *Etude* (op. 10, no. 3), 178; "intuitive" design, 183–185; mazurkas, 62, 109; *Nocturne in E*, 106; opp. Plate 5; phrase, 146–147; *Polonaise* (op.

53), 191; *Preludes*, 239–240; rubato, 62
choral ensemble, 118–121
chorale, 200–201, 273, 274; opp. Plate 3
chorale prelude, 200–201, 244; App. II, no. 27
chords, 78, 83, 84, 85; harmonic function, 84–89, 96; in homophony, 112; in monody, 114–115, 158; inversion, 84, 87; recurring pattern, 193–194; tonal function, 94–103
chorus, 47, 120–121, 252, 255, 272, 273; App. II, nos. 43, 44
chromatic scale, 66, 181, 198
chromaticism, 14, 72, 89, 92, 98, 119, 128, 270
church sonata, 207–208–210, 217, 218; App. II, no. 29
circle of fifths, 89–90–92, 93, 95
clarinet, 38, 40, 90; Plate 10
Classic Era, 13, 14, 16–19, 45, 105, 107, 113; App. II, nos. 16, 21, 31, 34; motive, 142–143; phrase, 146–147, 180, 203; Plate 4; scoring, 121–125, 127, 128; sonata cycles, 214–218, 226, 230, 235; versus Baroque, 115, 118
clavichord, 45
clavier, 45
clef, 69–70, 91
climate and music, 110
climax, 73; finale, 220; fugal, 164–165, 177, 185, 193; harmonic, 112, 162; "sonata-allegro" form, 230, 270, 293
closed form, 23, 151, 157, 181, 237
closing theme, 224, 226, 227
coda, 61, 178, 180, 183, 194, 199, 224; "sonata-allegro" form, 229–230, 231
codetta, 164
comic opera, 253
community songs, 172–174
composition, 102
compound meter, 51, 53, 56, 149, 205
concertino, 211
concerto, 75, 76, 211, 213, 215, 220, 231, 241; App. II, no. 34
concerto grosso, 210–212, 213, 217;

App. II, no. 30; opp. Plate 3
conducting, 59–62, 252
conflicts in opera, 257–260
conjunct melody, 72, 195–197, 289
consonance and dissonance, intervals, 78–84; modern harmony, 98–101, 103; polyphony, 117–118, 135, 159, 165, 209
contrabassoon, 40
contrapuntal devices, 141, 142, 165–166
contrast and repetition, hierarchic designs, 172, 178–179; principles of form, 134–135, 140–141, 151–152; variations, 186–187
Copland, Aaron (American, 1900–), 17, 58, 143, 146–147; App. II, no. 5
Corelli, Arcangelo (Italian, 1653–1713), 17, 35, 194; App. II, no. 29; *Church Sonata No. 5* (op. 3), 208, 209–210, 213; opp. Plate 3
counterpoint, 115, 140
countersubject, 162–163, 164
Couperin, François (le grand) (French, 1668–1733), 17, 25, 167, 169, 179; App. II, no. 18
courante, 205–206, 207
court sonata, 207–208
Cowell, Henry D. (American, 1897–), 103
Cowper, William, 275
Credo, 265, 269–270, 271; App. II, no. 43d
cursive form, 141, 151, 156, 167, 247, 249, 259
cycles of movements, 137, 153; choral, 263–279; instrumental, 202–224
cyclic theory of music history, 12–25
cyclical treatment, 143, 204, 222–223
cymbals, 43
czardas, 57; App. II, no. 4f

da capo, 176, 178
dance music, 108; App. II, nos. 4, 5, 28; Baroque, 204–207; opp. Plate 3; regular phrases, 146, 167; rhythms, 57
dancing and music, 68, 136
Debussy, Claude (French, 1862–1918), 22, 58, 100, 128, 240, 241,

248, 254, 259; App. II, no. 36; Impressionism (*Nuages*), 242–243, 244
deceptive cadence, 88, 141, 164
Delius, Frederick (English, 1862–1934), 241
Dent, E. J., 174
Des Prés, Josquin (Flemish, c. 1440–1521), 17, 268
development, 142–143, 165, 224–225, 227, 228–229, 231
diatonic, 72, 270, 274
Dies Irae, 266, 267, 271–272; App. II, no. 42
disjunct melody, 72, 101, 195–197, 289
dominant, 85–86, 90, 165, 168
Donizetti, Gaetano (Italian, 1797–1848), 120
dot, 53–54, 55, 56
double flat, 66, 68, 71
double fugue, 162, 214
double sharp, 66, 68, 71
double stop, 37, 197
Dowland, John (Irish, 1563–1626), 17, 75, 247
drama and music, 135–136
Dreiser, Theodore, 151
Drink to Me Only with Thine Eyes, 148–149, 150, 174, 188, 189
Drinker, Henry S., 249
dualism, 225–226, 230
Dufay, Guillaume (Flemish, c. 1400–1474), 17, 247
Dukas, Paul (French, 1865–1935), 245
duo, 122, 215, 230; App. II, no. 9
Dvořák, Antonin (Czech, 1841–1904), 17, 58, 217, 231, 241, 266; App. II, no. 4e
dynamics, 45, 93, 102, 138, 211

Early Christian Era, 13, 14, 16–19; App. II, nos. 40, 41, 42; monophony, 105, 108; motive and phrase, 142–143, 146; plainchant, 263–268; Plate 1
Early Romantic Music, 16–19, 24, 96, 118, 241; App. II, no. 32
ecclesiastical modes, 67, 98, 266
education in music, 47–48, 284, 285; America, 295–297

electrophonic instruments, 44, 103
Elgar, Edward (English, 1857–1934), 200, 241
embouchure, 39, 41
"endless" melody, 72, 76, 260
English horn, 40
English music, 190, 204, 247; App. II, nos. 3, 15, 44; madrigal, 160–161; opera, 252–254
enharmonic, 65–66, 71, 82, 90
ensemble, 119–126, 141
episode, fugue, 161, 162, 163–164; rondo, 179–182; "sonata-allegro" development, 228–229
equal temperament, 43
eras, 12–25, 142–143, 146–147
Eschman, Karl, 72
ethnomusicology, 107
ethos styles, 16–25, 107, 116, 146, 235–236; App. II, no. 1; Plates 2, 4, 6, 7b
etude, 148, 239
evaluation, 286–294
"evolution," 11–12
exotic music, 14, 107–110
exposition, fugue, 161–164, 165–166; "sonata-allegro" form, 224
Expressionism, 243; App. II, no. 7; opp. Plate 6; Plate 18

Falla, Manuel de (Spanish, 1876–1946), 241, App. II, no. 4d
false return, 181
fantasia, 151, 181, 190, 200, 205, 237–240, 291; App. II, no. 35
Farina, Carlo (Italian, c. 1600–c. 1640), 244
Fauré, Gabriel (French, 1845–1924), 248, 272; App. II, no. 19; *Elégie*, 177, 291
fifth, 85, 86–87, 89–93
figuration, 193
film music, 102, 237
final cadence, 86, 144, 150, 165, 180
finale, 180, 194–195, 206, 220, 261
first movement, 205, 209, 212, 218–219
flat, 65–68, 70–71, 89–92
flute, 32–33, 39–40, 122, 126, 206; Plate 10

Folia, 194
folk song, 87, 100, *106*, 109, 172, 263; App. II, no. 11
foreign tone, 87, 117–118
form, 7; general principles, 133–155, 156–279; review, 290–292, 294; tonal influence, 93–95, 98, 107, 108
Franck, César (Belgian, 1822–1890), 17, 143, 180, 217, 223, 241
French horn, 38, 41, 126; Plate 10
French music, 204–206, 248; App. II, nos. 2, 8, 18, 19, 28, 36; chanson, 160; opera, 252–254; suite, 204–205
French overture, 124, 204, 210, 276
Frère Jacques, 52, 53
Frescobaldi, Girolamo (Italian, 1583–1643), 17, *106*, 239
fughetta, 165
fugue, 14, *142*, 152, 154, 167, 168, 179, 190, 191–193, 206, 209, 210, 220, 269; App. II, nos. 16, 23; opp. Plate 3; procedures, 161–163–166
function of music, 108, 125, 287

Gabrieli, Andrea (Italian, c. 1515–1586), 17
Gabrieli, Giovanni (Italian, 1555–1612), 17
gallant style, 118, *169*; opp. Plate 4
galliard, 203
Gallus, Johannes (Flemish, ?–c. 1543), 17
gavotte, 176, 205
German music, App. II, nos. 6, 9, 20, 21, 23, 24, 26, 27, 31, 32, 38, 43; art-song, 248; opera, 252–254; polyphonic lied, 160; suite, 204–205
Gershwin, George (American, 1898–1937), 17, 102, 204; App. II, no. 4h
Gesamtkuntswerk, 252; opp. Plate 5
Gibbons, Orlando (English, 1583–1625), 17
gigue, 204, 205, 206, 207, 210
Gilbert and Sullivan, 252
glissando, 220
glockenspiel, 42

Gloria, 265, 267, 270; App. II, no. 40
Gluck, Christoph Willibald (German, 1714–1787), 17, 253–254
Goethe, 248, 249
gong, 43
Goudimel, Claude (French, c. 1514–1572), 17
grand opera, 252
Greek music, 14, 64
Gregorian chant, 14, 68–69, 75, 108, 142, 156, 244, 263–267–268, 270–271; App. II, nos. 40, 41, 42; opp. Plate 1
Gregory, Pope, 17, 263; opp. Plate 1
Grétry, André (Belgian, 1741–1813), 17
Grieg, Edvard (Norwegian, 1843–1907), 17, 226, 231
Griffes, Charles Tomlinson (American, 1884–1920), 67, 248
Guido d'Arezzo (Italian, c. 995–?), 14, 17, 69
guitar, 37

half cadence, 87, 144, 150, 165, 168
half-phrase, 148–149, 175
half step, 65–68, 80
Handel, George Frideric (German, 1685–1759), 17, 22, 208, 213; App. II, no. 44; "Largo" from *Serse*, 72, 89; *Messiah*, 60, 275–278–279; opera, 254, 261; opp. Plate 3; versus Bach, 22, 277
harmonic rhythm, 61, 62, 87, 113, 141, 289; Baroque versus Classic, 115, 219
harmonica, 44–45
harmonics, 31, 36, 198
harmony, 78–104, 112–113, 115, 116, 117, 158, 289
harp, 29, 37–38
harpsichord, 45, 118, 121–122, 169–170, 190, 206, 207, 294; App. II, nos. 18, 28; Plate 15
Harris, Roy (American, 1898–   ), 291-292
Hasler, Hans Leo von (German, 1564–1612), 17, 160
Haydn, Franz Joseph (Austrian, 1732–1809), 13, 14, 17, 166, 176,

231, 268; App. II, no. 16; Classic sonata, 214–217, 219, 221, 226, 227; *The Creation*, 162, 163, 164, 275, 291; "Emperor" *String Quartet*, 72; opp. Plate 4; versus Mozart, 22, 75, 146–147, 215–216
Heine, Heinrich, 248
heterophony, 78, 108; App. II, no. 10
hierarchic design, analysis, 171–185, 224, 230, 257, 261; phrase grouping, 145, 148–149; types, 152–154
Hindemith, Paul (German, 1895–   ), 17, 81; App. II, no. 9; harmony, 103, 125, 213, 217, 220; opera, 253–254, 275
historical charts I and II, 14–25
history and music, 12, 19, 24; Plates 1–6
Holst, Gustav (English, 1874–1934), 125
homophony, App. II, no. 22; accompaniment, 111–115, 126; defined, 105–106; phrase grouping, 144–145, 147, 159, 199
Honegger, Arthur (French, 1892–1955), 245, 275
hymn, 87, 200, 266, 275

idée fixe, 143, 244
imitation, 116, 141, 157–158–161
imperfect consonance, 81–83
Impressionism, 16–19, 24, 118, 240, 241–243; App. II, no. 36; opp. Plate 6; Plate 17
impromptu, 237
incise, 148, 267–268
inductive approach, 6
d'Indy, Vincent (French, 1851–1931), 17, 241, 275
instrumental music, 16, 23; App. II, no. 3; groupings, 121–127, 145, 152, 167, 244; opp. Plates 4, 5
instruments, App. II, no. 3; families, 29–48; groupings, 121–127
integrated form, 23, 112, 137, 153, 171, 172; rondo, 179–182, 220
intellectual appeal, 20, 115
intensity, 30, 32, 40, 45, 93, 137
interlude, 252
interpretation, 138

intervals, 78–84, 93, 108, 114
intonation, 40, 43, 121
"intuitive" design, 182–185, 257; App. II, no. 22
Inversion of chords, 84, 87
Isaak, Hendryk (Flemish, c. 1450–1517), 17
Italian music, App. II, nos. 17, 25, 29, 30, 39; madrigal, 160; opera, 253–254; suite, 204–206
Italian overture, 210
Ite missa est, 265
Ives, Burl, 109
Ives, Charles (American, 1874–   ), 110

Jannequin, Clément (French, c. 1485–c. 1564), 17, 160
jazz, 40, 57, 68, 92, 102, 176, 204, 229, 284; App. II, no. 4h
Jennens, Charles, 276
Jomelli, Nicolò (Italian, 1714–1774), 254
jota, 57; App. II, no. 4d

Keats, John, 151
kettle drum, 29, 42
key, 89–97, 145, 168, 221, 227
key signature, 91–92
keyboard, 33; harpsichord, 169–170; instruments, 43–46; piano, 239–240; white and black keys, 64–68, 69–71, 102, 118, 122, 140
keynote, 66, 89
Khatchaturian, Aram (Armenian, 1903–   ), 231
Kipnis, Alexander, 248
Kokoschka, Oskar, 243; Plate 18
Křenek, Ernst (Austrian, 1900–   ), 100
Kuhnau, Johann (German, 1660–1722), 17, 244
Kyrie, 265, 270; App. II, no. 43a

Landino, Francesco (Italian, 1325–1397), 17
Larsen, Jens Peter, 276
Lassus, Roland de (Flemish, 1532–1594), 17, 22, 121; "Adoramus te," 158; App. II, no. 14

leading tone, 85
ledger line, 64, 69, 70, 71
Lehmann, Lotte, 248
leitmotif, 143, 260
libretto, 252, 253, 255–257, 272, 273
lied, App. II, nos. 21, 38a, 38b; art-song, 176, 248–249, 251; polyphonic, 160
ligature, 268
linear counterpoint, 118
listening to music, 7–8, 15, 55, 107–108, 137, 203, 272; App. II
Liszt, Franz (Hungarian-German, 1811–1886), 17, 74, 113, 143, 183, 198, 223, 241, 266, 269, 273; App. II, no. 35; "Au bord d'une source," 239–240; opp. Plate 5; *Piano Concerto in E-flat,* 231
literature and music, 18, 49, 134, 135, 136; open and closed form, 151, 241; opera, 255–260; opp. Plates 1–6
liturgy, 202, 208, 264–265
Loeffler, Charles (Alsatian-American, 1861–1935), 248
Loeillet, Jean-Baptiste (Belgian, 1680–1730), App. II, no. 28; *Suite in G Minor,* 206, 207
Lorenz, Alfred, 261
loure, 205
Lully, Jean-Baptiste (Italian-French, 1632–1687), 17, 205; opera, 254, 258, 259
lute, 37, 75, 247
Luther, Martin, 274

MacDowell, Edward (American, 1861–1908), 17
Machault, Guillaume de (French, c. 1300–1377), 17
McKinney, Laurence, 48
madrigal, 14, 75, 152, 156–161; App. II, no. 15; opp. Plate 2
Mahler, Gustav (Bohemian-Austrian, 1860–1911), 17, 123–124, 137, 183, 217
major and minor, chords, 84–85, 87; intervals, 79–82; keys, 89–93, 107; scales, 67–68, 71
mandolin, 37

march, 113
masculine and feminine rhythms, 146
masculine and feminine themes, 224
Mason, Lowell, 275
Mass, 263–272; App. II, nos. 40, 41, 43; opp. Plate 2
mathematics and music, 31, 67, 75, 79–80, 83, 102–103, 286
mazurka, 57, 109; App. II, no. 4a
measure, 51–57, 159
mediant, 85
Medieval-and-Renaissance Era, 14, 16–19, 33, 37, 45, 50, 52, 66, 74, 79; App. II, nos. 14, 15; instrumental music, 202–203, 247–248, 263, 268, 272; modality, 97–98; motet and madrigal, 156–161, 182; motive, 142–143; phrase, 146; Plates 2, 8; polyphony, 116–117, 127
Meistersinger, 111
melismatic style, 257, 260, 266, 267, 278; App. II, no. 41
melody, 72, 73, 74–76, 93, 98, 99, 100–101, 108, 109; in textures, 111–118, 139, 140, 141, 150; Modern, 152–154, 191; variations, 195–198, 218, 268, 274
memory, 136–137, 140, 221, 293
Mendelssohn, Felix (German, 1809–1847), 17, 76, 125, 166, 179, 217, 220, 231; App. II, no. 26; *Elijah*, 121, 275–276; opp. Plate 5; *Songs Without Words*, 112, 178, 179, 236; *Variations sérieuses*, 74, 112, 199–200
Menotti, Gian Carlo (Italian-American, 1911–   ), 253–254, 256, 257
Menuhin, Yehudi, 294
meter, 159, 161; Baroque suite, 205–206; Modern, 153–154; motive versus phrase, 141, 145–146; types, 49–59, 117
metronome, 51, 59–60
microtones, 102, 108
middle C, 65, 69, 70, 71
Milhaud, Darius (French, 1892–   ), 17, 125, 213, 217, 254; App. II, no. 8; polytonality (*Sonate*

in C), 100–101
minnesinger, 110
minstrelsey, 110, 146, 247
minuet, 172, 173, 176; design, 178; sonata cycles, 217, 218, 219–220; suite, 207
modality, 14, 67, 97–98, 152, 156, 158, 266
moderate movement, 219–220
Modern Era, 14, 16–19, 23, 105, 109, 123, 128; App. II, nos. 2, 3 5, 7, 8, 9, 13, 33, 36; form, 152–154, 166, 213; motive, 143; opera, 253–254; phrase, 146–147; Plate 6; rhythm, 57–58, 60, 62, 66, 81; tonality, 97–103
modulation, 150, 152, 161, 164, 168; App. II, nos. 6, 32; "sonata-allegro" form, 224–225, 229; types, 93–97, 101, 103
Monet, Claude, 242; Plate 17
monody, 114–115, 121, 252, 258
monophony, 14, 78; plainchant, 265–266; types, 105–106–111, 144–145
monothematic form, 140–141, 154, 187
Monteverdi, Claudio (Italian, 1567–1643), 17, 254
mood, 128, 238, 240–243
Morales, Cristóbal (Spanish, c. 1500–1553), 17
mordent, 118
Morley, Thomas (English, 1557-c. 1602), 160; App. II, no. 15
Mossolov, Alexander V. (Russian, 1900-   ), 103
motet, 14, 121, 152, 156–158–162, 269; App. II, no. 14; opp. Plate 2
motive, as generator, 140–143, 146, 148, 150; in motivic play, 157–159, 161, 162, 168–169, 189; Modern, 153; "sonata-allergo" form, 227–228, 229
motivic play, App. II, no. 23; Baroque cycles, 205, 211; forms based on, 156, 157, 161, 164, 165, 168–169, 180; in variations, 188–190, 194; influence on form, 7, 133, 139–142, 146, 150–154; review, 290; "sonata-

allegro" form, 227, 229

mouth organ, 44

movements, 194–195; Baroque cycles, 203–204, 209–210; Classic cycles, 217–224, 241

Mozart, Wolfgang Amadeus (Austrian, 1756–1791), 13, 14, 17, 22, 23, 117, 122, 125, 166, 198, 231, 232; App. II, no. 34; Classic sonata, 214–217, 219–221, 226, 227; *Don Giovanni*, 120, 219, 254, 258–259; "Jupiter" *Symphony*, 124; *The Magic Flute*, 172, 259; opera, 253–254, 261; opp. Plate 4; phrase, 146–147; *Piano Concerto in A*, 60, 107, 176, 180; *Rondo in D*, 181; sacred choral music, 268, 272; singing-allegro, 113, *114*, 226; versus Haydn, 22–23, 75, 146–147

Munday, John (English, ?–1630), 244

music drama, 252

music printing and publishing, 209, 283, 284

musicology, 297

Mussorgsky, Modest (Russian, 1839–1881), 17, 254

mute, 36, 41

mystic chord, 100

narrator, 272

Nationalism, 16–19, 60, 253; App. II, no. 4

natural, 71

Neapolitan music, 24

neoclassic music, 14, 23, 153; opp. Plate 6

neume, 68–69, 267

Niles, John Jacob, 109

nocturne, *106*

notation, pitch, 68–70, 107; rhythm, 49–50

note values, 49–59, 117

"numbers" in opera, 253, 259, 276

oboe, 40; Plate 10

octave sign, 69

Office, 264

Okeghem, Johannes (Flemish, c. 1430–c. 1495), 17

open form, 23, 108, 151

opera, 14, 23, 244; App. II, no. 39; ensembles, 120, 127, 241; general, 252–261, 272–273; melody, 76; opp. Plates 3, 4; Plate 16

opéra-comique, 252

opera in English, 256–257

operetta, 252, 259

oratorio, 120, 244, 263, 272–279; App. II, no. 44; opp. Plate 3

orchestra, 231–232, 252; App. II, no. 12; Baroque, 211, 218; instruments, 32–35; make-up, 122–125, 128; opp. Plate 5; Plates 13, 16

orchestration, 102, 113, 123–*124*, 125–128

order of accidentals, 91–92

Ordinary, 264–267–271; App. II, nos. 40, 43

organ, 32, 43–44, 118, 165, 191, 200–*201*; Plate 11

organum, 78, 108

oriental music, 42, 107–109; App. II, no. 10

ornamentation, 108; Baroque, 118, 176; variations, *197*–198, 206, *207*, 267

overture, 210, 215, 238, 252, 260

Paganini, Niccolò (Italian, 1782–1840), 189, 194; App. II, no. 25; opp. Plate 5; *Variations on "Nel cor più*," 196–*197*–198

painting and music, 19, 20–21, 68, 133, 134, 135, 136, 138; Impressionism and Expressionism, 241–243; Plates 17, 18

Paisiello, Giovanni (Italian, 1740–1816), 197

Palestrina, Giovanni Pierluigi da (Italian, c. 1525–1594), 11, 12, 14, 17, 22, 117, 121, 268

parallel minor, 92

partials, harmony, 79–80, 102, 103, 126; timbre, *30*–31–32, 38, 46

passacaglia, 190–*192*–193, 271; App. II, no. 23

Passion, 273, 274

pathos styles, 16–25, 107, 235–236; App. II, no. 1; Plates 1, 3, 5, 7a

pavane, 203, 205
pedal point, 165
pedals, 44, 46, 165; Plate 11
pentatonic scale, 108
Pepusch, Johann Christoph (German-English, 1667–1752), 253
percussion instruments, 33–34, 42–43, 108
perfect consonance, 81
performance, 115, 138, 292–294
Pergolesi, Giovanni Battista (Italian, 1710–1736), 253, 256
philosophy and music, 18; opp. Plates 1–6
phrase, 117; as generator, 139, 144–147–150; in phrase grouping, 173–175, 183; in variations, 188–190; review, 290
phrase grouping, 7, 72, 86; App. II, no. 19; forms based on, 171, 173–175, 183, 227; influence on form, 139, 144–148, 149–150, 151–152; review, 290
piano music, 113, 122–123, 126, 215; opp. Plate 5
piano quartet, 122, 215
piano quintet, 122, 215
piano trio, 76, 122, 215
pianoforte, 31, 45–46, 64, 65, 70, 137; App. II, nos. 22, 34, 35; opp. Plate 5; Plate 12
piccolo, 40
Pierné, Henri (French, 1863–1937), 275
pipe organ, 43–44
Pirandello, Luigi, 12
pitch, instruments, 29–30, 32, 35, 36, 43; keyboard and staff, 64–76, 289
pizzicato, 36
plainchant, 14, 68–69, 75, 108, 263–267–268; opp. Plate 1
playing by ear, 87–88
point of imitation, 157, 158, 159
polka, 57; App. II, no. 4e
polonaise, 57; App. II, no. 4b
polyphony, 14, 230, 253; App. II, no. 16; forms, 156–160; motivic play, 140–141, 142, 146; opp. Plate 3; styles, 105–106, 115–118,

119, 126
polythematic form, 145, 180, 227
polytonality, 101; App. II, no. 8
postlude, 249
Poulenc, Francis (French, 1899–), 269
Praetorius, Michael (German, 1571–1621), 17
prelude, 166, 205, 237–240, 249
primary triad, 86–89
primitive music, 42, 107–109, 143
programme music, .14, 151, 167, 180; App. II, no. 37; sonata, 223; tone poem, 240–243–245, 246; versus absolute, 235–237
progression, 138–152, 179, 239, 290
Prokofiev, Sergei (Russian, 1891–1953), 17, 125, 217, 231, 275
Proper, 263–267–269, 271; App. II, no. 41
proportion in form, 74–75, 134
Prout, Ebenezer (English, 1835–1909), 73, 99
Pryor, Arthur, 86
psychology and music, 286, 294
Puccini, Giacomo (Italian, 1858–1924), 17, 259; *Gianni Schicchi,* 256; *La Bohème,* 76, 120, 137, 254, 261
punctum, 267
Purcell, Henry (English, 1659–1695), 17, 191, 254; App. II, no. 3

question-answer relationship, 144, 148–150, 164, 175, 183

Rachmaninoff, Sergei (Russian, 1873–1943), 178–179, 194, 231, 266
radio, 284–285
Rameau, Jean Philippe (French, 1683–1764), 17, 167, 169, 179, 254, 274
range, 33–34, 47, 64, 67–68, 72, 73, 100, 117, 120, 121, 162
Ravel, Maurice (French, 1975–1937), 17, 22, 81, 100, 126, 231; App. II, no. 2; *Bolero,* 196; *L'Heure espagnole,* 256; *Piano Concerto in G,* 76
realism, 253
recapitulation, 154, 225, 226

recitative, 257–*258*, 259, 272
recorder, 39
recordings, 8, 138; App. II
recurring bass line, *188*, 190–*192*, 193; App. II, no. 23
recurring binary melody, *188*, 195–*197*–198; App. II, no. 25
recurring harmonic pattern, *188*, 193–*195*; App. II, no. 24
reed organ, 44
reference books on music, 9–10
refrain, 161, 179–182
relative minor, 92
repeat signs, 167, 178, 199, 224, 230
repertoire, 231, 255–256
repetition, motivic, 140–141; sectional, 151–152, 186, 224, 225, 238–239, 259
Requiem, 271–272; App. II, no. 42
rests, 55
retransition, 181–182
rhythm, App. II, nos. 4, 5; in homophony, 145, 266; in polyphony, 117–118, 141, 154, 159, 164; meters and patterns, 49–62, 93, 98, 112; percussion, 42; review, 289, 293
rhythmic patterns, 49; App. II, nos. 4, 28; Baroque, 205–*207*; Romantic and Modern, 57–58, 108, 112, 139, 154, 161, 168, 192, 193; simple and compound, 52–*54*–*55*–56
Rinehart, Mary Roberts, 137
Rimsky-Korsakov, Nicolas (Russian, 1844–1908), 114, 128
Rococo music, 16–19, 24, 118, 169, 180; App. II, no. 18; opp. Plate 4
Romantic Era, 14, 16–19, 22; App. II, nos. 1, 4, 6, 12, 19, 20, 22, 24, 25, 26, 32, 35, 37, 38, 39; dance patterns, 56, 57, 58, 74; forms, 175, 176, 177, 180, 214, 220, 224, 225, 230; harmony, 92, 96–97, 98; motive, *143*; phrase, 146–*147*; Plate 5; programme music, 235–236, 240–241, 244; texture and sonority, 105, 107, 110, 112, 126, 127–128
rondeau, 172, 179–181, 205
rondo, 152, 153, 179–182, 212, 220, 228, 237, 266; App. II, no. 21

root, 83–85
Rore, Cipriano de (Flemish-Italian, 1516–1565), 160
Rossini, Gioacchino (Italian, 1792–1868), 17, 21, 125, 254, 261, 266
round, 116, 179
rubato, 62
Rubinstein, Anton (Russian, 1829–1894), 175
rumba, 57

Sachs, Curt, 20, 21
sacred music, 23, 146, 200; Mass, 263–279; motet, 156, 157
Sailing, Sailing, 56
Saint-Saëns, Charles Camille (French, 1835–1921), 17, 125, 231, 266
Sanctus, 265, 271; App. II, no. 43g
Sandburg, Carl, 109
saraband, 205, *207*, 210
saxophone, 33, 40
scale, 66–68, 71, 72, 84–85–86, 87, 89, 90, 92, 100–102, 107, 108, 193
Scarlatti, Alessandro (Italian, 1660–1725), 17, 24, 254
Scarlatti, Domenico (Italian, 1685–1757), 17, 167, *169*–170; App. II, no. 17
Schenker, Heinrich (Austrian, 1868–1935), 94–95
scherzo, 172, 173, 176, 218, 219–220
Schiller, Johann, 248
Schillinger, Joseph (Russian, 1895–1943), 102
Schoenberg, Arnold (Austrian, 1874–1951), 14, 17, 24, 98; App. II, no. 7; opp. Plate 6; *Wind Quintet*, 99
Schubert, Franz (Austrian, 1797–1828), 14, 17, 22, 75, 113, 128, 217, 248, 269; App. II, nos. 4f, 32, 38a, 38b; *Ave Maria*, 172, 174, 249; *Erlking* and *Death and the Maiden*, 249–250–251–252; *Quartet in D Minor*, 95–97, 251; *Quintet in C*, 75
Schumann, Robert (German, 1810–1856), 17, 22, 60, 72, 166, 175, 176, 183, 217, 231, 236, 248; App. II, no. 20; *Dedication*, 178; opp. Plate 5

Schütz, Heinrich (German, 1585–1672), 17, 273
Schwarzkopf, Elisabeth, 248
score, 123, 124, 159, 209
scoring, 118–128, 215
Scotch snap, 58
Scottish tunes, 58
Scriabin, Alexander (Russian, 1872–1915), 17, 100, 218, 230
sculpture and music, 19, 136; Plates 1–6
Seashore, Carl, 295
secondary dominant, 89
secular music, 23, 146, 157, 273; madrigal, 160–161, 247
sequence, App. II, no. 42; plainchant, 75, 266, 267; repetition, 96, 142, 161, 164, 194
Sessions, Roger (American, 1896–), 76
"seven classic arts," 135
sharp, 65–68, 71, 89–93
Sharp, Cecil, 109
Shaw, Bernard, 242
Shostakovitch, Dmitri (Russian, 1906–), 217, 240; App. II, no. 33; *Fifth Symphony*, 73, 101, 114, 220; *Seventh Symphony*, 196
Sibelius, Jean (Finnish, 1865–1957), 17, 72, 217, 241
siciliano, 61, 278
side drum, 42
"simple" meter, 51–52, 205
sinfonia, 210; App. II, no. 44a
singing, 46–48, 160–161, 253, 257; App. II, nos. 38a, 38b, 39; Plates 8, 16
singing-allegro style, 113, 115, 226
singspiel, 252, 259
slow introduction, 205, 219, 220, 224
slow movement, 176, 205, 209, 212–213, 219, 221
Smetana, Bedřich (Bohemian, 1824–1884), 241
snare drum, 42
social music, 287
soli ensemble, 118–122, 211–212, 213
sonata, 14, 24, 76, 153, 154; App. II, no. 31; Baroque, 167–169, 203, 206–210; Classic, 214–232; opp. Plate 4

"sonata-allegro" form, 143, 178, 214, 218–219, 220, 224–232, 269; App. II, no. 31
song cycle, 248
song-form, 176
sonority, 119, 127–128; App. II, nos. 13, 36
sound, 29–32, 81
Sousa, John Philip (American, 1854–1932), 113
Souzay, Gérard, 248
square notation, 69, 266–267–268
square phrase, 58, 145–147, 169, 179, 190
Stabat Mater, 266
staff, 64, 65, 68–71, 266–267–268
standardized design, 111, 133, 134–135, 138–140; App. II, no. 19; review, 290–291; rondo, 182–183; "sonata-allegro," 214, 224–225, 287; types and trends, 150–154
Stockhausen, Karl Heinz (German, 1928–), 103
Stradivari, Antonio (Italian, 1644–1737), 35; opp. Plate 3
Strauss, Johann (Austrian, 1825–1899), 113, 177; App. II, no. 4c
Strauss, Richard (German, 1864–1949), 14, 17, 24, 183, 236, 241; *A Hero's Life*, 246; App. II, no. 37; *Der Rosenkavalier*, 76, 254, 261; *Don Quixote*, 200; *Till Eulenspiegel*, 107, 180, 236, 245–246
Stravinsky, Igor (Russian, 1882–), 14, 17, 100, 117, 125, 128, 213, 253, 275; App. II, no. 13
stretto, 165
string quartet, 75, 122–123, 126, 215, 217, 230; App. II, no. 32; Plate 9
    See also sonata
string quintet, 122, 215
string sextet, 122, 215
string trio, 122, 215
stringed instruments, 32–38, 90, 118, 126, 128; Plates 8, 9
strophic form, 157, 172, 249, 257–259
structural result, motive and phrase, 134, 138–139, 144–146, 149, 153–

154, 162, 167, 183, 224, 235, 287; review, 290–291
style, 6–7, 157, 197–198, 215–216, 277–278; motive, 141–143; phrase, 145–146; texture, 105–*106*–107, 111–118; tonality, 94–95, 96–97
subdominant, 85–88, 168
subject and answer, 161–*163*, 164–*166*, 209, 227–228, 270
submediant, 85
subordinate triads, 86, 88–89
subtonic, 85
suite, 14, 146, 203, 204, 207, 210, 213, 217, 218; App. II, no. 28; opp. Plate 3
suspension, 117, 159, 209
syllabic style, 257, 266, 267, 274; App. II, no. 40
symbolism, 160, 244, 271
symphonic poem, 236, 240–246
symphony, 194–195, 215, 216, 220, 221, 241; App. II, no. 33
See also sonata
syncopation, 56, 58

tablature, 68
talent, 294–296
Tallis, Thomas (English, c. 1505–1585), 17
tambourine, 43
tango, 57; App. II, no. 4g
Tartini, Giuseppe (Italian, 1692–1770), 17
taste, 5; melody, 72–73, 74–75, 285–287
Tchaikovsky, Peter Ilyich (Russian, 1840–1893), 17, 112, 125, 198, 217, 231; App. II, no. 12
technique, idioms, 239, 240, 244; instruments, 36–48, 169, 193, 197; performance, 292–294, 295
Telemann, Georg Philipp (German, 1681–1767), 17
tempo, 59–62, 138, 219
ternary design, 152, 230; A-B-A, 174–179; App. II, nos. 19, 20
text, 142, 149, 151, 238; art-song, 247–252; motet and madrigal, 157–161; sacred, 266, 269, 274
texture, 7, 93, 105–*106*–*112*–*114*–

118, 194, 204, 209, 226. 289; motive and phrase, 140–141, 144–145, 154; motivic play, 162, 164; review, 293; scoring, 118–128
Teyte, Maggie, 248
thematic relationships, 221–222–223, 241
thematic transformation, 143, 223, 241
theme, 199, 224–226, 227–229
theme-and-variations, 172, *188*–189, 198–*201*; App. II, no. 26
thorough-bass, 14, 115, 121–123, 206, 253
"three B's," the, 15, 231
through-composed, 247
tie, 54, 55–56
timbre, 30–33, 39–42, 44–46, 102, 117, 119, 126, 137; App. II, no. 2
time and space arts, 134, 135–138, 151, 187
time signature, 51–59
timpani, 29, 42
toccata, 166, 238–239
tonal plateau, 144–145, 169, 226–227
tonality, 14; App. II, nos. 6, 9; cursive forms, 161, 164–165, 168; hierarchic designs, 173, 177–178, 181, 190; influence on form, 93–103; motive and phrase, 140–141, 144–145, 151–154; opera, 260–261; sonata, 226
tone, 29–32, 71, 92, 94–103, 292
tone poem, 240–246
tone row, 99
tonic, 66, 85–88, 94–96, 98, 164, 168, 227
tonic minor, 92, 95
Tovey, Donald, 74
Tract, 271
traditional harmony, 79–84, 86, 93, 98, 100, 103
transcriptions, 127, 191
transposing instruments, 34, 38
treble clef, 69–70
triad, 83, 84, 85–89, 90
triangle, 43
trill, 118, *169*, 207
trio section, 176, *178*, 219
trio setting, 122, 206–207, 208, 211
trio sonata, 206–210

triplet, 54, 113
tritone, 100
trombone, 38, 41, 69
troubador, 110
trouvère, 110
trumpet, 29, 38, 41, 198, 270
tuba, 41
tune, 72, 195–*197*, 198
turn, 118, *207*
tutti, 211–*212*, 231
twelve-tone technique, 99
two-against-three, 113–*114*

um-pah-pah, 76, 113, 259
upbeat, 56

vamp, 259
Varèse, Edgar (French-American, 1885-   ), 103
variation form, 76, 152, 172, 186–*188–201*, 219
variety within unity, basis of form, 133–135, 140–141, 144–145, 151; cycles of movements, 203–204; hierarchic design, 171–173; opera, 261; variation form, 186
Vaughan Williams, Ralph (English, 1872–1958), 17, 110, 125, 217, 248
Verdi, Giuseppe (Italian, 1813–1901), 17, 173, 253–254, 261, 272; App. II, no. 39; *La Traviata*, 120, 259
vibrating agent, 29–34, 36, 43
vibrato, 36, 39, 43, 45, 48
Victoria, Tomás Luis de (Spanish, c. 1548–1611), 17
vielle, 37; Plate 8
Villa-Lobos, Heitor (Brazilian, 1887–1959), 73, 202
viol, 37
viola, 35–37, 69, 122; Plate 9
violin, 29, 30, 35–37, 76, 122, 123, 206, 239; App. II, nos. 9, 25; Plate 9
violoncello, 35–37, 69, 121–122, 123, 177, 206; App. II, no. 19; Plates 9, 15
virginal, 190, 244

virtuosity, 181, 197, 212, 231, 239; opp. Plate 5
Vivaldi, Antonio (Italian, c. 1675–1741), 17, 35, 208, 210; App. II, no. 30; *Concerto No. 8, op. 3, 212–213*
vocal music, 16, 23, 74; groupings, 118–121, 123–124; Plates 8, 16; polyphonic, 156–*158–160*, 161, 244
voice, App. II, nos. 20, 39; singing, 46–48, 118–121, 260, 261; texture, 114, 157–160, 162, 165
voice-leading, *101*, 114

Wagner, Richard (German, 1813–1883), 12, 17, 22, 40, 117, 125, 137, 241, 252, 253, 254, 257; App. II, no. 6; *Das Rheingold*, 120; leitmotif, 143, 260; *Mastersingers*, 72, 76, 111, 261; opp. Plate 5; *Parsifal*, 96, 105; *Tannhäuser*, 121; *Tristan*, 112, 254
Walton, William (English, 1902–   ), 275
waltz, 57, 113, 177; App. II, no. 4c
Watts, Isaac, 275
Weber, Carl Maria von (German, 1786–1826), 17, 125, 241, 254
Webern, Anton von (Austrian, 1883–1945), 100
Wesley, Charles, 275
white and black keys, 64–66, 67, 102, 108
whole step, 64–68
whole-tone scale, 66–67
wind instruments, 29, 32–34, 38–42, 108; Plate 10; scoring, 122–124
Wipo (Burgundian, ?–1048), 75
Wolf, Hugo (Austrian, 1860–1903), 248
"woodwind" quintet, 122; App. II, no. 7; Plate 10
"woodwinds," 32–34, 38–40, 125
word painting, 159–160, 244–246, 278

xylophone, 29, 42

Yankee Doodle, 67
Yasser, Joseph, 102

COLOPHON BOOKS ON LITERATURE, DRAMA & MUSIC

Svetlana Alliluyeva	ONLY ONE YEAR. Russian Language Edition. CN 182
Svetlana Alliluyeva	TWENTY LETTERS TO A FRIEND. Russian Language Edition. CN 122
J. Bronowski	WILLIAM BLAKE AND THE AGE OF REVOLUTION. CN 164
John Brooks	THE BIG WHEEL. CN 162
John Cheever	THE ENORMOUS RADIO AND OTHER STORIES. CN 48
Thurston Dart	THE INTERPRETATION OF MUSIC. CN 25
George Eliot	DANIEL DERONDA. CN 102
Henry Anatole Grunwald, Ed.	SALINGER: A Critical and Personal Portrait. CN 13
Leo Gurko	THE ANGRY DECADE: American Literature and Thought from 1929 to Pearl Harbor. CN 124
Luis Harss and Barbara Dohmann	INTO THE MAINSTREAM: Conversations with Latin American Writers. CN 167
Ihab Hassan	RADICAL INNOCENCE: The Contemporary American Novel. CN 85
Aldous Huxley	BRAVE NEW WORLD and BRAVE NEW WORLD REVISITED. CN 101
Bill Kinser and Neil Kleinman	THE DREAM THAT WAS NO MORE A DREAM: A Search for Aesthetic Reality in Germany, 1890-1945. CN 166*
Marshall McLuhan and Harley Parker	THROUGH THE VANISHING POINT: Space in Poetry and Painting. CN 161
Ved Mehta	DELINQUENT CHACHA. CN 141
William S. Newman	UNDERSTANDING MUSIC. Second Edition. CN 109
Jean-Paul Sartre	WHAT IS LITERATURE? CN 60
Erich Segal	PLAUTUS: THREE COMEDIES. The Braggart Soldier, The Brothers Manaechmus, and The Haunted House. CN 142
Aleksandr Solzhenitsyn	THE FIRST CIRCLE. Russian Language Edition. CN 156
Stephen Stepanchev	AMERICAN POETRY SINCE 1945: A Critical Survey. CN 110
Mark Twain	THE WAR PRAYER. CN 197
Thornton Wilder	THE LONG CHRISTMAS DINNER and Other Plays in One Act. CN 41